The Fire Watchers

JOHN CRAWLEY

authorHOUSE®

AuthorHouse™
1663 Liberty Drive
Bloomington, IN 47403
www.authorhouse.com
Phone: 1 (800) 839-8640

Published by AuthorHouse 07/14/2017

ISBN: 978-1-5246-9900-0 (sc)
ISBN: 978-1-5246-9899-7 (e)

Library of Congress Control Number: 2017910564

Print information available on the last page.

This book is printed on acid-free paper.

PREFACE

I'm going to piss you off…....hopefully, in a good way, so you can use the energy creatively and help me fight the "fire" that has been growing, ever so steadily, in our Nation. The title of this book: "The Fire Watchers" is a metaphor referencing the lack of "continuum of care" for our mentally ill and substance addled folks; often one in the same person. Much of my focus is on the veterans, returning from harm's way in various parts of the world. They have a high rate of mental illness (PTSD {Post-{delayed, sometimes for months or years} Traumatic Stress Disorder} and other maladies like Major Depression, Bi-Polar Affect Disorder) and TBI (Traumatic Brain Injuries). There are many effective treatments for these issues that are not being used as frequently or as effectively as they should. Why not? I will document and discuss major reasons why much of our treatment services delivery system is flawed and, in many places, broken. We need a major effort in this country to repair what's broken. I will take us through, step by step, ways in which we can all work together to provide an efficient, less costly, and model system that rivals any in the world.

My intent is not to denigrate nor castigate the majority of our dedicated people who serve the treatment professions; the doctors, nurses, psychiatric therapists, social workers, and others who provide for the care of our mentally ill and substance abuse folks. But, there are some major issues with bureaucratic malfunctioning and greed (Big Pharmaceuticals, Big Medicine, and Big Insurance) where the Hippocratic Oath (remember?"…do no harm") seems to have been set aside for personal/corporate profit. We all know this is true; but, we seem to accept it as "status quo"; that's the way it is and there's little we can do about it. Well, I'm here to relay to you all there IS something we can do about it and, I will name names and programs that are, now, in fact doing something to change the system for the better.

For example, one person who has been working to change things, for many years, with some success, is Dr. Paul G. Harch, out of the University of Louisiana, a medical practitioner, international lecturer, and expert on Hyperbaric Oxygen Therapy (HBOT). In fact, I have used his writings and research (with his permission) for much of what you will read in this book. Dr. Harch has fought an uphill battle to get HBOT, as Hyperbaric is called, into more of a mainstream therapeutic application; mostly, as an adjunct therapy to standard treatment applications for diseases like Multiple Sclerosis, Alzheimers /Dementia, Parkinson's, Autism, Spinal Cord Injuries, Birth Injuries, Carbon Monoxide Poisoning, Substance Abuse Damage to the brain and nervous system in general, Vision loss, Near drowning, Stroke, and many other diagnoses. Hyperbaric chambers have been used for many years to treat divers for the bends (where they rise to the surface too fast and the blood is infused with Nitrogen, causing extreme pain and discomfort), for burn patients, and to prevent amputations; especially where diabetes is concerned. HBOT is based on a simple fact: Oxygen promotes healing. I would strongly recommend you read Dr. Harch's latest edition of "The Oxygen Revolution" after you've read this book. You will clearly see why it is necessary and, a duty to humanity, that we all become "fire fighters."

In addition to what I'm telling you here, is the fact I've documented that the average taxpayer can save anywhere from $5,000.00 to $12,000.00 on his/her tax bill (depending on which area of the Country you live in; tax rates vary as do "average" area incomes from $35,500 to $47,500 {from U.S. Bureau of Labor Statistics/ I.R.S. 2015}). Each year, if we all get behind pushing Congress to treat mental illness and substance abuse as "diseases", which they are, the "fire" will be quelled a bit, and to where we can catch our collective breaths and formulate a more effective agenda. Congress needs to pass a "parity" bill where these ailments are finally accepted on the medical diagnostic spectrum and treated as such. Right now, we're shooting in the dark. We have a heroin/prescription narcotic epidemic throughout the U.S.A. (2016 Center for Disease Control) and, we're spending way too much money building prisons, jails, costly social services network systems, welfare misuse, use of emergency rooms in hospitals by the homeless (often drug-addicted and/or mentally unstable folks), waste/ criminal negligence in the Veterans Administration (in some areas), and misuse of resources by Government (State and Federal) to where the taxpayer is throwing money down a black hole that grows larger by the month. This too is part of the "fire" of which I speak.

We can and we have a duty, to our continued existence on this planet, to fix this. There are "fire fighters" working at this fix as I write these words. Dr. Harch is one of those people who is, I consider, a "fire fighter," because he is advocating for treatment protocols that not only work, but are much more effective than some of our "standard" medical applications.

Currently, as of 2016, resistance to his applications is only partially reduced by some in Congress; but supported by other medical personnel who have replicated his phenomenal results many times over, for many years. Unfortunately, large conglomerates of the "Establishment" (read International Pharmaceutical Cartels, Big International Insurance Corporations, and Large Medical consortiums {Humana, Providence Medical Group. Blue Cross, etc.}) have previously discredited Dr. Harch's results by misapplying his methodologies in order to skew results into an abyss of what they determined to label "anecdotal" results and "unscientific and unsupported clinical trial results."

Dr. Harch has debunked these claims, over and over, through the careful analysis of the claimant's misapplications and untoward results. For example, in one study, a U.S. Government agency (Department of Defense application of HBOT clinical trials on patients diagnosed with PTSD, 2004) used subjects who were not qualified (did not meet the clinical tests) to be subjects; thus, nullifying the results of the trial. They concluded that Harch's significant cure rate for PTSD (at an average of 83%) was an anomaly, an "anecdotal" result, and "not in the norm of rational results." Harch later refuted these findings by demonstrating the erroneous application of his methods and protocols. More recently, some are paying heed to his claims and, they are signing clinical trial notes to support more studies.

It's really difficult to attain credibility and scientific authenticity when large corporations are unwilling to support your efforts. They know they stand to lose significant profits if some of Dr. Harch's applications are approved by the Federal Government, FDA, and Department of Defense. Ironically, Dr. Harch is not advocating disuse of current methods; he's suggesting that HBOT be used as a supplement to current methods, right along with current practices. His efforts are not a threat to current medical practices; they are a boon, an enhancement. As in many "new" ventures, fear of the unknown or having to adjust the "status quo" sometimes causes corporate leaders to shy away or find excuses not to support something. As one doctor once told me, after my youngest daughter had been looked at by some 26 different "specialists" who finally diagnosed her with: "severe viral infection, unspecified;" he said, "John, medicine is the study of what it's not." So, I guess medicine, and treatment, advances in starts and fits, failure, misapplications, and political obstructionism until somebody breaks down the door and says, "Enough of this shit! This is what works and we are going to implement it because it's the right and humane thing to do." Of course, before one does this, he/she should have all the ducks lined up (clinical trial proof, some Congressional supporters, the press, journalistic and historical precedence, and colleagues in the medical profession who acknowledge that what is proposed does, in fact, work because they've done it, etc.)

Another source of information I found very informative and enlightening was Patrick Kennedy's book titled "A Common Struggle." Patrick is, of course, the son of the late Senator Teddy Kennedy. He served the State of Rhode Island as a Congressional Representative for 16 years before quitting to initiate the Kennedy Foundation which is dedicated to serving to eradicate the stigmas we all see in mental health and substance addled people. Kennedy has first hand knowledge, and he documents it in his book, about how big corporations go to extremes to stifle the efforts he and others attempted to gain "parity" legislation passed that would have provided a desperately needed "safety net" for our mentally ill and substance addicted sufferers, often one in the same person. Kennedy's struggle parallels mine in many ways; although, he was "on the firing line, while I was more of a support person who struggled with our own Legislature in Washington State and Department of Corrections Administrators in the fight to gain better treatment for the mentally ill and substance dependent folks who were part of our jail and prison system. I found very similar barriers to what Patrick Kennedy found in the Nation's Capitol. The unwillingness of leaders to even address these issues is astounding. They often "shine it off" as something that doesn't really have a priority. Kennedy's book not only details his own personal struggle with Bi-polar disorder and subsequent prescription addiction, and his on-going battles to overcome same, it also details Patrick's time as a Congressman and the battles he had within his own constituency and outside the "beltway" of Washington D.C. in trying to get "parity" laws passed. Parity would be: defining mental illness and substance abuse as recognized "diseases", and including them in the lists of medical acknowledgment, journals, and defined criteria to give diagnostic validity to same. As it stands, as I write these words, mental illnesses and substance addiction ARE NOT recognized as "diseases" (in the truest sense) by the Federal Government or any Agency affiliated with the Federal Government. This desperately needs to change. Why? Because we, as taxpayers are getting the shaft: having to pay for treatment, emergency rooms, institutional placements (this includes jails and prisons), mental health facilities, social/psychiatric caseworker salaries, Veteran's Administration misplacement and "loss" of records (to meet an Administrative quota so the managers could receive a bonus for the people they actually did not "process"-read 2014-2015 V.A. scandals VFW report and others), referral after referral, bureaucratic merry-go-rounds that provide little, if any, solutions to issues we may have with loved ones who are "caught up" in a dysfunctional system, and leaders who seem to want to "shine it off" because there are bigger problems to solve; or, they just don't care or, they have no vested interest (read: monetary and/or political gains) in finding solutions. Believe me, I've spoken to, written to, and tried to sway a number of people in high places, over the course of a 37-year career as a Parole/Probation Officer and Supervisor to know what I've written above is true.

We currently, throughout this Country, have mentally ill persons, substance addled folks, in jail and in our prisons who shouldn't be there. Why? Because someone didn't have the gumption or fortitude to go to bat for them and get a qualified person to provide the Courts with a diagnosis. I will give you a very good example of what I'm writing about:

For the past 15 to 20 years, depending on which judiciary one uses, the Washington State Superior Court System has been held in contempt of court, by the 9th District Federal Court System, because they are holding people in jail without the "due process" right to seek an evaluation to see if they are mentally competent to aid their attorney(s) in their defense. Some of these folks are clearly incompetent and/or so mentally impaired, either by mental health issues and/or substance abuse issues, that they should be in a close-quartered treatment program. Our jails/prisons DO NOT fit the definition of "treatment programs." I know this because I worked in and around them for many years. These people are sometimes kept in "solitary confinement" cells because they are considered to be a danger to themselves (suicidal) or, they will become a "punching bag" (or worse) for those in the main population of the jail/prison. I know this is going on throughout the United States, in various forms, because I can read, hear, and see media reports of same. In other words, I've documented it.

Prosecutors say their hands are tied because the evaluation provider, in Washington State's case, is Western State Hospital; itself under Federal indictment for various maltreatment practices, failure to provide staff with a safe working environment, and delays in record keeping, treatment applications, and efficacy issues. The turnover rate of staff and administrators at this facility is mind boggling. One thing I do know about institutional "flow" is 'when the barrel has "leaky" seams, the "water" doesn't stay inside.' In other words, very few people are going to stay on a sinking ship if things don't get fixed. And, to add to this dilemma, bed space is almost non-existent due to over crowding and constant referrals from other agencies, jails, and hospitals.

Part of this issue is historical. In the 1970s, the psychiatric community of this country felt it more appropriate to treat folks closer to their homes, or in communities within which they were most familiar. As a result, our major mental health institutions were either closed or vacated. Hence, "community-based" therapy clinics were advocated, adopted, and funded by most State legislatures. This all worked well until financial crises, recessions, or economic downturns prevailed. Guess what got "cut" from the budget?.....If you guessed the "community-based" programs you get the brass ring.....or, in this case, the tax bill, because most of this has now transitioned to us, the tax payers. We are paying for those homeless, mentally ill, substance abusers, who go to the local hospital emergency rooms to get treatment (hospitals are mandated, by Federal Law, to treat indigent people but, only to the extent that their potential loss of life or limb are not imminent). After minimal treatment, people are released "to the street" where they may fall victim to the Criminal Justice System for, say, peeing in public.

I can recall a number of folks I had on my caseload, as a Parole/Probation Officer, who were minor offenders, but had mental health and/or substance abuse issues, who, in the cold winter months, not having a warm place to stay because all the "inns" (Missions) were full, and who were hungry, would deliberately do something innocuous (to people), like breaking a storefront window, just so they could get arrested and have "three hots and a cot" in the local county jail. Believe me, this is more commonplace than you'd expect. They may have mental health issues, or be "whacked out" on meth, but they are bright enough to know how to get shelter and food, even if it's by being incarcerated. It's a vicious cycle and one, as "firefighters," we can greatly reduce IF certain laws get passed and "parity" is finally recognized as a legitimate course of action.

The Family / Parts Unknown

Part of the old family history, on my father's side of the family, goes back to old England during the later part of the 13th century and forward. Being that I have an avocation and a desire to know from whence I came; coupled with my inclination to discover new resources and get accurate information (I loved statistics in college, so much, that I took three semesters of it), I dove into Ancestor's dot com, the local library, the Internet, and other sources: like my cousin, Camille Anderson (an avid student of genealogy) to learn more of our family history.

In researching jolly old England, I found that there exists a town named Crawley. It's about 85 miles south of London, near the Channel that separates Britain and France. This town is now a fairly "modern" city due to the extreme destruction, during the Second World War, when the German Luftwaffe bombed the area to pieces. My parents, on one of their worldly excursions, visited Crawley while staying with mutual friends who lived in London. They found an old estate, now a township park, comprising approximately 13 acres, surrounded by an old rockery "fence", or boundary if you will, and the remains of a 13th century abbey. This particular piece of property was once the grand location of Crawley Manor, where many fine buildings and a small enclave of people worked, worshiped, played, loved, lived and died. They found the remnants of an old cemetery on the grounds. And no, there is no relation here (that I know of) to the fictitious, but wonderful television series named "Downton Abbey", where a family, named Crawley, practiced the art of British aristocracy prior to WW1.

In my research on Crawley, I found that the land had changed hands a number of times. Specifically, during Henry VIII's reign, a bishop was granted the parcel as a gift for doing the King's bidding. This man was "disappeared" by some nefarious means that no one seems to know about. Perhaps he gained disfavor of the politically omnipotent Henry. I could not find out what actually happened or why. Perhaps further research on this topic needs to be done. During this era, many land owners were subjected to taxes, and 'offers they could not refuse' like: "Your land or your life." There were many forces practicing subterfuge, chicanery, deceit, and political maneuvering. There were many subjects who were beheaded, outright murdered, and people disappeared without ever being seen or heard from again. People were being imprisoned, without trial, or not knowing their accusers, for something as inane as saying they did not like someone in the Royal court. After reading a lot about these tumultuous times of killing, mayhem, and back-stabbing people, I decided to leave well enough alone; for fear I may find one of my distant, shirt-tail relations was a henchman or worse.

My journey is still in progress. My mother's is not. Angie (Anje' as her nom du pen artist's name was) passed away on February 25, 2014; two days before my 70th birthday. 'Happy birthday "J.P." (my nickname in the family), I'm checkin' out.' In all fairness, she had a wonderful life, a loving, loyal companion in my father, John L. (who recently passed on October 6, 2016, at 99 years young), and, at her 96 years, was well traveled and gracious to everyone she ever met. I doubt there was a bone of hate in my mom. She conquered you with love and kindness, an unbeatable tag team if there ever was one; almost always a winning combination. I know a little rubbed off; otherwise, I wouldn't be writing this book.

My father was a U.S. Navy man who met my mother through a mutual friend whose husband was also in the Navy. The story goes that this handsome guy, from Texas, with a steely look and a "slow hand" drawl, was introduced to this beauty queen (mom was the Marysville, Washington State Strawberry Queen in 1936, the year of her graduation from high school), who he immediately was drawn to. One could say it was Kismet; love at first sight. I digress, but it's fun to recall what happened. They went out on a date, arranged by folks who would eventually become my godparents, Olive and Bill Baca (both now deceased). They danced into the wee hours of the morning at the Tree-anon Ballroom in Seattle, while John L. had shore leave. It was during the Second World War and my dad was in flight training, in Pensacola, Florida, where he trained to be a pilot in Stearman bi-planes. He later flew PBY (amphibious) troop/cargo carrier aircraft during the War. John and Angie were soon married and, as my mother related it, she was very nervous when going to meet John L.'s family in Texas. He'd been raised by two maternal aunts. His parents died when he was just a child, being the youngest of four children. Mother had learned that the Crawley family in Texas had some rather well-known linage. My great, great grandfather, John L Goodman, on my grandmother's side in Texas, was a U.S. Congressman for Texas, from 1900-1902. He'd originally moved from Georgia. As a young man, he was conscripted into the Confederate Army, where he fought in the Civil War. His movement west was probably wise, because he eventually was involved with the Union Army to the point of his election to Congress. It was said that he'd married a half-breed Western Band Cherokee Indian (I've often wondered how that went over with his fellow Congressmen, some of whom fought in the Indian Wars). So, I may have some "Native" blood in me after all. John L. Goodman was also one of the first U.S. Congressmen to be involved, with 4 others, in establishing "old soldiers homes" in the South. Many Confederate soldiers had no family to go to, following the Civil War. Many were malnourished, sick, wounded, and without resources. John L. Goodman and four fellow Congressmen were instrumental in initiating these homes for all the veterans, including Union Soldiers and other non-military conscripts. {note: you will see later why I am a strong proponent of correcting wrongs in our current Veterans Administration where, in my opinion, in some cases, criminal negligence has occurred}. John L. Goodman is buried in a family plot where my father was born: Heath, Texas. (From Ancestor's.com and family archives)

On my mother's side of the family, she was the youngest of five children born to Angela and Stephen Philipp. The family name, on this side, had been changed for a number of reasons; the least of which was what was about to happen in Europe (WWI). I've been told that Grandpa Philipp's actual spelling of the last name may have been "Fillippe," a family closely affiliated with the Hapsburgs, but more research is being done by me on this one. He may have changed the spelling when the family immigrated and, because he did not want his family looked down upon. Often times, as is the current state of affairs (2011-2017), certain ethnicity and cultures are singled out when their religious beliefs, customs, or mores seem to be in conflict with the "majority" culture, or, the political "climate" is swayed toward rejection (i.e. Japanese internment camps during WW2). We are seeing this in today's world (2017).

Two of mom's siblings were born in Germany before their father had the foresight to see where the Kaiser was going (starting World War 1), and he and his family were able to secure documents to travel to America. They settled in Pennsylvania, into an enclave commonly known as "the Pennsylvania Dutch" which basically took in people from many European sources during the early 20th Century. Stephen's skill was badly needed. He was, by education, a skilled electrician and he was hired by the Pennsylvania Railroad System. He made a good living; enough to support his family. When times got tough, during the Great Depression, and work was sparse, the family ran a small "truck farm" and sold produce to the local community.

One of my mother's sincere wishes was that she could record my grandparents' efforts at learning the English language, a far cry from the 5 different languages each parent spoke, fluently. My grandfather was born into aristocracy in Munich (pronounced: 'Meunchen'), Germany. My Grandmother, part Polish and part Viennese, was a millinery seamstress who crafted beautiful dresses and hats. They, my grandparents, met and were taken with each other. However, at the time, in Europe, it was looked down upon to marry beneath one's class or station in life. Grandfather's family did not approve of this union. So, Stephen Philipp, related to the Hapsburgs, took his bride, four children, and left the country for America. This was a very courageous move on my grandfather's part. No one knew what one would face in the New World. They had five children, my mother being born in the U.S.A., and a loving relationship throughout their lives. That doesn't mean there was not, at times, turmoil or disagreement. For example, I specifically recall, while living in my grandparent's home, my mom's two sisters would come to the house and speak in a hodgepodge of

English, low German, Polish, Czechoslovakian, Russian, and Hungarian. This would drive my grandfather nuts. He would stomp out of the house, cussing (I think) in High German. He insisted on speaking the "pure" languages, without adulteration or slang. He spoke High German, but his command of the English language was always elusive to him. My mother wrote down some of the common conversational "gems" that I will share with you here. Note: these are not meant to insult or denigrate my grandparent's memory, nor anyone else who struggles learning the English language. We, as a family, found them delightful, funny, charming, and entertaining:

Mom took grandpa Philipp to see a Mycological (wild mushrooms) Show at the Seattle Science Center. Grandpa was around age 80 at the time:

Mom introduced her father to Dr. Daniel Stuntz, a renowned botanist, professor at the University of Washington, and President of the local flora and fauna society, "Dad, this is Dr. Stuntz...he's in charge of the show and a very good friend; we've hunted mushrooms together."

Grandpa: "Do not disturb-et me, now, I take-et the mushrooms, they are more important." Mom told me that Grandpa didn't miss a beat, never looked up from the specimens he was examining and strolled away, ignoring everyone. He was always a really focused man.

Later, looking at a cluster of mushrooms with a sign saying (as to edibility): 'Caution-Uncertain', Grandpa announced to all those within earshot, "These mushrooms I like-et best...I eat-ed them very much...mama, she know-et how to cook-et them!" Some folks smiled I'm sure.

On the new hearing aid:

Mom: "How is the new hearing aid working Dad?"

Grandpa: "Oh...so it work-et. Today I hear-et a beerd (bird) sing. He did not sing-et vell, but he sing-et!"

Going to a new doctor for the first time {more diplomacy}:

5

"Doctor, I am now like the oldt Ford car...is vit me the trouble vit the heart (angina) and the vater (prostate)"

"The vater need-et fixing first...If you do-et good job on the vater I will give you the Rhododendron you vill like-et. But if you make-et bad job you get-et exactly nothing(Grandpa was an expert grafter of plants. He was often called upon to help people with their trees, "Rhodies", and garden landscaping. At one time, he had a Rhododendron with 8 different species grafted to a common stalk. It bloomed in different colors and floral shapes like a bouquet.)

To the ophthalmologist:

"Now doctor, you make-et good investigation on me. Ven you finish-ed, you vill tell me how much you vant for the eye glasses. I know-et they are not too cheap, yes?"

When a bear visited the back orchard:

"Come-et a bear by mine house by nite unt eat-et all mine epples (apples) unt mine honey. He break-et mine hives unt break-et the fruit trees...So, all he leav-et me was a bear pie (crap)."

Another example of grandfather's diplomacy; to a neighbor lady who was a size 18 or more:

"Mrs. G, she like-et to bring-et me some epple pie, but (she) was a leetle too beeg to fet for mine gate.

I say, Now, Mrs. G, I fix-et the gate, so you can now come easier through-et."

From the garden:

"I like-et very vell potatoes. Best I like-et bum-pet (boiled and drained) potato...is better than smashed (mashed)."

More about potatoes:

"Mama unt I not fry-et the potatoes. We cook-et them in vater. They are not on your stomach like a big lump."

Grandpa goes for a walk:

"I vill now go-et backwards to the orchard. Mama? You vill maybe make some strootzel? (apple strudel) Yes?"(He went to pick the apples...the strudel was a forgone conclusion).

"Mama she plant-et the full daffodils. I pre-fer the empty ones (conical as opposed to "lacy" centers)."

More about the garden:

"Vell, it don't look-et like much, but it seems it always pay-et." (In all modesty, my grandparents grew beautiful gardens and, in fact, remember? They had a "truck farm" in Pennsylvania, during the Depression, to make ends meet.) 'Green thumbs' were common to this generation of folks.

Buying shoes ("shoots"):

"This is not right to make-et shoot that press together the fingers off mine feet. Young mand, (sales person) you are a good salesmand, but do not know-et that I care-et nothing about the new styles. You vill please order-et me a vide pair! The men who make-et these shoot know that the foot is not point-et."

About a man grandpa knew in town:

"He is not so dumb as he look-et."

At Snoqualomie Falls (a beautiful area in Washington State): At the time, water was being held in reserve so the falls were but a trickle:

"I vill now look-et upon the falls. Oh! You know Stephen (son)?, is everything here but the vater!"

At the symphony as his daughter-in-law Dorothy adjusts Grandpa's hearing aids. Just as the conductor raised his baton, there was the usual moment of silence when Grandpa suddenly remarks, in a voice heard throughout the venue:

"Dorothy, I hear-et nothing!" (audience snickers).

Dorothy replies: "Papa,... is nothing!"

Sometimes, Grandpa could be a stern old Prussian; as when correcting his wife:

"Mama, don't talk in advance!"

And, sometimes, Grandma had a retort:

"Papa, you read-et and read-et and you know-et nothing. Better you help me broom the porch."

One day, two garlic eating old prospector neighbors came to help eat some of Grandma's prune bread. Grandma, as an aside to the rest of those present:

"My, my these oldt men, they smell-et so much. Ve open the vindows and door und I vill "viff" (whisk) the air vit mine apron when they go-et home."

And after a hard day's work around the house, garden, and other chores:

"Papa, he nap-et. I go too much, is enough!"

Reassuring Mama that her first airplane ride, to visit me and my folks in California, was not going to crash:

"Mama, do not vorry. The airplane it vill not crash...not yet. Jesus he still need-et a little rest!"(From all the souls he's saving every day, no doubt).

Upon finding newspapers laid out under a chandelier in their living room:

"No! No! Do not take the paper up. I leav-et the window open so the mama swallow fly-et in. She hav-et this nest in the light. She vill not go-et anywhere before the babies com-et."(By god, there was some compassion in him after all.)

Being a master electrician by trade, Grandpa knew a thing or two about wiring. He also knew who to talk to at the local hardware store: (To his son, Stephan, who was going into town)

"Vhen you buy-et for me this viring, go by Bartlett Hardware Store, but be sure you ask-et for Mr. Fox...he vill know-et vhat I vant. The black one (dark Irishman owner), he know-et nothing. He only sing et vell." (Mr. Bartlett sang in the church choir; he had an excellent tenor voice; more "diplomacy" from Grandpa.)

A neighbor, Mrs. Kendall, who often came to visit, came over to Grandpa and Grandma's house one day to introduce her mother-in-law, Mrs. Snodgrass:

Grandpa: "Ah, How are you Mrs. Candle?"

Upon being given the correct pronunciation by Mrs. Kendall, Grandpa replies:

"How do you do Mrs. Snapgrass?"

Mrs. Kendall:

"It's Snodgrass Mr. Philipp."

At this point, Grandma chimes in:

Papa, you cannot say-et right... is 'snotgrass.'

Mrs. Kendall:

"Oh dear, please let us talk about your garden and change the subject a bit."

Grandpa:

"You lik-et the Rhododendron?...I can 'bump-et' (pick, I think, in this context) one for you."

And on it went; each day, a new joy in how to murder the English language. Funny thing, even though my parents and my grandparents are gone; I sometimes think and hear, in my imagination, these colorful and wonderful conversations. I will cherish them, as I hope you do, for as long as I live. They make life worth living to any of us who have heart.

Grandpa Philipp passed away, peacefully, following a Thanksgiving dinner at my Aunt Helen's (Lindquist) home in Arlington Heights, Washington. I was in the United States Air Force serving my country (Vietnam Conflict era). It was said that Grandpa got up from his meal with the family (Helen, one of my mom's older sisters, always put out a grand spread for the holidays), said something about going out on the adjacent porch to "smoke-et mine pipe," fell asleep and never woke up again. This was in 1967. Some say he chose his time to die. A nice way to go I think...great meal with most of the extended family present and, go to sleep. So simple, so peaceful. He was 87 when he passed away.

Grandma Angeline wasn't so lucky. She had suffered a bi-lateral stroke some years prior, which affected her ability to walk and speak in complete sentences. We cared for her as best we could, in her home, until it was almost an impossible task because of her incontinence and constant discomfort in the bed she demanded to stay in (it was the original bed, broken down mattress and all). My grandparents were "resourceful" people, as were many from The Great Depression era. So, she spent about the last ten years of her life in a care facility in Marysville. We would go and pick her up (literally, I was playing football in those days and, at 4 foot, 10 inches, weighing all of 95 pounds, she was a feather weight to me), take her to the homestead and spend the weekend together. What I do, fondly, remember of her was her sitting on the back porch of the house, looking out over the beautiful view of the marshland, waterfront, with the Cascade mountains in the background, feeding humming birds that would come to her and land on one of her fore fingers to take honey nectar that she held in a thimble in her other "working" hand. Somehow, these delicate creatures knew my grandmother's kindness.

She loved music (Vienna waltzes), cooking (she was a great cook; especially "gwumpkies" {cabbage rolls stuffed with fresh-cooked ground pork and beef, mixed with cooked rice, covered with home made sauerkraut, left to sit for about 24 hours, fried quickly (2 minutes per side) in butter, and served, piping hot, with a strip of bacon and dollop of sour cream on top}... Are you hungry? I am. They were my favorite. And the fresh baked bread. The smell of fresh baked home-made bread is a hard thing to beat. I know of few smells that bring on such heavenly desires. With a dollop of fresh home-made strawberry jam (butter was superfluous), at ages 12 through 16, I WAS in heaven. I guess I remember grandma's cooking most because my mom, God rest her soul, was never an excellent cook. Her skills lay in public relations and art. Mom did, however, make some rather fine casseroles. She could also do a pretty fine job on a lemon pie, meringue and all (my father's favorite) and a pecan pie. She learned how to make this pie, with fresh-picked, off of the ground surrounding the massive pecan trees on the property, thin shell pecans found on my uncle Ed's farm in Texas. John L.'s aunts taught mom how to make this pie. They would mail us a box of pecans, every Christmas, just in time for a pie to be made. If you've ever had fresh thin shell pecans, you'll know they'll make any other substitute pale by comparison….delicious!

Earlier (1930s) my uncle, Steve Philipp, mom's older brother, traveled West, working his way, via the railroad system, doing whatever it took to earn his way to the State of Washington. There, he found some property, on the Tulalip Indian Reservation (Tyee Tract) that was for sale. It was approximately 14 acres of waterfront property where the Quil Ceda Creek and the Marysville Slough co-joined; 1 ¼ miles west of the town of Marysville, Washington; approximately 36 miles north of Seattle.

My grandfather paid a little over $10,000.00 for the property; a lot of money in the late 1930s. The rest of the family moved to the property as my uncle began building homes. He was a skilled wood craftsman/ boat builder by trade; having apprenticed in Hamburg, Germany's large boat yards prior to the family's move to America. He was age 16 when he first learned the trade. Steve built houses as if they were boats. Large beams and planks were used for structural soundness. The two homes he built on the property were still standing well after the deaths of all my relatives from the Depression Era.

I recall, with fondness, how my uncle Steve became a surrogate father to me. My father was still in the United States Navy when we lived with my grandparents (late 1950s-early 1960s). This was when my father could be stationed at Sand Point Naval Air Station in Seattle or, the Whidbey Island facility, further North. As I've previously mentioned, my father was a pilot for a time. He fought in World War Two in the Battle of the Coral Sea (Pacific Fleet), and he was highly decorated for his bravery and valor. How do I know this? It was related to me by my mother, who was told by the men who served with father on an aircraft carrier and, later, in a PBY (a seagoing airplane) squadron.

One of the stories relayed was when a Japanese Kamikaze suicide bomber struck the ship, near the conning tower, and blew up. My father was said to be one of the first men to grab a fire hose in an effort to put out the ensuing inferno. At one point, as John L. struggled with the high pressure fire hose, he yelled in the direction of another man who was standing nearby. He yelled for help. The man just stood still, as if transfixed, not moving. It was later determined that John L. was yelling at the ship's Commanding Officer who, like a deer caught in the headlights of an oncoming vehicle, was mesmerized and, probably, in shock from what he was seeing. At another point, as this story unfolded, an ammunition magazine exploded, sending pieces of hot, searing shrapnel and debris in the direction of those fighting the fire on deck. My father was hit in his left ear by a piece of shrapnel. He continued to battle the fire. Two inches to the right, I wouldn't have had a father.

The ship's company wanted to award my father a Purple Heart and Silver Star for his bravery and valor, under fire; but, as the story goes, sailors told my mother that John L. turned these awards down, stating something to the effect: 'Give them to someone else who really deserves them.' I tend to believe the previous quote, knowing how my father's quiet, understated manner was a joy to behold. And his great wit was a thing to witness. He could "set someone up" and take them off without them catching on until some time later. The only thing that gave him away was the beautiful smile he had when the other person finally caught on to his joke. This is one of the many things, I was told, that endeared my father to almost anyone he met, worked with, and with whom he had family relations. He always had a kind, gentle, but resilient manner.

My mother, as I've previously mentioned, was an artist. She studied art since she was a child, often doing murals and posters for her high school functions. She formally studied art, following marriage, when John L. was stationed in Corpus Christi, Texas where I was born (so, she didn't do "Art" all the time…. just my dad; I know, it's corny). Her instructor was a fairly well known artist by the name of Diego Gomez, who originally hailed from the art world around Chicago.

Toward the later part of my father's 20-year Navy career, we were in Hawaii (mid-1950s) when Angie (Anje') studied at the Honolulu Academy of Fine Arts with Joseph Fairer and a fellow named Stampher, who was said to be of old Prussian heritage. I remember my mother coming home from her commercial art classes, crying, because Stampher had torn up a piece of her work, demanding that she do it over again. At times, she was so upset that it brought on migraine headaches. At age 9, I wanted to defend my mother's honor and, I really wanted to kick Stampher's ass. But I didn't. Probably a good thing, looking back, he might have stabbed me with one of his paint brushes. Mom hung in though, because her desire to be a gifted artist drove to her core.

Back in Washington State, following John L.'s retirement from the Navy (1957), Angie studied with Leisal Seltzer (Edmonds, WA), a well known portrait artist in the area. My mother's focus, by this time, was on portraiture. More specifically, Native American portraits and depictions of indigenous ways. Angie had a ready-made gallery of potential subjects to paint. Her family was well-known on the Tulalip Reservation. Her father was appointed the County Justice of the Peace and he would often preside over the marriages of Tulalip Tribal members, and, sometimes, the ensuing divorces. Over time, she painted some 35 elders and members of the Tribes. Her other works entailed other tribal members around the Northwest and some Southwest tribal subjects. Angie also painted persons of European and African extraction when she and John L. traveled. She was able to have a showing of 41 of her paintings at the Frye Museum in Seattle (1980), and, in 2009, her art traveled to Goa, India as part of the Xandev Foundation's international cultural exchange programs. "Anje's" artworks were part of an exchange between the Goan people (at the very southern tip of India) and the Tulalip Tribal members who accompanied a close family friend, Joyce Mitchell (originally, of native India herself), and shared their history, music, traditional ceremonial customs, and art with the Goans. Anje' worked in oil/canvas and casein mediums. Her style was "old world" like Rembrandt or Michael Angelo. In fact, as she and my father traveled the world, she went to many of the world's finest art museums (Spain's Prado, The Louvre (Paris), Rome's Galleria, Germany's Berlin collections, etc.) where she would sit for hours and sketch great masters' works. She always told me that she was seeking, not so much "perfection," but "reality." I guess I'm probably biased, but I consider my mother's depictions to be right up there with many of the "great ones." She sold some of her work to various doctors, lawyers, and such who were, in my opinion, getting a really good deal at anywhere from $700 to $2,500 per painting.

A business woman, my mother was not; although, from her commercial art training in Hawaii, she was hired to become an advertisement/bridal consultant for the Bon Marche' Allied Stores (now known as Macy's). They wanted her to promote to executive level, move back to New York, and become an industry icon. My mother had no intention, as she put it, "to become someone I'm not." She was promoted anyway, in Everett, Washington to Junior Executive, with a "suspense account" (major store discounts, higher pay and perks, including mileage/travel/ and meal expenditure reimbursements, and credit accounts under the stores brand). It was a time when my mother's income, aside from John L.'s Navy monthly retirement, was the primary support for our family. My father was in the process of finishing up his Sociology Degree at the University of Washington, commuting every day from our home on the Tyee Tract (same area as where Uncle Steve built family homes), and my attendance, finally, at a full-time school where we didn't have to move every two-three years or so, as part of John L.'s U.S. Navy commitment.

More recently, during the Summer of 2015, and posthumously, the Tulalip Tribes honored my mother by sponsoring and hosting an art show of her works in their newly crafted Hibulb Museum and Cultural Center. In all, the curators and I were able to locate and borrow 39 paintings. Some of the works were brought to this wonderful, catered gathering by their owners, from as far away as Toronto, Canada. Since Anje's work, literally, hangs around the world it was not an easy task, locating and retrieving art pieces for the show. We still have some "original" pieces in the family (one is of Chief Dan George, the actor, {"Little Big Man" and "The Outlaw Josie Wales"} who mom painted from a real life sitting when she was invited by Robert Redford {posthumously, I found letters she'd written back and forth with Mr. Redford...she found his environmental work inspiring} to visit a Pow-wow in Montana and, she was introduced to Chief Dan by Mr. Redford. She sent a print of this painting to Mr. Redford as a thank you for his graciousness and candor).

The Hibilb showing was only supposed to last one week, but so many people showed interest that the show was extended for an extra week. I had 3 prints of Mom's work framed and set up for auction at this event. My intent, subsequently discussed with the Tulalips, was to set up a 501C3 non-profit to sell limited prints of her work. The proceeds of the auction and subsequent sales of the prints went to and, are going to the Hilbub Center, for their language/ arts program.

Many people do not know the history of how the mission culture tried to discourage the Native American from speaking his own language. Boarding schools were set up and the indigenous children were forced to go and learn the "white man's tongue." In fact, children were beaten for speaking their language in class. This happened to some of my family's friends on the Tulalip Reservation. For example, Stan Jones ('Scho Hallem', as his Lashootseed name is), who now (2017) is well into his 90s, a highly decorated United States Marine Corps veteran from WWII, told my family of how he and his brothers and sisters were herded together and placed into the "mission" school by the (as he calls them) "invaders." Stan, who was re-elected Chairman of the Tulalips over a 28-year span, told of how he and his two siblings, after contracting Tuberculosis, were sent to a hospital, off their reservation, where one sister and one brother died at the hands of the "white man's peril" (diseases the indigenous people succumbed to because they'd never been exposed, nor inoculated) all for the sake of "assimilation" into the "stronger and smarter" culture.

Funny how some of the Native ways were also adopted by the "white man." For example, the plant that we make aspirin out of was used by indigenous people many years before it was "discovered" by the "greater" culture. Many things can and should be learned from these people, whose time-honored methods and cultural lessons have merit, and, in my opinion, even in today's world. For example, conservation of resources was a common practice with the Native Americans; they took only what they needed and left plants and animals to propagate and thrive instead of "clear cutting" a total forest of old growth cedar, as we've learned, isn't a very sustainable practice. What cedar we now get in this country comes, mostly, from Canada, at very high prices.

During a discussion with a Tribal friend and acquaintance, James Madison, who is a 'talking stick' story teller and a totem craftsman, I asked him where his cedar poles came from. He told me, "We buy them from Canada, John...we don't take any of our own unless they are windfalls (literally blown down by a wind storm)...to us, the cedar is sacred because it provides us, to this day, with materials for baskets, ceremonial clothing, and construction of dug out canoes that are used by the Tribes in their cultural events." I know this to be true because I've watched an elder weave an intricate basket; one so tight that it will hold water and not leak!

I should note here that the Tulalip Tribes have done rather well for themselves. I recall taking a Business Law class from a man who was later hired, as the Tribes' attorney, and who negotiated settlements, long overdue, and compensations, out of Washington D.C for the Tribes' benefit. The

Tulalip people now are self-sustaining, with their own water treatment plant, construction and aquatic marine fisheries programs, elder care, clinics, doctors, nurses, schools, and they pay for college tuition to any Tribal member who wants to go forward (as long as that person keeps his/her grades up); and, if one wants to work for the Tribes in their destination resort casino, fisheries, or construction trades, they must be "clean and sober." If one is not, the Tribes will pay for treatment until a person is rehabilitated. They also have their own law enforcement and Court system on the Reservation. They have an ongoing partnership with the Marysville Police Department and, they have donated over $250,000.00 a year to local law enforcement to aid the partnership and enhance public safety. More recently(2016-17), the Tribe's Tarro Program, a constructions trade training program, built and donated "small houses" to a homeless outreach program in Seattle. These units are about 12 feet by 10 feet with a bed, a sink, a toilet, and a closet. They can house up to two homeless people per unit if a bunk bed is included.

I recall a recent conversation I had with a man who was losing badly at the local casino. He was griping about how the "damn Indians don't pay no taxes..." and so on. I finally got tired of this man's irksome, drunken attitude and leaned over and quietly stated: "I'm sorry you feel that way sir, but the rest of us are tying to enjoy the game....I think what you're really mad about, besides losing, is that the Indian is beating the White Man at his own game!" At this juncture, the guy got up from the table and left. Everyone clapped, and the rest of us went on with a fun game of Ultimate Texas Hold Em' (by the way, I won that night).

As I was helping plan the art show, I met with and spoke with Inez Bill, a Tulalip lady who works with the Hibulb Cultural Center. We somehow drifted into the topic of this book and when I told her that I was focusing part of my book on veterans and PTSD, she commented that she felt the indigenous people (Native Americans) were probably the first sufferers of PTSD in this country. I think, as a student of this culture, she has a point.

One of the things I'm most proud of, here in Washington State, is the fact that a recent legislative session, in 2015/2016, passed a requirement that Northwest Native American History, from the native's perspective and historical facts, be taught in our school system. What's more, the instructors will be tribal members who either have first-hand knowledge or recorded history of events, times, and a true understanding of what it's like to be "assimilated" into another culture. Personally, I've been told that the word "assimilated" isn't held in high regard among Native Americans. I don't blame them; especially, if one knows the history of what happened, how it happened, and why. If someone really understands this perspective, one can only come to one conclusion: power, control, and the greed of the "settlers" which drove the Native Americans from their lands and onto, in some cases, god-forsaken reservations, was a primary motive of the "invaders." The indigenous people's plight goes on today (read: Keystone Pipeline). There isn't one treaty that was fully honored by the "white man." Each successive administration nullified what had happened or what was agreed to in the previous administration's term. I digress, but I would encourage the reader to attend a Native event, speak with an elder, and learn the Indian ways. In this manner, we may all learn to survive the oncoming issues of global warming, and, maybe, just maybe, all work together to avert catastrophic Armageddon.

My uncle Steve's influence was very instrumental to me during my formative years. He found a man, Mr. Hugh Causey, who was fairly well-off financially and, who wanted a boy to help maintain his 47 foot yacht, moored at the docks where uncle Steve worked. This boat was a beautiful piece of art to me. It was built in Holland as a "ketch" sailing vessel. The name on the stern of the boat was "The Devon," probably taken from the same township, by the same name, in England. Mr Causey's father had been a steamship Captain who sailed many an ocean liner in the day. The "Devon" had twin 190 hp. Mercedes Bends diesel-marine engines, inlaid teak decking with rubber strips in between each slat to aid in footing while walking on top side during foul weather, a complete galley, (the interior was also done in teak; a very durable wood for salt water exposure) stateroom, three bunks and a master bedroom in the bow. I had a small cabin near the galley with my own toilet. There were many brass and stainless steel fittings that I had to polish to mirror finish. My "job" as a "cabin boy" was to care for the basic maintenance and appearance of the boat (wash the dried salt off the decking, polish and polish some more, clean the galley after meals, wash dishes and china, make sure the bedding, towels, etc. were fresh for each trip {the Causey's maid would come to pick up soiled linens and laundry items from the boat}, etc.). I was paid $8.00/hr. for the tasks I performed for Mr. and Mrs. Causey. She was the daughter of the founder of the Simpsom-Lee Paper Company. So there was a lot of money and wealth here. They lived on a bluff in Everett, Washington, in an upper-end "cottage-like" home (actually about 3,000 sq. feet of house) that looked as if it could have been in story book England. I also ran errands for Mr. Causey. To do this, since I was age 16, he let me drive his 230SKL Mercedes Sport convertible, gray with red leather upholstery. Another part of my "job" was to go with the Causeys on the weekends, when weather was good, to sail the Puget Sound and San Juan Islands. And, yes, I was paid throughout the trip! Mr. Causey taught me how to sail, literally. They had no children, so, I guess, I was also fulfilling their desire to have a son, without all the financial responsibility that attaches to raising a child. I was a "surrogate" son. One of the things I observed about these older, cultured people was how gracious and kind they were. Their money was not inherited as much as they were able to manage their wealth rather than some I've seen who let money "manage" them, and not in a good way. The Causeys treated everyone they met with respect and good manners, including their hired help.

I recall one sailing trip to Friday Harbor, San Juan Islands (near Canada), in particular, where I was given a lesson in good manners by Mrs. Causey. We usually ate together in the stateroom dinning area. On this particular occasion, we had a lunch, pre-prepaired by the Causey's chef (yes, they had an in-house chef). The lunch consisted of roast beef sandwiches with the crusts cut away, chutney, celery sticks filled with cream cheese and caviar, fresh peach tart, and lemonade punch, and tea. After eating my fill, I was asked by Mrs. Causey if I wanted more food. Thinking I was proper in saying, "No Thank you mam, I've had enough," Mrs. Causey stated, "Young man, never say 'I've had enough.' Always say, 'I've had sufficiency.'" So, that was my very first lesson in proper English etiquette.

Back to Uncle Steve. He would take me fishing in the Puget Sound. We would use "long lines" which were held by hand while trolling for salmon, dolly-varden (aka bull trout), and sea-run cutthroat trout. When there was an extreme low tide forecast, we'd leave on the outgoing tide, early on a foggy morning, and travel the 'banks' (shallow waters) to Mission Beach, some 3 miles away, where we would catch Dungeness Crab (limit: 12 apiece). As the slack tide came about, we'd row (yes, we rowed a two-man long boat) some 2 more miles, across the Mission banks to Hat Island, where we'd dig two buckets of steamer clams. By this time, in the early afternoon, usually in the Summer months, the westerly winds came up. Steve had rigged a canvas sail to a simple right-angled device. Placing the vertical pole into a precisely cut hole in a forward seat bench, we'd sail toward home on the incoming tide. We'd stop at the mouth of the Snohomish River to catch "shakers" (as Steve called them), young Silver salmon (also know by their native name, "Coho"), about 18 to 22 inches in length.

We'd then sail up the Marysville Slough to the big ditch at the mouth of the Quil Ceda, and into the slip that Steve had built, years previous, and where he kept his boat house and other sea craft paraphernalia that caused one to stare with awe.

Steve also gave me my first "real" drink of hard core alcohol, 151 proof rum. We'd just returned from a "mid-night" low tide clam run, rowing the two-man long boat some 5 miles to Hat Island to dig, by the light of a full moon, our two buckets-full of 'steamers". It was in early January and, although I'd dressed in warm layered clothing, I still felt extremely cold. Steve was able to start a fire on the rocky beach, using some locally requisitioned dry (where he found this is anyone's guess) firewood. I warmed myself and Steve, being the resourceful uncle, found an old, rusty gas can. He took out his "trusty dirk" (This is a wooden-handled German steel knife that was willed to me, about 7 inches in length) and fashioned out the top of the can so he could place hot rooks into the can. This can sat between my spread legs while we rowed home that night. It offered some warmth to the front of my body, but, at approximately 5 degrees Fahrenheit (with a wind chill factor), it didn't offer much to my back and extremities. When we arrived back at the house, Steve handed me a glass that looked a lot like the sacramental glasses they use in church, for the Eucharist. He filled this glass with Hudson's Bay 151 rum and told me to drink it down in one gulp, saying, "This'll warm you up J.P." And Boy Howdy! Sure did! In fact, it felt like someone was sticking the blade of a hot sword down my throat. I coughed and gagged a bit, caught my breath, and immediately ran to the sink for a glass of water. I recall this event so vividly because it was my "first" for very hard liquor. I was 13 years old, and still a "virgin" in many respects.

This grand occasion, to the "banks" and back, was usually planned ahead, with all the family members and relatives coming for a big pot luck feast. The event was usually held outdoors in the Summer months. Steve's wife, Dorothy, had a nice fire started in a brick fire pit nearby. A large 5 gallon canning pot, filled with boiling seawater was on a grate that covered the flames, and the crabs were placed inside to cook, for about 15 minutes. Near to this were stakes of wood, driven into the ground at an angle, where the fillet side of the Salmon were skewered and placed near the Alder wood flames, mostly hot coals, to "smoke-cook," Indian style. The clams were also steamed in the same container as the crabs. Two long picnic tables (hand-built by....you guessed it!) were set with checkerboard oilcloth table coverings (washable with a hose) and we were were ready.

Potato salad, fresh green beans, summer squash, fresh-picked corn on the cob, compote, casseroles, puddings, pies, home-made bread and rolls, usually a green salad few people ate, various libations (non-alcoholic, out of respect for Dorothy's religious belief system; she was a devoted Christian Science member all of her life), and whatever else someone would bring to the fete', provided a fine late afternoon supper for all. We told stories, laughed, ate til our guts could hold no more, and, if we were "lucky" (sic) Steve would get his accordion from the house and he'd play songs for us. Steve also played the mandolin. In fact, he collected them. He had a fine collection at the time of his death in 1991. I bought one of his finest, from Aunt Dorothy, as a remembrance of all these wonderful family times.

One thing I should mention about Steve's "attempts" at music. He could carry a tune; but, his timing was atrocious. I'd studied classical violin, and, subsequently, the guitar. I would try to accompany Steve at times, but I finally gave up trying to keep up or slow down, at his whim. For example, Steve would start a waltz, in ¾ time, as it should be, and finish in 4/4 or 6/8 (double-time). He was not lacking in verve, exuberance, feeling, nor soul when he played music. I think that's one of the other qualities that endeared him to so many people.

Aside from being a master wooden boat builder (Steve worked most of his adult life at the Andersen Boat Yards in Everett, Washington), he was a member, as was Dorothy, of the Mountaineers and Snohomish County Chapter of the Mountain Rescue Squad. During his lifetime, Steve saved 5 people from sure death or a lifetime of crippling injuries.

In one harrowing occasion, a man had fallen over a dockside railing, near Steve's place of work (this was in the 1950s). The man fell, striking his head, rendering him unconscious, into the water. Steve was alerted by a boy who'd seen the man fall. Steve came running to the man's aid and fished him out of the water with a pike pole (a tool with a long wooden handle and a "pick-like" end, used by loggers, to push logs apart and direct them forward, while floating logs down a stream to lumber mills, throughout the Northwest, in those days). It was a time before CPR and Steve did what he knew from his First Aid Mountain Rescue training. He placed the man over a railing and pulled the man's arms in a forward motion, while the man's torso bent forward. Apparently, this method was effective, because the man vomited water and was revived.

By the time the fire department and ambulance arrived on the scene, and a crowd had gathered around, the victim was sitting upright and joking with Steve.

Steve went on with his daily routine, but some two or three days later, an envelope came to him. Inside the envelope were 5 brand new $100 bills and a thank you note from Hon. Chas. Moody, who happened to be the CEO and President of the Sea-First National Bank, at the time; the victim of the fall off the dock. In those days, $500 was a lot of money; probably equivalent to $3,000 in today's currency. So, I guess the lesson here is to always try to "play it forward" and help others; you never know what good fortune may come your way as a result. At least, it'll make you feel good. The account of Uncle Steve's heroism was all over the Everett Herald Newspaper and the Seattle Post-Intelligencer; but Steve, being a modest man, never looked for accolade or fame; even though, in many people's eyes he deserved much more favor than he received in life. He and Dorothy never had children of their own, but they helped raise my younger cousin, Billy, into a fine, hardworking young man. Billy became, eventually, a railroad yardman supervisor. Our family never seemed to stray very far from the rail lines.

Steve and Dorothy also helped many other family members, financially and otherwise, throughout their lives. They were loving and truly loved by all those who came in contact with them. Steve even helped me build my first row boat and, he decided to retire from the boat yard when "tupper craft", as he called fiberglass boats, came into vogue. He had a small wood shop near his home where he'd repair and build bird houses, furniture, cabinets and other items. He relished making miniature boxes, figures, and such to give to folks and family members as gifts and keepsakes. He would often decorate them with Tyrolean art to honor where his father came from, the Austrian Alps. Our family had a "connectivity" that, I feel, is so lacking in today's modern "wi-fi" world. Wi-fi is not nearly as "personal."

So Uncle Steve and Aunt Dorothy were very dear to me, as second parents, who lived within a stone's throw from our house on the banks of the Quil Ceda. When Dorothy passed away, in 2014, some 22 days after my Mother's passing (they were "like sisters" she'd told me), I learned that Dorothy had made me co-executor of her will, along with her niece (on her side of the family), Mary "Midge" McDonald. Dorothy, before she moved to a retirement center in Marysville, had sold the land that Stephen, her father-in-law, had purchased. She sold the land back to the Tulalip Tribes. She had told me it was her intent, and my grandfather's wishes, that the land return to its rightful owners, The Tulalip people.

Dorothy and Steve were very frugal, practical, self-sufficient people. They grew most of their food and, what Steve didn't glean from the waters, they would learn to make. The estate was substantial. They both took great pains to learn the Native Culture and they befriended many of the tribal families on the Tulalip "Nation" (as I like to call it). In fact Steve and Dorothy learned the indigenous ways so well (weaving baskets, how to braid cedar bark hats, articles of clothing, and nets for catching fish, making deer antler halibut hooks, sleeping mats from cat tail reeds, etc.) that they were giving hands-on demonstrations, and talks to outside folks (those who lived off the Reservation) and various organizations. At one time the University of Washington ethnic archaeologists came to see their works and compare it to artifacts in their possession; commenting that the workmanship was excellent and a true representation of the Northwest Tribal Culture. Good friends of both my parents and Steve and Dorothy, Stan and Joann Jones (Stan was Tribal Chairman for many years, saying, "They keep electin' me….guess no body else wants the job!") told these esteemed folks, "you should have come to us, we would have saved you a lot of time….we know how Steve and Dorothy do this and it's authentic."

Stan had taught Steve, in the early 1940s, how to make a one-man dug out canoe. Steve diligently hand-crafted the vessel and was invited to a one-man race with the Lummi Tribe, north of the Tulalips. The object was to paddle out, about 200 yards, in the bay, tip the canoe over, rock it back and forth until most of the water was out, get back in and paddle back to shore. The fastest one back won the race. Guess who won? Yep, you guessed it... Steve. The Tulalips made Steve an honorary Tulalip Tribal Member after that race. The tribes were very proud of the way Steve had honored them and how his casual, discreet manner always showed respect for the Tribes (I say tribes because the Tulalips comprise an amalgam of 5 basic local tribes around the Snohomish River Delta and surrounding area). These stories and facts were related to me by my Uncle Steve, Aunt Dorothy, The Jones Family, and other family members who witnessed same. I was personally present for some and, Stan and Joanne Jones are dear, long-term friends of both Steve and Dorthy as well as my parents, who related some facts. I have personally spoken with Stan and Joanne on many occasions, having Stan tell of the "old ways." Some of the cultural information was gleaned from the Tulalip Hibulb Cultural Center, Stan Jone's published Autobiography, and the University of Washington's Northwest Native American History web site.

WHAT IS MENTAL ILLNESS?

I think most of us know what drug addiction or dependence is. We surely know the difference between "street" drugs (those illegally sold by near-do-well wannabee "pharmacists" or more commonly termed "pushers.") They too often have their own habit to support. Drug dependence and addiction can successfully be treated, in the right setting, and with the right anti-agents in place. This can sometimes take place in a fairly short period of time.

With mental illness, after one has been correctly diagnosed, it usually takes a lifetime to learn how to manage the illness. Let's break it down: "mental", meaning having to do with the brain, nervous system, how we think, reason, compute, and function as a "normal" human being (I use the term "normal" in the sense of how most people behave, in their culture, most of the time; how we eat, sleep, make love, work, play, interact, feel, exhibit emotions, or act in common). When one is mentally ill, one doesn't act "normal." Often times, behavior is compromised by the chemical-electrical impulses in his/her brain to where acting "normal" cannot be achieved. I say "cannot" because certain receptors in the brain are either blocked or made to malfunction in a way that causes the sufferer to act out or act in a manner unacceptable to his/her peers or family members. It's not that person's fault. It's just that there is a chemical imbalance in the brain and nervous system of those who suffer. With the proper medications, interventions, and "continuum of care," people who suffer from mental illness can lead productive, "normal" lives. They can be contributors to society.

One of my more recent research sources, "Infectious Madness" (copyright 2015), written by the esteemed Dr. Harriet A Washington (Ph.D.), a recognized authority in psychology, brain research, disease pathology, and causal factors related to the "parthenogenesis origins" of mental illness holds that much of mental illness derives from patho-genetic sources. Supporting Dr. Washington in this research are medical research Doctors E. F. Torrey, R.H. Yolken and a French doctoral candidate Herve' Perron, who jettisoned his thesis to study retroviruses (viruses that change RNA into DNA, such as AIDS). Coupled with their research on pathogens that "infect" people and have now been proven to contribute to such mental illness diagnoses such as schizophrenia and bi-polar, Perron's discovery was the nail on the coffin that Torrey and Yolken were looking for. With their combined research, modern psychiatry was introduced to new methodology that now embraces pathogenic sources (pgs.61-71, "Infectious Madness"). In addition, these researchers also found a significant correlation with "seasonal" incidence related to, for example, the "flu season" in winter. People seem to indicate more schizophrenic behaviors and diagnosis in the winter and early spring. This has been documented worldwide (Ibid. "Infectious Madness").

Torrey and Yolken also found a high incidence of schizophrenia in children whose mothers had handled cats. It seems a parasite, *Taxoplasma gondii,* is responsible for infecting and causing aberrations in brain tissue that manifests as schizophrenia later in the child's development. These doctors have replicated studies that confirm *T. gondii's* causative factors and how it infects ("Infectious Madness", pgs. 66 -71) the genetic structure of a fetus. This creature is also responsible for the disease Toxoplasmosis which has flu-like symptoms, at first, but eventually infects the brain causing mental retardation, seizures, retinal damage, deafness, and microcephaly (a small head, disproportionate to the growth of the rest of the body), and inflammation of the brain, also known as encephalitis. Gone unchecked, this parasitic infection can cause major damage to other organs in the body: heart, eyes, liver, inner ears, and kidneys. Doctors continue to warn pregnant women to stay clear of cats during their pregnancy, to wash their hands thoroughly, and disinfect counter tops and other surfaces where the family cat may walk. Due to the aggressive nature of *T. gondii,* Torrey has estimated that one in four adults in the United States is probably infected with the parasite. In France, where a lot of food is consumed "raw," the estimated infection rate is 50% of the adult populace. African countries also have very high rates (some as high as 80%); especially in West Africa where raw meat and unsanitary food preparation techniques abound (Ibid, pg. 67).

It seems, our ancestors, sometime around the time the Dinosaurs went extinct, inherited retroviruses that, eventually, and by chance, ensconced themselves into the humanoid reproductive systems; thus, guaranteeing co-existence in perpetuity. (Ibid. p.62)

So, what we now have, as a definition of mental illness, is based on a combination of environmental, chemo-electrical effects, pathogenic, and genome sources that cause significant behavioral changes in human beings. These facts all add up to one conclusion in my book: Mental Illness is a disease and should be treated and recognized as such by all our esteemed medical/ pharmaceutical/ insurance and Congressional Representatives. We should have "parity" in acknowledging this fact and full funding for treatment and continuum of care. But, alas, we do not because, the "profit margins" of these large corporate behemoths gets in the way.

Some of the world's greatest people suffered from mental illnesses: Alexander Hamilton was said to suffer fits of extreme depression and anxiety when faced with decisions he had to make. Jean Paul Sartre, the great French philosopher, was said to have extreme mood swings that might be diagnosed as Bi-polar I in today's psychiatric world. Don Quixote, the famous character who was a creation of Cervantes, has been said to be the very persona of Cervantes' ego and quixotic personality, running off to save fair maidens, chasing the demons in the watch tower (the infamous windmill) and having, at his side, Sancho Panza (his conscience, guide to reason, and benefactor of sanity), fighting in the lost age of chivalry and gallantry. In fact, Don Quixote is used in psychiatric training as an example of someone who suffers from delusions or illusions of grandeur or multiple-personality syndrome. Abraham Lincoln suffered bouts of extreme Depression and Anxiety. Vincent Van Gogh, the famous French artist, was said to be schizophrenic. Winston Churchill had what could be described as Bi-polar 2 in today's psychiatric jargon. There are many more examples of famous, and not so famous people, who I could name. But, my point is that the "mentally ill" are us, we are them, or some of us will be at some point in our lives. To stigmatize them is to stigmatize ourselves. Also, in my opinion, Dr. Washington and her cohorts in "Infectious Madness", are all "fire fighters."

Speaking of sanity, I often hear people compare mental illness with being "insane." This couldn't be further from what is, in reality, a legal term. Insanity can be "temporary" as in the nature of a "crime of passion." For example: a man who, inadvertently, walks in on his wife having a tryst with a paramour, picks up a knife and stabs both of them. In the "normal" world, this defendant would have no inclination to behave in such a manner. So, his attorney may claim that his client was "temporarily insane" (without reason and good judgment: to withhold violence and what he, at the time, perceived to be retribution.) Insanity can be relegated to "foolish" or "unreasonable" behavior and, I have found it not included in the DSM IV or V, the psychiatrist's "bible" for diagnoses, for this very reason. It is not a diagnostic term. Insanity is a legal term. Personally, I like the definition of insanity that Martin Luther King gave when referencing what we were doing in and to Vietnam in 1967. On April 4, 1967, in a less famous, but just as poignant speech as the one he gave later ("I have a dream….") at the Lincoln Memorial in Washington D.C., Dr. King said, "insanity is doing the same thing, over and over and expecting different results." We tend to get ourselves embroiled in wars that are quagmires and fraught with no end in sight unless, we just "quit" as we did in Vietnam. I believe our involvement in the Middle East is a good example of what Dr. King was referencing.

Unfortunately, mental illness has taken a "bad rap" in our modern society. It has been stigmatized, relegated to those who "go crazy and commit mass killings' (actually, 1/100th of 1% of those diagnosed actually commit a violent act on others {National Institute of Mental Health (NIMH) and the Center for Disease Prevention and Control (CDC),{2013/2015 respectively}. In fact, diagnosed people are more prone to commit an act of violence on themselves than others (same statistical source as above). But, those who do commit these violent acts are sometimes said to have had a "mental illness" issue in their past and, thus, they get all the press and hoopla which only adds to the negative "stigmas" we face today.

Many of those I spend time with in the Depression and Bi-polar Support Alliance (DBSA) relate how they've been shunned, castigated, and targeted by bullies and people who don't have a clue as to what mental illness really is. Often, those who stigmatize are often the sufferer's own family members.

So, part of my task here, in authoring this book, is to also enlighten, educate, arouse, and motivate people to bring mental illness out of the shadows where it can be, once and for all, understood and embraced as a "human condition."

The NIMH has also documented, over many years of clinical reviews, how our modern day societies have relegated workable treatment modalities and solutions into some backwater swamp where they languish in perpetuity. Dr. Paul Harsh's HBOT applications are a good example of this; but, Big Medicine, Big Pharmaceuticals, Big Insurance have historically relegated such viable approaches to the back room, labeling them as "anecdotal," coincidental results, where the light of day is unreachable and negated. Only recently have such treatment modalities been able to resurface with some clout and backing from folks who are adamant to have what's workable, beyond what's foisted upon the public now, as acceptable, relevant and efficient. I fear, with the current political climate (2017), we may move back into the "dark ages" of profit taking to protect the "Biggies."

According to the NIMH and the CDC, 1 in 10 people will have a mental health diagnosis in their lifetime. One in three will have a "mental health" episode at some point in their lives; some will recover from their episode; others, maybe not. These are precursors of the "fire" I speak of. It will not be of any less tenure in years to come. If left unabated, it will continue to grow, as it does now.

I recently met with two Natural-path doctors who are forming a partnership with an engineer friend of mine. They are starting up a hyperbaric/natural-path/holistic therapy group, focusing, primarily, on veterans who have been diagnosed with PTSD and other ailments (including mental illness and Traumatic Brain Injury {TBI}). These providers intend to use healthy exercise, dietary changes that benefit the body (no more burgers and fries gang), good, clean mountain air (as clean as one can get it),constant hydration with filtered water to wash the toxins from one's body, flora maintenance (where good gut bacteria are interjected into a person's metabolic balance) and, emotional support groups that include family, friends, community members who will volunteer as "peer supporters" (much like Alcoholic Anonymous Sponsors), and they will provide an in-house environment, at minimal cost to the patient. They are also seeking grant money and Veteran's Administration financial support to pay for their patient's treatment and stay at the facility. As of 2017, they are in the process of remodeling an old house near Snoqualomie, Washington to fit the patient's needs. Part of this approach is for continued research and clinical trials that some in our medical professions and U.S. Government now support.

When I interviewed these doctors (who shall go nameless here for their own privacy and protection), they told me about some of their colleagues who were "run out" of the business by the Government "tag teams", sponsored by the "Biggies," (Big pharmaceutical conglomerates, Big insurance consortiums, and Big medical corporations) who have lobbyists on retainers in Washington D.C., just for this purpose. One doctor told me a close colleague of hers was "disappeared" for a period of time. When she spoke to this person, after months of no contact, she was no longer interested in practicing her trade. She opened a health supplements store and chose not to speak of her ordeal again. So, as I claimed in the Preface of this book, I'm going to "piss off" a lot of people….some in very high places; but, this story is way past the pull date. It needs telling, and I fully intend to tell it.

We desperately need a "continuum of care" in this country; a system that provides 24/7 care availability to anyone diagnosed with either a mental illness and/or substance abuse issues. This "safety net", if you will, will provide access to help, immediately, when necessary. Instead of having to wait in a jail cell because someone broke a window or peed in public, and was known to have a mental health issue by arresting officers, this person would be placed into a triage assessment protocol and have a program available to them, medications if necessary, and someone to monitor their progress on a, at first, daily basis. Over time, this approach, I have documented, will save taxpayers the costs of building more jails, prisons, infusing now overburdened social network systems and caseloads, and offer those who suffer a pathway to success.

I should emphasize here that those who are placed into such a system do not get a "free ride." The plan I will delineate in later chapters requires significant involvement, work, and commitment on the part of the participant/patient. In turn, once rehabilitated and in control of the self-management of his/her ailment and/or addiction cycle, the recipient/patient will be expected to act as a sponsor/ advocate for those coming after him/her in the program (i.e. "play it forward."). The monetary savings of this program are substantial, when calculated over time. It certainly will be much more effective and productive than what is currently being done in our broken systems.

One asks: How would my system marry with what currently exists? I would suggest that we already have a framework (Medicaid and Medicare) to build upon. All we need do is expand the core to include the "continuum of care" structure and protocols. In return, cost savings could be phenomenal: not building more jails or prisons, no more expanded and overworked social services programs and staff, no more welfare systems that are abused and unkempt in terms of overall financial accountability, nor a V.A. system that has been broken (in many locales), and other Government waste that just puts more money into programs that don't work (i.e. The War on Drugs, etc.). Many of these "programs" are just a rat hole for more bureaucracy and fiscal mismanagement because some Congressman/woman had an epiphany soundbite but didn't think far enough ahead to put a fiscal note to their Bill and, as a result, it cost the taxpayers millions of dollars; with nothing to show for it. These things happen; they're happening today, as I write this.

If you want a running score of the previous claim, I suggest you read Patrick Kennedy's recent book, "A Common Struggle." As a sufferer himself, he tells how he got caught up in a system that treats its patients as if they are cattle in a coral, plodding along, treating some and avoiding others ("selective intervention"= if you have the $ or insurance coverage, you get treatment; otherwise, you are outta' luck Jack). It happened to him and he's from a fairly well-known family.

It happened to me too; except the medical team screwed up and didn't find my insurance coverage for about a month. A month wasted on a space in a hospital I never should have been in in the first place! Or, maybe they did find the coverage early on and "milked the system" for all they could get. All I know is I was given 23 different medications over a 19 week period that were supposed to help me with Major Depression. None of the medications worked; but I sure had the side effects (diarrhea, headaches, sweating, chills, muscle cramping, vision issues {blurring or trouble focusing}, confusion, palpitations, loss of appetite, no motivation, no libido, loss of sleep, I could go on but I think you get the point). I was a guinea pig for some big pharmaceutical company to do clinical trials upon. I can prove this because when I asked the contracted psychiatrist (most major hospitals contract psychiatric work; it's cheaper than keeping them on staff), "Which pill works Doc?" He just stared at me and didn't have an answer. Shit happens. But, it doesn't need to happen to me or anyone else for that matter!

So, by investing in a system that provides a potential lifeline to people, when they need it, and by funding said program, in perpetuity, the U.S. Government and the taxpayer would save, in the long run, billions of dollars. By passing legislation that, once and for all, acknowledges that mental illness and substance abuse ARE, in fact, diseases, with symptoms, indices, and physical, mental, and physiological manifestations, and viable treatments, we would go a long way toward correcting an ill that has festered for many years in this country. Our Medicaid and Medicare programs would be greatly enhanced by having this system in place, where anyone who is a citizen, green card holder, visa holder would qualify for care.

"Socialized medicine" you say. You bet! We've been teetering on this precipice long enough. It's about time we take the plunge. Many other modernized countries, besides those in Europe, have done so: Canada, Australia, Philippines, in some form, Japan, China and Russia, of course, and India is now in the process of revamping and modernizing its social health care systems to make them more efficient and streamlined (USA Today, June 2016). A healthy country is a successful country. It thrives; and it prospers. Its citizens are more willing to work for the betterment of all, rather than bitch and complain, as we saw in the recent, contentious 2016 elections in this (U.S.A.) country.

In this regard, many countries in Europe are way out ahead of the curve on this one. Sweden, Finland, Denmark, Great Britain, Germany, France, and Switzerland, all have programs similar to what I've mentioned above. And, what's more, THEY WORK! We, as a Nation that prides itself in innovation, technology, ownership, and modernity, are failing ourselves by allowing sick people to roam our streets, homeless, begging for food and shelter, and seeking medical care, when they can, in our overburdened emergency rooms of every major hospital in this country (NIMH and CDC statistics 2007-2016). These folks also "panhandle" for money. You can see them, now, on almost every major on-ramp of our Nation's highway system, street corner, and sidewalk.

I would only ask that you NOT give these folks money. Many have mental health, drug dependency issues, including alcoholism. Gift them a clothing voucher at a local Good Will ($10.00 will outfit a person with slacks, shoes, a shirt, and sometimes, a coat or a dress, jeans, slippers, a jacket or robe); some food or a voucher to buy some food at a local grocery; water (many are poorly hydrated; hospital staff see this when these folks come into the ER {CDC annual stats}), and, if you are ambitious, as some friends and I were last year (2016), you can make up 3 x 5 note cards with the name, address, phone number and contact person's name written on them for local food banks, shelters, emergency care facilities, hostels, churches (wrap these cards in cellophane tape to waterproof them) or, any place you know of that's willing to help the "down and out." Hand these cards out. These people will thank you for caring. I know this. I've done it. Try to remember the old adage: "ask not for whom the bell tolls...it tolls for thee." In other words, some of these folks could be us, if not for a stroke of bad luck (job loss, death of a breadwinner in the family, illness, etc.) we could be out on the streets too. This conflagration "fire" isn't getting smaller folks, it's growing daily and it will, eventually, consume everything we have, resource-wise, in this Country. Unless, we do something pro-active, sustainable, and massive to stop it or slow it down.

We already have a social welfare system that's inundated, has overworked staff, and caseloads that are impossible to manage in an efficient and effective manner(U.S. Bureau of Social Work Statistical Reporting, 2007-2015). Our prisons and jails are overcrowded, with more on the way, each day (U. S. Department of Justice annual reporting 2007-2015), our hospitals (to use one of my grandfather's sayings) "runn-et over" with too many people seeking, if not care, then shelter from the cold and wet, a hot meal, and someone to talk to (CDC annual reports 2007-2015). Criminal behavior is on the rise (mostly property crimes and white collar crimes like identity theft, computer theft of data, etc. (U.S. Brueau of Criminal Justice and Records 2007-2015); although, violent crimes have dropped, nation-wide, they have risen in some urban areas (Chicago, for example 2014-2016),

I don't mean to be the harbinger of bad news here, but these statistics and facts need to be brought into the light where we all can see them, clearly and without the (to use a recently coined phrase after the 2016 elections) "alternative facts" (coined by Kellyanne Conway, the President elect's counselor, 2017). Facts are facts. They speak for themselves. You don't change them just to fit a political paradigm or a personal agenda. So, here are some REAL facts, in regard to the topic of this book:

On average, per year, since 2010, 22 veterans commit suicide, each day, in the United States of America (source: Department of Defense {although the D.O.D. only counts "active duty" personnel at "2" per day, D.O.D. 2013 Annual Report), but the CDC says it is twenty-two per day(2011-2016 statistical reports from the Center for Disease Prevention and Control). These deaths ARE preventable and a "continuum of care" would provide the "safety net" we desperately need to make this frightening statistic go away. The Veterans Administration, whose scandals and failure to "keep watch" over those we put into harm's way (since the Vietnam Conflict) {all I've been able to document} because Veteran Administration records only "go back as far as the veteran is still alive", I was told this by a senior V.A. Administrator {this claim might not be true, I'm also researching this for a follow up}.

Doctor Paul G. Harch has documented an average 83% success rate in treating veterans using HBOT (Hyperbaric Oxygen Therapy) coupled with the more traditional forms of therapy and intervention (Harch, "The Oxygen Revolution" copyright 2016, 3rd edition). This means: no more night sweats, nightmares, tremors, hallucinations/flashbacks to gruesome experiences, no more alcohol or street drug abuse, less anxiety and psychotic manifestations, better cognitive orientations, better family relationships, less divorce, more employ-ability and, if desired, return to active duty or employment. And, no more pills! (Hence, why Big Pharma doesn't want it in the mainstream of therapy).

One thing I wish Clint Eastwood had done with the movie "American Sniper"(2016) is delineate, at the end, the PTSD that the main character was suffering from. I can understand why he didn't; because, that would have been a whole new story, with another main character. But the indices of someone suffering from PTSD were finely depicted in this movie. They did a superb job (both actor and director, etc.). The story still needs to be told about these folks...they ARE us! They suffer, bleed, get put on a "medication roulette" merry-go-round, agonize, beg for acknowledgment, and ask for our help, and sometimes, reject our offers of help (that's the illness talkin' here...remember that, if you are tryin' to help!); even when they cannot recognize they need our help. So, I'm telling the rest of the story.

Dr. Bennet Omalu, a distinguished forensic pathologist, in 2010, was able to isolate and correctly diagnose CTE a form of protein plaque that forms in the brains of, mainly, professional athletes who suffer repetitive hits to the head in games such as football, soccer, and hockey. These proteins cause the synaptic transfers in the neurons of the brain to misfire or not fire at all and, reroute to an area of the brain that causes aberrant or illogical behavior. The movie "Concussion", in 2016, by Will Smith, who played the part of Dr. Omalu and co-produced the picture, gave rise to an intensive legal battle, between retired NFL players and the NFL, over successive concussions they received and subsequently suffered from. A settlement was reached in 2016.

Dr. Omalu's research was instrumental in why we now have a "concussion protocol" in all professional sports today. We also need to invoke this protocol in pee-wee leagues, high schools, and semi-professional sports where head-to head or head to ground contacts are common. This is being done, sporadically, as I write this. It needs to be done, legislatively, in all of the United States of America, and the world (I can only speak for my country, which I desperately defended in Vietnam, and still love to this day!). Dr. Omalu was able to autopsy some rather famous NFL football players who committed suicide shortly after they "retired" (due to mental health or physical impairment concerns) or they died as the result of "tau protein" buildup in the brain. (Sports Illustrated, 2016 and, Journal of Pathological Medicine 2015-2016).

I'll be giving you verifiable facts throughout this book. But, this book isn't just about facts and figures. It's a REAL story, about REAL people. People like you and I, loved ones, your husband, wife, child, uncle, aunt, sister, brother, co-worker, or close friends who suffer from something we CAN and SHOULD do something about fixing. The steps to take in contacting your legislature are simple. The hard part is "sustainability"; staying with the effort until it is changed; and then "getting involved" so no 'near-do-wells' (read: people out for profit at the expense of others) fuck it up again.

Too often, we hear some politician boast about this program or that program they've foisted in some bill before Congress. Often times, the rhetoric looks good; the "soundbite" and the press build up are awesome. We feel good that we are solving what ails the society; especially, if we supported it. However, oftentimes, no "fiscal note" (how to pay for it) is included with the legislation or, it's attached to some other bill that siphons off the money that would have gone to repairing the very thing we thought was going to get repaired. This happens all the time in Congress. How do I know this? I read the Congressional Record and, I have a second cousin who worked for the GSA (Government Services Administration) in Washington D.C. in the 1970s and 1980s. This 'crap' goes on all the time, just to make someone "look good." We currently have a President (2017) who relies on prevaricating to "look good." I will try to refrain from political commentary, because that is not the intent of this missive.

Remember "Tailhook"? The sexual abuse scandal where, in 1992, more than 100 U.S. Navy and Marine officers sexually abused and assaulted more than 80 women during an aviation convention in Las Vegas. As a result, the then Secretary of the U.S. Navy, Sean O'Keefe, was forced to instill programs to ward off such demeaning behavior in the future. Many of the victims of this ordeal suffered PTSD-like symptoms for years. That, in my opinion, was something the media should have followed-up on but didn't.

So, now, some 25 years later, we're learning than not much has changed. In a scathing expose', by Paula Coughlin, the woman who first broke the story of "Tailhook" in the early 90s, another report of lewd pictures of Marine Corps women are being circulated, on Facebook, without their consent. What's more, accompanying these pictures are degrading commentary, abusive notations, and outright suggestions of rape and sexual assault.

The military commander in charge has called for "mutual trust and respect" and he called for every Marine "to demonstrate the highest integrity and loyalty to fellow Marines." (Robert Neller, Commandant)

Unfortunately, this kind of rhetoric pales, by comparison, to the potential damage it does to the morale, readiness, and fitness of those who serve. It compromises the "spirit du corps." We cannot afford to have a military command so complacent and negligent that it allows "boys will be boys" to prevail over military discipline and codes against sexual harassment. This sort of behavior creates a sexually hostile work environment. Negligent commanders. who turn their heads the other way, need to be disciplined.

Those who cultivate such a climate, need to be Courts-Martialed and put in the stockade or, drummed out of service with a Dishonorable Discharge.

Of those cases brought before Command, in 2014, some 44% of victims were encouraged to drop the issue, and 41% said no action was taken. Only 13% went as far as a courts-martial action. Coughlin has documented over 20,000 service members, in 2014, who were raped or sexually assaulted. Many of these cases were mishandled or, obvious actions of gender discrimination were committed when commanders "washed" them under the rug, so to speak, and tried to deliberately hide the fact from public scrutiny. How does Coughlin know this? She's an attorney now and, she was in the military when "Tailhook" broke out. She was part of the investigative team that brought the scandal to light.(U.S.A. Today article, 2-9-2017).

We need more "fire fighters" like Paula Coughlin who are not afraid to uncover a culture of misogyny and discrimination against service women. We have a moral obligation to do this. The psychological damage this sort of behavior doe is mammoth; it feeds right into the "fire," Big Time!

MY STORY

The other day, a woman, upon learning my last name (Crawley), asked me if I was related to the "Crawleys of Downton Abbey" (a recent television series in 2015-2016 broadcast by the Public Broadcasting System {PBS}, but alas, a fictitious account of jolly old English aristocracy prior to World War 1 in Britain, with a Manor, butlers, handmaidens, cooks and waitstaff, chauffeurs and such). The program was a big "hit" with some folks and, it had been well-acted, well researched and vetted as to factual trappings of the era. I didn't have the heart to tell her 'no.' So I politely told her, "Not that I know of." But, I did inform her that she could visit Crawley, on the Internet, and find an old abbey and site of what once was an estate, now a township park, named Crawley. There also is a college there and a town modernized in the aftermath of German bombings during World War Two. Crawley is directly across the Channel from France, about 89 miles south of London, and during this War, it was in direct line of fire from the Luftwaffe who continually bombed and strafed the town to pieces.

I did not go into darkness willingly. I would consider my childhood to be "average." I think, considering the fact I was a "service brat" as all children of military personnel were called in the day, the only "advantage" we had over other children is the fact we were exposed to other cultures, belief systems, languages, and traditions which widened our perspectives of the world. Personally, I think all people should travel and learn about other cultures around the world. Perhaps we would have much less conflict as a result.

In1944, I was born February 27 in Corpus Christi, Texas at the Spahn Hospital (I always found that word "spawn" to be rather odd for a Hospital name. One usually "spawns" before one goes to the hospital to have a baby, oh well). My father was in the United States Navy and, we were soon transferred to Pensacola, Florida where my dad was training to be a pilot. He was flying Stearman bi-planes (the two-wing jobs that had a reciprocating, prop engine, with 9 cylinders). His job was to land said aircraft on a rocking and rolling aircraft carrier, at night, with limited sight parameters. Obviously, a lot of potential pilots "washed out" of this program due to what was called "visual acuity" night vision issues. My dad was one of them; although he was able to fly PBY seagoing aircraft, later on, during daylight hours. If the aircraft needed to "ditch" it could land on water because the fuselage was made like a big boat, and the wings had "sponsons" (Large metal flotation chambers, hanging down from each wing, about midway down the length of the wing, that allowed the aircraft to stay stable in the water). These were uncertain times, World War Two was in full swing. The Japanese had bombed Pearl Harbor (1941) and our Nation was at war, mostly in the Pacific. We didn't get fully engaged in Europe until almost the end of the War.

I don't remember much of my childhood before age 5; however I do remember being taken to a "root cellar" at my aunt and uncle Ed's place in Texas when a tornado came through the area. A "root cellar" was used as a cold storage area, dug into the ground, where natural preserves and canned vegetables, fruit, and other items were kept. All I remember was the sound, like a locomotive, roaring through at close range with a howling sound and the crashing of trees and buildings above me.

Later, around age 6, I also remember being bitten on the right side of my head by one of the neighbor's German Shepard dogs. I still have a scar where this dog bit me. I don't know what happened to the dog, but I don't remember ever seeing him again. I was not afraid of dogs after that. Our family, to this day, has had dogs as pets; currently, it's a mutt (Lab mix) named Simba, and a Corgi, named Cisco. Dogs are very loyal companions, unlike many humans.

When my father was stationed in Long Beach, California and San Diego, I remember playing with my good friends, Ann Seavold and David Bills.

Ann's father was a pharmacist's mate in the U.S. Navy and, David's father was a Navy doctor, a gynecologist to be exact. It seemed everywhere our parents were transferred, the other families would transfer too. We kind of "grew up" together: California, Hawaii, Japan, and back to the good 'ol U.S. of A.

In Long Beach, I remember Annie and me hunting tigers and lions in the high grasses of a field near our Navy housing project. To kids 5 and 6 years old, these were imaginary beasts, but, all the same "real" in our creative intellects. The hills above the field were dotted with oil pumping stations (Signal Hill) where the big "horses heads" (as I liked to call them) would dip and pull the oil up from the ground. We always saw these big machines as if they were dinosaurs (in a way, we were correct because that's where a lot of oil comes from, the remnants of long decayed animal carcasses and floral decomposition) and, we never ventured up onto the hill. It was "off limits." And, to make sure, it was fenced with concertina wire and "keep out" signage. Ours was a giant fantasy and, a world of wonder and excitement. We didn't have I-pods or television to distract us. We made the best of what we had...using our own fertile imaginations. We made up games and challenges. Often, we'd take an existing game like "hide and seek" and merge it with another, like "find the hidden treasure (usually a candy bar)" that one of our friends would hide for us to find; but we couldn't find each other first or we'd be disqualified from the find. Annie usually won this game. A lot. She was small and could hide really well, and she seemed to have a "sixth sense" for candy. Personally, I think her "smeller" was just as good as a dogs. Dogs' sense of smell is about 16 times more efficient than a humans (United States Veterinary Association Journals). The only humans that may come close are the bush peoples of Africa and the Australian outback. It's said that both of these cultures can "smell" where water is located, dig a hole in the parched ground, and find enough moisture to drink. That, I did see on television, on a National Graphic special.

We did not have a television in our home until I was well passed my 16th year. My father believed in education and reading. He devoured books. I was allowed to go up the road, when we lived at Tyee (Tulalip), to my Aunt

Jean (Morgan) and Uncle Bob's place to watch their television, provided I'd finished my homework from school, did my chores, and promised my folks I'd be back home no later than 10:00 P.M. because the next day was usually a school day. I usually had to "endure" a session, nightly, of Lawrence Welk and his troubadours. "A one-a and a-two-a, and a-three-a... da dada da dada...da da." Watch the bubbles come out of the bubble machine, supposedly representing champagne. It was alright, because I grew up liking music, but nightly servings of "One-a, and Two-a, and Three-a" sometimes got a little old, for an hour each night. I wanted to be there because Bob usually fell asleep in his easy chair (he was a delivery truck driver for the Rainier Brewing Company), and Jean would go back to the kitchen. This allowed me "free reign" to watch programs like "Gun smoke" or "I Love Lucy."

One thing I didn't like about going to the Morgan home, though, was that they always seemed to fight with each other. I remember going to their place one evening and, as I was about to open the screen door to their kitchen, an uncooked potato came sailing right through the netting, barely missing my head. Jean would yell and scream at Bob in a very accusatory manner. Bob was a pretty "laid-back" sort of guy. He didn't say much; but you could get his "Irish" up if you pushed too far. And Jean knew which "buttons" to push. This usually went on for about 15-20 minutes and then it was quiet....very quiet. Sometimes I'd peek around the corner, from the living room, to see if someone had killed the other or not. It was verbally violent, then it was over....just like that. The rest of the evening was calm and "relaxed", except for "One-a an a-Two-a..." Well, you get my point, I'm sure.

David and his family had a black and white television set and, we'd go over and watch Hop-along-Cassidy or the Lone Ranger on television. Once in awhile, we'd view a game show, but we found television boring and, we'd soon leave to play outside and invent our own stories and games. Unlike children of today, it didn't take much to stimulate our imaginations or satisfy our curiosities. We weren't over-stimulated or "baked" with so much information that we "shut down", nor did we give in to temptations like pizza commercials and the sugary cereal commercials that children of today's world seem to be inundated with. Ours was a simple world, a naive world to be sure, but, all the same, pretty safe, unassuming, but fun because we made it that way...(Note: We also did not have the epidemic proportions of youth diabetes that now exists in today's world. This can be directly attributed to poor diet and lack of exercise of many of today's youth. From American Diabetic Association publications).

I never thought any thing I did or felt was out of the ordinary. I was a "normal" kid with "normal" emotions and actions. I "fit in" with my peers. I didn't see anything wrong with feeling "down" or "moody" at times. It was "just a phase" my mother would say; "everyone goes through the blues now and then." She was so good at explaining stuff and I bought it, hook, line and sinker. Unfortunately, it wasn't until my junior year in high school that I learned about Major Depression and what my periodic moods, in fact, were.

When Dad was stationed in Alameda, California (NAS, Naval Air Station), I had just began the second grade (1954). They gave me some tests and told my parents I was doing third-grade work. So, I was skipped to the third grade. At the time I thought, "Wow, this is great, I will finish school a year sooner than others." But, there are social and "rite of passage" penalties for being skipped to a higher grade. One doesn't usually experience them until puberty (all the kids in your grade are at least one year older than you are). I had to wait an "extra" year to get my driver's license because all the other kids had theirs. You are the brunt of many jokes like: "Hey Crawley, how's it hangin?"...(Knowing I'm still, most likely, a virgin). I'd only kissed one 'girl', and that was Annie. We'd seen people kiss on T.V. and in movies; and, "ugh!" we'd seen our parents kiss. But, I made the best of it (the teasing and "bullying"), because that's what Mom and Dad expected of me… "turn the other cheek, and press on."

I was also tested in California for musical aptitude. They set up "tone stations" and listening booths where students would be asked to tell the difference in tones, speed of the piece of music being played into their earphones, or try to tell the difference between two very similar passages of music, usually about 8 bars of score. I guess I scored high on these tests because, soon thereafter, I was offered the choice of taking drum or violin lessons. I chose the violin, at age 7. To this day, the only reason, I think, I chose for the violin was because my mother and grandparents liked Viennese waltzes by Johann Strauss or, music from other famous composers like Mozart or Beethoven. One would venture to ask why a seven-year-old, very active, almost to the point of being ADHD (Attention Deficit Hyperactive Disordered...can't sit still or looses attention very easily) kid would not want to beat the holy shit out of a drum set. Go figure!

I excelled at the violin, taking private lessons right through the time we spent in Hawaii, when father was transferred there toward the sunset of his U.S. Navy career (20 years worth). I took lessons and played for 8 ½ years; right up until the time just before entrance into the 9th grade in Marysville High School. I was in the grade school orchestra and, through a wonderful Italian music teacher named Gene Nastri, beloved throughout the Northwest and known for his devoted dedication to the Youth Symphony and school music programs all over Snohomish County, I was able to give wonderful recitals and play in the local Youth Symphony.

Then, girls, cars, and guitars came along. My violin took the back seat because something, at age 13, was happening to my body. I woke up one day with my penis very rigid and hard. At first, I thought something terrible was going on, but I remember some of my guy classmates talking of how they got a big "boner" when certain girls walked down the hallways at school. And they also bragged about "stickin' it" to some gorgeous thing (as a fantasy of course) who all the guys wanted to date but were usually afraid to ask. I soon learned, that folks who brag about stuff like that, usually don't "get any."

I was also introduced to "dirty pictures" that a couple "jock" friends brought to school one day. They were pictures, black and white, of what appeared to be soldiers, on leave, in Japan and they were in all manner of undress and making love with women. Some of these pictures were very graphic, showing everything! So, this is how I, initially, learned about sex. Not by doing it, but by seeing it depicted on black and white, 4 by 5 snapshots, rather "grainy" ones at that.

My father, always the gentleman, told me never to force myself on girls, I learned to treat women with the common respect and dignity one would expect for oneself. I practiced congeniality and kindness, a lot. It did pay off, eventually.

I was dating girls in the lower grades because those in my own peer group, save for two, very good friends, were not inclined to go out with a guy who still had "peach fuzz" for a beard. That didn't hold me down though. I was "horny" and ready for bare....uh!, I mean bear.

My first sexual experience with a girl was in the 9th grade. She was known, by my fellow players on the high school football team, as a "tease." Her reputation was that she'd get a guy all "worked up" and hot and then tell him to take a hike. She "pissed off" a lot of guys this way. It's a wonder she didn't get raped. But, in those days (late 1950s, early 1960s), there was a "code of ethics"; one did not force oneself on another. It wasn't "cool." But, it didn't stop most guys from trying to get to "second base." Most of us respected the word "No."

Anyway, I decided to ask this girl out on a date.(I'll call her Gena, not her real name, but those who'll read this book and went to school with me know who I'm writing about). It would be a stop at the local burger joint and a movie. Then home. Pretty simple and pretty "safe", right? NOT!

When I got back to my seat in the movie theater, Gena told me she wanted to leave and go somewhere "more private." I was somewhat taken back. Here I was, with this good looking girl who seems to be all "hot to trot", but whose reputation as a "cock teaser" preceded her, but she wants to go somewhere "private" with me. I was confused, but I stammered out a meek, "Okay" (I think I said something like that....it was a long time ago, but I do remember, very vividly, parts of this night with Gena).

We wound up at her uncle's beach cabin on Mission Beach (remember the crab banks, earlier?). She drove her car, I was not driving yet (except for my friend Kenny and I taking out an old 1950 Buick from his dad's garage for midnight runs down Rainwater road, just for "practice," lights off by the light of a full moon….we never got caught! And, we always put gas back into the gas tank so the gauge was "on the money" in case Kenny's dad saw less gas than he'd remembered. We had all the bases "covered.")

We ate breakfast at a local Denny's that morning. I was voracious, having expended myself to sheer exhaustion over the past 24 hours. I asked her if she thought I had good potential as a lover. All guys secretly want to know this from the women they sleep with. She told me, for being my "first" time she thought I had, "great potential." That's the words I remember... "you have great potential John," she said. A person doesn't forget words like that. It was the greatest compliment anyone had ever given me. And, I cherish it to this day.

We never "dated" again, but we remained friends throughout high school. My team mates would snicker and kid me about "Gena, Gena, won't do ya beana," and shit like that. But they never knew. I was a loyal subject who would never, until I write this missive now, tell what she and I did on that glorious Spring night and morning in Uncle Charlie's beach cabin at Mission Beach.

Gena went on to marry some stock broker in New York City. She wrote me a couple letters and she told me the guy didn't want a family. He was too selfish to have kids. I knew this broke Gena's heart. They, eventually, divorced and I never heard from her again. So, Gena (you know who you are and I am sure you remember me), I hope you are well and happy in what ever station you now find yourself in life. I will NEVER forget you and, I will always be here for you, when ever or whatever; because that's what loyal friends do.

There were other women, of course, but a man never forgets his "first"; especially if he found an awkward situation to be turned into a glorious experience as was my good fortune to have early in my life. It paved the way for future, healthy relationships, that broke off in friendship; and eventually led to a marriage that has lasted some 44 years as of June, 2016.

I went to college after my graduation from high school. I wanted to "earn my own way," so I never asked for money from my parents. I worked summers at Scott Paper Company, various jobs from "re-mill" where paper products that are defective get "reprocessed," to helping the millwrights in various maintenance jobs from welding to operating a D-12 Caterpillar pushing sawdust into a conveyor belt that went directly to the furnace to heat water and mix it with wood chips that eventually went to the "digester." There, sulfuric acid broke the chips down to what eventually became "pulp," the preliminary ingredient of paper, in all of its forms from toilet paper to fine bond sheets.

I also worked for the Weyerhaeuser Lumber Company as a "green chain laborer." This job really helped a person stay in great physical shape because I was lifting boards off the mill line and stacking them into vertical, uniform, symmetrical stacks. There was an art to this job; one slip up and your stack would fall over. The motions were like a ballet, even cadence and fluid motion without stagnant or radical divergence. The "stacker" had to balance each stack of lumber with "stays" (pieces of wood that balanced the stack to make it even and uniform; otherwise, the stack would veer to the left or right and eventually skew over. The lift operator would not pick up a stack that was uneven for fear that the stack would fall over or collapse.

After working and military service, I met and married my wife, Susan. We have had a successful marriage, by my accounts, with minimal strife and want. Our relationship was bonded by friendship, love, understanding, and compassion. It wasn't until I became mentally ill that our relationship became strained and incongruous.

Unfortunately, my marital partner, has now decided to leave me. I think my illness and alcoholism had a part to play in this; but I really don't know because I'm well into the roads of recovery and reclamation of my life; after a lot of soul searching, tears, and support from self-help groups, therapy, and friends who really care and have learned to put the stigma of mental illness and pretext behind them. Go figure...now that I've paid all my debts (except the home mortgage which is used as a tax deduction), become sober as a church mouse, and healing from my "darkness," surviving my

Depression, in control, having learned how to "manage" my illness (as is the case with most patients...we learn how to "manage" through diet, exercise, the right medications {the fewer the better}, interaction in groups such as the Depression Bi-polar Support Alliance, and use of as many resources as we can muster), my significant other now claims the marriage is "irretrievably broken" (a legal term for "I quit."). I never forced her to be with me, nor was I ever physically abusive. We both drank, she still does (in moderation, always), and things were sometimes said, in haste and in the heat of the moment; but, apologies were always made and, we had one rule: 'come back later and talk it out.' Now, hardly a word is spoken between us, and like the old Righteous Brothers song: "You've lost that lovin' feeling... now it's gone, gone, gone....." Go figure!

Well, I've come too far, sacrificed too much and, I've developed a safety network I can use as a "continuum of care" for myself. I have promised myself that I will never go back into that "dark void" again. I've described severe Major Depression as if it was a dark, long tunnel with a light at the other end. Only problem is, each step you take toward the light, which you desperately need to get to, the further away it is. It's a deep, deep blackness that takes a lot of work to climb out of. Medications, if you play "medication roulette" long enough, will help. I was lucky, my treating physician, Dr. Howard Lichtenstein found what works for me (Mirtazapine, a sleep aid and an anti-depressant). None of the psychiatrists and psychiatric social workers I saw over a two year period were very helpful to me, say for one psychiatrist, at Northwest Hospital, when I was put into a "loony bin" (think "One Flew Over The Cookoo's Nest, the movie Jack Nickleson did such a superb job of acting in). This psychiatrist, who shall go nameless to protect his stellar reputation, called me into his office one day and told me, "You don't belong here do you?" There was hope for psychiatry yet! This gifted man saw to it that I be placed in an out-patient therapy group who met at the hospital each week, where I could demonstrate my skill sets and, not be treated in the in-patient wing where all sorts of negative karma and outright mistreatment of patients was taking place.

For example, while sitting in the day room one day, sounds were broadcast over the P.A. system. These sounds were annoyingly loud, then soft, then

48

loud again. They were meant to disorient or rattle the paranoid patients who would go shrieking down the hallway, only to be met by orderlies, who would give the patient a shot and drag him to bed. I saw this happen, many times; and, if you "acted out" too severely, you'd get "disappeared" to somewhere else, by tie-down straps, in an ambulance. I don't know where they took these people. The only State facility I knew of was Western State Hospital in Southwest Washington State, an over-crowded, overburdened staff, an archaic-methodology psychiatric hospital that is currently under Federal Contempt of Court citations, for many years, and whose "corrections" have been superficial and marginal at best; claiming there is no money, legislatively, to correct all the issues that have been extant for years. How do I know this? I can read and, I know a former staff person who worked in one of the wards of this hospital.

I had a 37.5 year career as a State Parole/Probation Officer. My college degrees were in Psychology and Sociology. I worked with and around psychiatrists, staffed cases with same, and I was very familiar with the "jargon" of the trade. So, in many respects, I knew more than some of my detractors in the facilities I stayed at. I "played" their game so I could get out and live my life again.

Believe me, the state of our mental health care in this country is barbaric by comparison to, say, Germany, whose "open door" system lets people walk outside of a "home facility", go to work if they can, and help them self-monitor medications and their daily routines. In other words, HELP PEOPLE MANAGE THEIR LIVES; as opposed to our system that uses people as guinea pigs for the big pharmaceutical conglomerates, keeping people incarcerated (in jails, prisons, institutions) who could learn to manage for themselves IF someone would just fully fund "continuum of care" programs. In those places where this has seen the light of day, great progress has been made. Congress needs to pass "PARITY LEGISLATION."

I've used the example of Dr. Harch's program. He has been very successful treating people with diagnoses such as Major Depression, Bi-polar 1,2, and 3, some schizophrenics (mild), anxiety disorders, insomnia, and other psychiatric maladies. His successes ARE NOT anecdotal results. They are sustained and permanent changes in patient's lives. He is a "fire fighter."

When I was in my mid-teens, I asked my mom why I was an only child. I was curious as to why I didn't have a brother or sister. I had noted, as I grew older, how my mother, especially, doted on me, was rather possessive and protective of me, and seemed to "spoil" me. I learned that she'd lost what would have been my little sister, in the late 1940s, due to a Rh factor in her blood. Medicine had not advanced in those days to where it is now. Doctors and medical staff can now do *in situ (in the womb)* transfusions that correct this issue and, as a result, a woman can have more children. I then understood why my mother was so over-protective of me.

I recalled one incident of her fierce instinct to protect, in particular, when we first moved to Hawaii. The elementary school on the base, Pearl Harbor Naval Complex, was full and, I had to go to the 4th grade at a local Native school, Punahoa Elementary. I remember walking about two blocks from the rental we had, (housing was also not available on base and we were placed on a waiting list) to meet my new teacher and my classmates. The school was old and surrounded by large Banyan trees, trees that have many niches and trunks one can play "hid and seek" in. I remember mango trees too. One could pick up ripe fruit and eat it on the way to school. And, Plumeria trees, with heavenly-scented cream-colored flowers with yellow centers; the ones the Hawaiian's make their welcoming "Aloha" leis out of.

The classroom was upstairs. I was introduced to my teacher, a big Hawaiian woman who was wearing a "mumu," a dress that drapes over one's body like a big tent. Only, this "mumu" was decorated in colorful floral designs. I was introduced to my classmates: "Dis is Johnnie Clawly, he's a howlee from da mainlan." ("Howlee" is Hawaiian slang for a white person from the States). I immediately noticed that all the kids were looking at my feet. I soon figured out why....I was the only kid wearing shoes. All the rest of the class was either barefooted or wearing flip-flops or, as I learned, in Pigeon English, "goheads." The teacher asked me to take off my shoes and remove my socks. I complied. She then told the class, "Dis is what you feet gonna look like if you wear da shoe all da time." I was embarrassed and shaken by this comment and I began to cry as I ran from the class back home. When I told my mother what had happened, she grabbed my hand and marched me right back to that classroom.

I'll never forget what happened next. My mother weighed about 110 pounds, dripping wet. She stood all of five foot two inches in height. The Hawaiian teacher outmatched mom's size by 6 fold. She was very rotund and big. I recall my mother wagging her forefinger at this woman, as she was looking up at her and reading her the "riot act" with words such as… "how dare you treat my son in this manner." I got along very well after that and, I had some very close friends from that school throughout our stay in Hawaii. Two of them taught me how to surf on a long board (there were no "boogie boards" or short 3-fin boards in those days {1950s}). I also learned what it was like to be in a minority. I was the only Caucasian kid in that class, and, probably, in the whole school. All the other kids I met, played with, and studied with were Hawaiian, Polynesian, part Japanese or Chinese, Samoan, Portuguese, Middle Eastern (Muslim), or of other ethnic extraction. They were definitely not Caucasians. My parents had taught me never to judge people by the color of their skin. It was a good lesson to learn early in life.

I think another reason I was singled out for "special" care by my parents was due to an incident that happened just before we moved: Alameda, California to Honolulu. Some of our "gang" of local Navy brats had built a fort out of old railroad ties in a nearby train yard. We had built it in such a way as to crawl under a beam and turn sideways to get into the "secret" middle chamber, a room with a dirt floor, approximately 10 feet by 8 feet in proportion. We had an old metal army surplus trunk in the secret chamber where we kept all our candy bars, pop, chips, and "girlie" magazines that the older boys liked to look at. I was still pretty young (age 7-8), so my interests were mostly centered on playing games and just "hanging out" with the guys.

One day, alone, I went to the fort to get something. As I entered the inner chamber, I found myself confronting two, older African American boys. As I recall, they both appeared to be about 14 or 15 years old. They had broken into the "stash box" and were helping themselves to our goodies. I remember one of these fellows asking the other if he's ever "had a white boy" before, I didn't know what he meant until one of them grabbed me and held me down while the other unbuckled my belt and pulled my bluejeans to my knees. What happened next was extremely painful and shameful. The one larger boy raped me, anally. The other just laughed and looked on. They left shortly after this incident, leaving me partly undressed, in the dirt, sobbing. I don't remember how long I just sat there, but I eventually got dressed and ran all the way home, about 5 blocks away.

My dad was just arriving from his duty on base and I told him what had happened. He took me by the hand and told me to show him where. I did so, but there was no sign of the perpetrators. I don't think my father ever told my mother about this rape. It would have devastated her. There wasn't much in the way of counseling in those days, early 1950s. And, we were soon scheduled to depart for Hawaii. I don't know if my father ever reported the incident to the police. I think he just wanted us to "forget" about it and move on. Not much was known, in those days, about PTSD or psychological trauma. In fact, PTSD was called "shell shock," what soldiers experience in war zones. As far as I've been able to determine, treatment was non-existent and what did exist was in the form of pills: tranquilizers.

Part of my education, in later years, prepared me for my career as a Parole/Probation Officer and, at one time, I was writing Pre-sentence reports, giving sentencing recommendations to Superior Court Judges and Prosecutors throughout Washington State and via the Interstate Compact for people we supervised from other jurisdictions and other States who resided in Washington. I was also a trainer for the Washington State Criminal Justice Training Commission on the topic of "Child Abuse: Awareness, Detection, and Reporting Requirements." All professional staff (teachers, doctors, social workers, probation officers, and others) are mandated, by law in most states, to report suspected child abuse and neglect to the local authorities. Part of my task and motivation was to make sure they did so and knew what they were talking about. In this manner, I believe my efforts over time, helped me heal from my own ordeal. I learned how to be a survivor rather than be a victim. There's a huge difference between these two poles, victim/survivor. I made sure, when I was teaching a class, that the participants knew the difference; because, at the end of the course, I used my own, personal experience to tell them what the difference is. It had an impact and, often, folks would come up, after the session, and disclose their own experience with abuse. We have many "silent victims" in this country (and, probably, around the world).

Many child victims suffer for years from such abuse, both physically and mentally. I know I did, and it probably contributed to my Major Depression and self-medication with alcohol. Although I never drank on the job, I waited until I got home to be a hypocrite. What this sort of crime does to a child's sense of worth and self-esteem is abominable and, it should be punished to the fullest extent of the law. Children do not lie about this kind of behavior. So, my advice to anyone whose child is trying to tell you about something someone did to them that hurt them, is to listen, ask open-ended questions, and you will know the truth. The main thing is to reassure the child that it wasn't his or her fault. And, by all means, file a police report. You may be saving a child from another victimization; even if it's one of your own family members who committed the act (s). It's hard, I know, but it needs to be done. The truth shall set you free from the guilt and shame of not disclosing; and THAT (non-disclosure), my friend, IS A VERY HEAVY LOAD TO CARRY throughout one's life.

One out of three girls will experience an improper touch by, usually, an older adult, before the age of 13. One out of four boys will experience the same. These statistics are reliable and constant (Sources: For Kid's Sake, Inc. and the Federal Criminal Justice Records from 2000 to 2015 were used to calculate averages noted above). During my career I wrote over 1,200 Pre-sentence reports to the Courts: Child Molestation, Child Rape, Incest, Communication With A Minor for Immoral Purposes and, Assault and Murder.

I have often wondered when my Major Depression could have been diagnosed. It certainly was not during the time of my childhood activities. I was a "very" active child, according to my parents and close friends. Looking back, I probably could have been Attention Deficit Disordered (ADD or ADHD, the Hyperactive part of another diagnostic paradigm).

I know that my parents took me to have a "brain scan" (EEG, where electrodes are taped to the top of the head and around the head, and a monitor measures the pulse of various brain waves, or how the synaptic profile is working). I guess I "passed" because the doctor told my mother, "He's just a very active boy, we see this all the time." My other doctor prescribed Phenobarbital, a hypnotic drug that, literally, "zones" you out. I didn't do well in school for about 4 months because of this. I kept falling asleep in class. Remember, this was in the 1950s; not much was known about childhood trauma; least of all, I've found, how to effectively treat it. As a result, a lot of kids grew up with unresolved neuroses. I was soon taken off of this drug and my schoolwork and alertness in class greatly improved. I sometimes think my "craving" for the "downer" effect of alcohol was somehow initiated through the use of the Phenobarbital; it's a very strong drug and, I now find it should never be used on children, whose brains are still developing (American Psychiatric Association Journals). I think the term, in today's world, would be "gateway drug" to alcohol abuse, or worse.

I was not officially diagnosed until shortly after my retirement in 2008. I knew I suffered from Depression, but I masked it by keeping busy with projects at work, teaching, committee work, staffing cases and, when at home, relieving the "stressors" of the day by consuming a couple glasses of vodka, about 6 ounces each; enough to get a really good "buzz" going. I remember my wife coming into the den, where I'd fall asleep watching television, at 2 or 3 A.M., telling me, "It's time to go to bed honey...you have work tomorrow (sic) today." This went on for years.

I was a good, providing husband and father. We raised two lovely daughters, Kimberly, now an adult, and classically trained in piano, stage managing on Broadway Shows in New York (her last position before coming home to live with us and help care for Susan and I, and my aged parents, who, by 2008, were fairly feeble and in need of care); and Christine, a couple years younger than Kim, who went on to become a successful attorney. Susan, my soon-to-be ex (as of 2017), and I have often commented that we did something very right in how we parented our children. Neither got pregnant early on in life; neither one got into the "heavy" drug scene in the late 1980s and 1990s.

I recall, when Kim was about age 3, she could not read yet, but she would sit on the floor of our pantry and organize cans by shape, color and size. Her organizational skills are brilliant; that's why she probably makes an excellent professional sound/lighting/stage manager. One has to be able to "multi-task" to do the job. It ain't easy! We've seen her in action, at venues she's worked at, professionally. She can do this job very well.

Christine, as I've mentioned went on to law school after working for Boeing Aircraft and, eventually, as an adjudicator for the Washing State Patrol until her most recent job offer came; she now negotiates contracts for the University of Washington, Issaquah Campus; better pay, perks, and a shorter commute; not bad.

During the time of raising a family, Susan and I worked our regular jobs: Me as a Parole/Probation Officer (the names been changed to Community Corrections Officer; now, anyone you mention it to thinks you work for the County jail...Not!) and Susan, as a Culinary Arts Instructor for a local Community College in Everett, Washington. In addition, we owned and operated a catering business, "Sue A Chez Vous" (loosely translated from the French: "Sue at you place"). We would go to the place/venue where the event (wedding reception, anniversary party, birthday, or retirement party) would be, inspect the premises, especially the kitchen area, see if it met with minimal health and safety requirements, and approve a contract based on the inspection. Kim and Chris also helped us in this business. We paid them the same hourly wage as the other workers we hired. All had current Food Handler Safety Certifications from the local Health Department. It was a great "learning platform" for how one manages one's money and work ethic.

We did weddings where 500 to 600 patrons and guests were present. It was a great gig for about 9 ½ years while we saved up to remodel our farm house in Arlington Heights, not too far from where Aunt Helen (Lindquist), mom's elder sister's family, lived. We did great work. We were told this by repeat customers. I had a photo album, with pictures of past events, so we could show it to prospective customers. We'd ask what the customer's budget was and, we'd provide them with menu options. They could pick and choose from, say, salmon and prawns, various salads, breads, jello molds, punch, and condiments (at $25.00 a plate) or something simpler like a casserole and various noshes to accompany the main course, to o'deuvre party favors that we'd bring and serve. People always asked why it was so expensive per plate. I explained that we had purchasing costs, transportation costs, labor costs (we were able to hire some of Susan's best students in the Culinary Arts Program, from the college, at $10.00/hr.... these kids would jump at this money because, in the early 1990s, this was a great wage!), prep and delivery set-up costs and.....cleanup. When I said "cleanup" it usually made the sale. Many catering outfits do not do cleanup. They do the event, pick up their stuff and leave. The bar was also included, but, as bartender, I reserved the right to refuse to serve anyone who I judged to be intoxicated and, I always asked to meet the "designated driver." The customer had to provide the booze and the "event license." I did not consume at these events. We wanted people to enjoy the events, not be falling down drunk or obnoxious. I also had a big brandy snifter on the bar for tips. My cousin, Gretchen (Lindquist) helped me tend bar at large events. We averaged over $100.00 per event in tips.

We discussed going on with the business following our retirements from our "regular" jobs. But, the investment (1.2 million dollars to set it up right, with a 3-partitioned venue, with a kitchen running the length of the back of the house, refrigeration trucks, tables, chairs, florist, distributors, etc. on call, as well as wait staff), at our respective ages, me 63 and Susan 61, prohibited us from doing it. I think, now, in retrospect, it was a wise decision. Catering is a lot of work, heavy work, where one is striving, 3 days before the event, almost 24/7 to bring everything together. We did beautiful events, 4-tiered carrot cakes (very heavy), wedding cakes and all. Average prices were from $2,000.00 to $10,000.00. People definitely got their money's worth and we, all of us, at the end of each event, were totally exhausted; but it's a good kind of exhaustion: knowing we all worked as a team, successfully, in unison.

Looking back, now, I believe all this "work, work" contributed to my eventual "breakdown." I remember, shortly after retirement from my State job, lying in our bed one morning and telling Susan I felt "lost.... like everything is going away, that we're about to lose everything we've worked for in life." She thought this statement, in 2008, was nonsense and told me I was just having a bad dream.

Well, three weeks later, I decided to pour the remainder of ½ gallon of vodka down the drain, thinking I needed to quit drinking, just like I'd done with cigarettes, in 1982, "cold turkey." Not a problem, right? Wrong! I now know I should have gone under a doctor's care, because, the body metabolism goes into a sort of "shock mode," where cravings and denial is predominate, and going into a "tailspin" is almost guaranteed. At least, it was for me.

One morning, a short time after "the pour", I felt extremely depressed, not wanting to live anymore. I remembered an old 33 1/3 phonograph record my mother had. On this record was the voice of an old, distinguished actor by the name of Charles Laughton (he was in mostly black and white Hollywood movies, back in the "glory" days, 1930s and 40s). In one of the pieces Mr. Laughton read from was the experience of Jack Kerouac, as a young man, when he spent the summer, in the Olympic National Forrest, on the Olympic Peninsula, the Northwest corner of Washington State. Jack, a revered "beatnik" existential philosopher and prolific writer of his time, 1950s early 1960s, described his stay in a fire watch tower Ranger station, all alone, with only the soaring eagles, among the wind-swept tree tops, soft breezes, gentle foggy mornings with the mist rising with the warmth of the morning sun and, at days end, the glorious sunsets looking out over the Strait of Juan De Fuca, the grand entryway into the Puget Sound. I tried to write about this "ending" in some type of meandering, confused note I left for Susan, on our kitchen table, before I left our home for "The Mountain." She was at work.

I drove my truck to a road I'd remembered as a young man, on Mount Pilchuck. The road, eventually went to a trail to Bordman Lake, a hike of about 1 and1/2 miles, on fairly level ground; easy for just about anyone to accomplish. Fishing was good in this lake; I'd done it with my friend Jim on many occasions. Prior to arrival at the trail head, there is a quarry where rock for the roads in the area were obtained. It was now an old, dilapidated site, in disuse. I stopped my truck, got out, and looked at the distant mountains and forested hills. It was a sunny day in late-June, 2008. In my left hand, I held a .36 caliber Rugger revolver with one bullet in the chamber. I intended to "end it." I remember feeling extremely distraught, demoralized, completely "in darkness" (emotionally), devoid of rational thought and (obviously) action, and without (I believed at that time) any way out other than to kill myself. Suicidal ideation (now, in my opinion) is very selfish. One doesn't think about the impact it will have on others. One doesn't "care." And, there, virtually, is NO feeling....I was numb.

I turned and looked back, away from the quarry, one last time, at the beautiful surrounds of this creation and, at that moment, something happened to me. To this day I do not know how it happened, but I think I know why. Some "one", the Source of my existence on this planet, in this infinitesimal universe of what I now believe are many universes that go on forever, came into my being and told me...... not in words, but by "feeling" not to do what I was intending to do. It was, I recall, an overwhelming warmth, a "presence," some "thing," or some "force" that was so overwhelming that I began sobbing like a baby. I, almost immediately, felt a "lifting" from my body, a feeling of relief and love like I've never felt before. It was almost euphoric. It certainly was transcendental and transforming!

I turned back to the quarry, lifted the gun, and I shot the bullet into the rocks, vowing never to do this again. Now, some of you who are reading this may think I was "around the bend" when all of this happened. Yes, I was ill with Major Depression; but, people who are suicidal usually DO NOT have such epiphany or "religious" experiences. And that's exactly what I call it. To this day, I feel as though I was touched by the hand of God. I was very sober. I got back into my truck, drove down the mountain, and went straight home to a wife who met me at the doorway, sobbing, along with my then son-in-law and his father, Mike Lavelle, a once retired police officer who now is the Manager of the Boeing Museum of Flight in Seattle. I met them, stating, "I need help", and I broke down in tears. Mike took the gun for proper disposal.

It was then that my nightmare of psychiatric hospitalization began. I've told you some of this story already but, that's not the half of it. At one point, after the hospital administrators found out that I had a "golden parachute" of a health coverage plan, I feel they "milked it" for all they could get. I was kept well past the usual stay at one facility. At one point, when I was under the influence of some experimental drug they were trying (I know this because I was administered 23 different drugs over a 19 week period of time {documented}…. "which one works, Doc?!!") and, at one point, they tried to get me to sign an Involuntary Commitment paper. I wasn't so far "under" to know that signing this document would, literally, take most of my legal rights away and put them into the hands of the person who had my Power of Attorney (my wife, at the time) and the Courts. I also knew I had the right of counsel before signing anything. This right was NEVER afforded to me at any time during my hospital stays. Now you know another reason why I believe our system of mental health care is REALLY FUCKED UP in this country.

It's not just my experience; I've talked to many people in my DBSA (Depression Bi-polar Support Alliance) who have gone through similar experiences, and worse. We are sorely lacking continuity, clarity, purpose, and "continuum of care" in this country; especially, where mental illness diagnoses, treatment, and referral/follow-up are concerned. I, along with my fellow DBSA folks, are living proof of this. Our defense: "We must be our own best self-advocates and managers." (from Ken, one of our facilitators…I've never forgotten this because it's SO TRUE!) Unfortunately, when one is in a "manic" state, or extremely depressed state and chemically-electrically (brain shorted) off balance, it is extremely difficult to think about self-advocacy and "managing" our episodes. This is another reason why we need the "safety net of continuum of care."

Big pharmaceutical conglomerates, big insurance corporations, and big medical consortiums are raking in the dough, while those of us, who suffer, are left to our own devices; often relapsing, because no "continuum of care" is extant. I wish I could have these folks, who I've secured releases from, be right here, in this book, to tell you, as they have me, how they've been cajoled, manipulated, and left to wallow in their own misery because no one took the time to take them in, comfort them, and help them find a pathway to success. They are forced to be their own advocates. But if you are confused and you don't know how, you're left at the mercy of the system and, the system, in my opinion, is really screwed up. Sure, it looks all "squeaky clean" and "hunky dory" on the surface, but if you're in it, as I was, it's a "friggin'" nightmare (fact). Learning how to "manage" one's illness is not an easy task. One does not "just get over it." One does not just "snap out of it." It is, in most cases, a life-long battle. We all need to be "fire fighters."

As I previously stated at the beginning of this book, diagnosed mental illness IS a disease of the mind, a chemical imbalance, that needs proper care, nutrition, exercise, and medications to manage. And even then, no one is completely "cured." Symptoms may be reduced or "extinguished" only to reappear later in life when a traumatic event occurs (death of a loved one, loss of a job, an injury, other illness, etc.). We all experience life. Shit happens, but it's how we deal with the "shit" that sometimes tells whether our systems (brains here) can handle it. Many people can't. Some are more prone to mental illness than others. In some cases, like Bi-polar (formerly called Manic Depressive Affect Disorder), a genetic propensity seems to exist (American Psychiatric Association, Journals of Pharmacology, NAMI and NIMH reports 2015, 2016). Many people who suffer from Bi-polar have family histories of in kind diagnoses; in other words, the mother, father, grandfather, grandmother, etc. have the same diagnosis. (NIMH. Et al.)

I have recently documented, via reliable Internet research, a new field of medical practice: Genopsychopharmalogical medicine. Scientists, since the early 2000s, have been studying the human genes and mapping loci (Indices that affect our, for example, hair color, bone structure, the color of our skin, our ethnic origins {try a DNA swab from Ancestor's dotcom}, our sex and sexual preferences, and, now, our behaviors, or propensity to behave, under measurable circumstances). Scientists in various fields have been able to find, for example, 5 loci in a genetic mapping sequence that indicate for Depression, Bi-polar, some types of Schizophrenia, Personality Disorders, Schizo-Affective Disorder, and others (Medline, American Journal of Medicine and Psychiatry, 2000 through 2016).

Now, the trick is to be able to pair the above with a persons "metabolic profile", their brain's ability to cognitively function{as best we can},and "design" a drug for that person's diagnoses that will not have the negative side-effects that many psycho-active drugs now do. (Journals of Psychopharmacology, 2016).

Personally, I'm sick and tired of hearing about people suffering, because their treating psychiatrist, doctor, or psychiatric social worker (they are legally allowed to prescribe) can't get off the "medication merry-go-round" that their patients seem to be continually going for a ride upon. It sucks! And, what's more, it's wrought with stigma and hyperbolic innuendo that keeps people in a constant state of anxiety about their disease. I know this because I suffered it and many others do too. It needs to stop. Again, another purpose to authoring this book. We need people to get mad. The energy created from anger, when focused into a constructive purpose, can do wonders to change a very badly broken system.

On top of this, you, as a taxpayer and a "fire fighter" who helped fix the system, will have saved thousands of dollars in future taxes, fees, surcharges, etc. that are now "wasted" on new jails, prisons, social worker systems that are overburdened and understaffed, huge caseloads, extra overtime for police, crippled emergency rooms in most of our major hospitals, and on and on it goes. This "fix" can and will be done. It's only a matter of time.

Perhaps, the current "shake up" in the healthcare system will bring this about; sometimes, things have to get worse before they get better. Our current Administration (2017) is about to learn this invaluable lesson; and some may lose their cushy political jobs over it. So be it; as I've suggested, "If he/she ain't doing the representative job he/she was elected to do, for ALL the people, then he/she don't belong in office." Politicians need a direct reminder once in awhile….it keeps them humble, I think, don't you? They, sometimes, forget from whence they came, right? "Ya gotta dance with the one that brung ya, right?" Don't go dancin' over there with that pretty pharmaceutical lobbyist." (sorry for the "countryfication", but it needed to be said, right?).

Okay, so here's what happens with sugar, yep, sugar, when it gets into the metabolic process of your and my physiological systems. It gives us a "high." I have just about eliminated sugar from my diet. I have to, now, because I was diagnoses with Type 2 Diabetes a couple years ago (2015). Sugar is, in one form or another, in just about everything we consume; especially fast food and pre-prepared foods (packaged/frozen deli or grocery items). How do I know this? Just read the ingredients listings on most food and drink packaging labels and you'll find out (dextrose, sucrose, refined corn syrup, etc. you name it, sugar's there). Sugar IS addictive. The body can change its metabolism to where, if we don't get a "sugar fix" somewhere during the course of the day, some folks actually go into a sort of withdrawal: irritable, hungry, without energy and pep, antagonistic, and some even get headaches. Chocolate, having some "healthful" properties, is very popular because it has a psycho-active effect of raising the "positive" (dopamine) levels in the brain and causes us to feel pleasurable sensations. Not unlike, on a very limited scale, like the "high" we get from a drug, like cocaine or methamphetamine (in my opinion, the most insidious drug that was ever created (Meth). It's harder to "kick" than Heroin. Fact, Jack! Believe it!. I had people on my caseload, when I worked as a Parole/Probation Officer, that had an easier time, in treatment, "kicking" the habit of Heroin than Meth. People always seemed to come back to Meth.

I remember one guy, "S." I'll save him the embarrassment, who, while on my caseload as both a probationer, and, eventually, a parolee (he was on my "load" for over 17 years, in total) who would, due to his Meth habit, go to the local Albertson's Grocery Store, shop-lift a couple of steaks, a six-pack of beer, while he was "high," call a cab, when store employees knew what was going on, and wait, in broad daylight, for the taxi to arrive at front of the store. Guess who came? The local police. This is virtually how "stupid" Meth makes people become, mentally, psychologically, and physically (dependent and addicted).

I would have to go into Court and explain to the Judge, that this person had an addiction issue and, in many cases, a mental health issue, that mitigated their potential sentence. The judges, in the main, were sympathetic, but they still, as elected people to office, had a duty to preserve the decorum of the office and abide by the "laws of the land." So, off ya go fella, to jail or prison (if the violation was felony level or, so serious that prison was the only other option), "flappin'" in the wind. So sad, because you knew this person was going to be, eventually, back on your caseload, a continual pariah, a reminder of how fucked-up the system really is. A "continuum of care" option, might be a more workable situation where the "incarceration" (read: jail time) is served in an in-patient treatment facility with 24/7 participation in "wellness' efforts. The incentive, for the violator? Shorten the stay by each day the person successfully participates. This "carrot and stick" method has worked for many people for many years. It is still used as a learning/motivational model in our education systems, and other places, in this country and around the world: Perform this task well and, you will get this reward (money, certificate, a promotion, "laid," etc.). It's just how most of us are "hard-wired" folks. It works for me.

I recently reflected on how lucky it is to be alive. So many things can happen to a person in his/her lifetime. The other day, in fact, the day after my 73rd birthday, February 28th, 2017, I was driving my 2000 Corvette (a belated "retirement" present; I retired in 2008 and got nothing; my wife retired two years later and she bought herself a brand new Hyundai Santa Fe. Somehow, that picture had to change, right? Answer: 'vette.) I was in the far right lane of the Interstate Freeway (I-5) traveling North, at approximately 60 miles-per-hour. Traffic was pretty heavy because the Boeing plant in south Everett, Washington had recently changed shifts.

There was a container/cargo semi-truck ahead of me, in the middle lane, about 100 feet separated us. I saw something come off the truck and heard a loud "BAM!." I had enough sense not to slam on my brakes; so, I coasted to the side of the highway and stopped. As soon as I got out of the car, I saw that my driver's side front tire had a gash in it. My tires are "run-flats;" made out of thick rubber with a little air in them. They are made to "run" flat so that a person can get to a repair shop.

When I looked at the left rear of my vehicle, I saw no tire; not even a remnant of a tire. The tire had apparently hit something, or, rather something hit it and it disintegrated. The tire rim and hub were also damaged. The hubs of my car are custom made rally wheels, made out of magnesium alloy (pricey to replace I've found out). Noting the amount of damage, I had the vehicle towed to a local repair shop and prepared to contact my insurance agent to file a damage claim.

The next day, after obtaining a rental car, I went back to the scene of where all this happened. On the grassy tarmac, just off the pavement, I found what appeared to be a very heavy (approx. 28 lbs.) piece of solid steel I-bar; the kind that is used for skyscraper construction framing. This piece, in the form of an "H" had been cut by a welding torch to a rough width of approximately 3 inches thick. It measured about 2 feet by 18 inches. On one side of the surface, I could see where this piece had been recently scoured, moving along the pavement of the highway. The scored metal was "fresh" with no rusty spots. I was almost positive that this was the piece that, in a split second, came off the container semi-truck and struck my car. I took this piece to show to my insurance agent.

I am very lucky, today as I write this, to be alive. Had the piece been lighter, or had it bounced up, it could have hit my windshield, gone through and killed me. My agent and everyone who saw and hefted this object agreed. It would have gone through the windshield like a big rock through wet paper.

I also thought about other times I almost "bought it." Two other occasions stand out: One was when, as a young lad in Hawaii, I went swimming and body surfing while my family was visiting friends on the windward side of Oahu at Makaha Beach. I made an almost fatal mistake of going into large surf alone. No one else was around. The waves here average 10 to 15 feet in height, so one must be a good swimmer to master them. I was a good swimmer, having swum almost every day of the week when my father was stationed at the Navy attachment, Hickam Field, Honolulu, Hawaii. After about 30 minutes in the water I became a little fatigued, so I decided to swim to shore to rest. Only problem was, the tide was going out and there was a very strong "rip tide" pulling me away from the shore. Exhausted, I began screaming for help. I was panicked (not a good way to be in an emergent situation). I had yet to learn that one should swim parallel to the shoreline and gradually work one's way to shore. Fortunately, a Native Hawaiian man, who had been walking on the beach, about 100 yards away, came running and he swam out to get me. He was strong and big and I was thankful that he was able to get me. He told me to climb on his back with my arms around his neck, and we "body surfed" to a point where we could touch the sandy bottom. He then scolded me, something like this, in Pigeon English: "Wat's wrong wid you boy?! You should know bedda dan go out dare alone...neva do dat again!" He then walked off down the beach. I didn't even get a chance to thank him for saving my life. I would have drowned. The next day, I was told, someone found the remnants of a human arm on the beach. The fate of another swimmer, no doubt, who had ventured out too far, drowned, or was attacked by a shark. Great White sharks do come as far as the Hawaiian Islands to breed and feed. Normally, they don't eat humans......but they are territorial and can be aggressive while breeding. (NOAA)

The other occasion, I recall, is much later in life. Having finished college and securing a job with the State of Washington, as a Youth Camp Counselor, some of my fellow counselors and I decided to "float" the mighty Skagit River on a beautiful Summer day. I think it was on our collective time off (we worked shifts on the same shift: 3.5 days "on" and 3.5 days "off") in July. The water in the river comes from glacial melt, so it's always cold. This was our first mistake. We should have worn surfing suits or the like so we'd keep warm if the canoe (second mistake: poor choice of water craft to go down this particular river in) capsized. There were four of us, including myself, to fit into a 20 foot, flat bottom fiberglass canoe. All of us had outdoor/camping/boating experience. It wasn't as if we were novices at this. Frank, our supervisor at work, had mastered the wilds of Alaska, usually going up each Spring to check out and operate his gold mining claim. He was the most experienced at river running. He would steer the canoe from the rear seat. I had an 18 foot canoe I owned and used for fly fishing in British Columbia with my good friend, Jim Johnston (a whole separate story later). I would be the front paddler, giving the canoe momentum to be just a little faster than the speed of the current and add stability to our quest. Our other two adventurers, Royal and Jim, were along for the ride and would offer "ballast" in the center portion of the canoe, as long as they sat upright and did not lean over the sides of the canoe. They both knew this. So, we were set. What could go wrong, right? Wrong again, John.

We started out just fine, enjoying the lazy current at a wide spot in the river. We soon came upon a log jam in the river, swinging the current in a "hard left" direction. Paddling like a trooper, I made a gallant effort to get us as far left as I could, as Frank was holding the rudder paddle to make us go left. It wasn't enough and we hit the log jam about 2/3 of the way to our escape destination. The canoe capsized and we all hit the drink. Boy! Was that a shocker. The water was very cold, icy cold! I remembered that I had tied a safety line, one length of sisal rope the length of the canoe. The rope was loose at one end. Now, the loose end had somehow wrapped itself around my left ankle, like a snake! The canoe, now filled with water, was sucked under the log jam with me being dragged along. At the very last moment, before I went under to surely drown, the "safety" rope came off and I was able to swim around the left side of the jam.

I found Frank sitting on a large boulder in the middle of the river, downstream from the log jam and where the river split in two, on a rocky prominence. The canoe, now with a large gash in it, was at his feet. As I got out of the river, I remember saying something like, "guess we're not going anywhere soon in that thing (pointing at the canoe)." I think Frank acknowledged me in some fashion. He had a gash on his forehead from when, he told me, his head had struck a log. He'd actually gone under the log jam!

I asked him if he'd seen either of our partners. He told me he had not. We were both worried that both or one of them might not have made it. Going under a log jam can be tricky because there are so many ways a person can get stuck and drown. I remember search and rescue teams finding swimmers in the summer who'd ventured too close to a jam and got sucked under to drown. The body would usually be retrieved by certified divers because it was usually wedged into some crevice of timber and debris.

About a half hour of drying in the warmth of the July sunshine brought us a glimpse of someone, in what appeared to be a rowboat, coming toward us. It turned out to be Royal. He told us he was able to climb up onto the log jam and find his way into a wooded area where he found this old boat, probably left by a fisherman for his season of fishing. What luck! We asked Royal if he'd seen Jim. He told us he thought he saw Jim swimming to the other side of the river. At this juncture, about 20 minutes had passed, we see a vehicle coming down the roadway on the opposite side of the river. It was Jim and the local Mt. Baker U.S. Forrest Ranger and a couple of his crew. They yelled, "Are you alright, is anyone hurt?!" Frank yelled back that we were all good. I knew he wasn't the kind of person to make a fuss about the cut on his forehead. It had washed "clean" in the cold water anyway and the blood had stopped running down the side of his face.

We were able, the three of us, to row the rowboat across the river to the waiting rescue squad. Once in the Ranger Station in Darrington, Washington, and drinking hot, fresh-made coffee and, munching on stale donuts (I recall, they tasted REALLY good!), we were able to rest and joke about our ordeal. But, now, looking back, that day could have been so tragic if it were not for "lady luck" and, a rowboat.

One other time comes to mind when I decided to go for a long postponed hike. My wife and I honeymooned on the Oregon Coast in 1972. We would stop for lunch at a nice little restaurant, The Pacific Way Cafe, in Gearhart, Oregon. During our stop I noticed a "mountain" (Tillamook Head) jutting out into the Pacific Ocean near Seaside. I had read about various hikes on the Oregon Coast, and the Tillamook Head trail to Cannon Beach, about 7 miles in length (one way) sounded intriguing. At the time, little did I know that my father would purchase a beach cottage in Gearhart in 1985.

So, in 2015, prior to my diagnosis with arthritic hips and Diabetes, I decided to make the trek, by myself. I was 71 years old, but I felt up to the task. What could go wrong? The trail, I was told, is well defined and easy to navigate, once one conquers the initial 2 miles of switch backs to the top, where "it levels out and you can see vistas of the rugged coastline for miles and miles, all the way to the mouth of the Columbia River to the North, and almost to Bandon (Southern Oregon) from the South."

At least, that's what my guidebook said. I wasn't a novice at hiking and preparation for same. I dressed in layered clothing. I had a small backpack wherein I placed a Hershey candy bar, a container of water, dry socks, a flashlight, and my cell phone (fully charged).

The weather was cooperative on the day I decided to hike. I started off at a slow, deliberate pace so I would "acclimate" to the climb and not get winded. I did well until I reached the plateau at the top of the "Head." There, I found that the trail branched and I chose the trail I believed would follow the coastline. I could hear the Ocean to my right, so I figured it would help orient me to the direction I needed to go. It was mid-morning and I felt I had plenty of time to reach my destination, as long as I held a steady pace.

Well. here's where the "best of laid plans..." falls victim to an elk trail. Yep, the trail I chose was an elk trail. How did I know this? I found their tracks and the 45-65 degree incline and valleys they traversed. Besides that, the pathways veered...a lot. I knew I wasn't lost because I could always find my way to the ocean. My only fear was that of falling and rolling off a cliff onto the rocky shoreline. I held on to fern fronds to aid the precipitous drops and inclines I had to use to move forward. I was determined to find the original trail. At one point, unknown to me at the time, I lost the Seiko watch my wife had given me, some 40 years prior, as a birthday present. So, dear reader, if you find yourself on an elk path someday, on Tillamook Head in Oregon, and you find my watch, you'll know who it belongs to. Like the old Timex commercial, "it took a lickin' and kept on tickin'" (maybe).

Finally, I became so exhausted from this ordeal that I decided to give up on finding the right trail and, I decided to go down to the beach and walk back to my car. Easier said than done. I had fallen, many times, into muck and swamp-like patches that the elk probably just jumped over. My climb downhill was more of a grab and hold on for dear life excursion. I did manage to find a meadow with a very large Sitka spruce tree in the center. These trees have very large, raised root systems. The one I found had a V-shaped system with what appeared to be tree cone shavings, most likely dropped by nesting squirrels, in the "V." It looked very inviting, so I sat down in this comfortable place. I had a panoramic view of the ocean in front of me. All I needed was a few moments of rest and I'd be okay. Well, a few moments turned out to be a nap. When I awoke, it was near dusk. When I looked out to the ocean, I saw what appeared to be spray shooting up into the air. Not once, but three separate times. It took me a moment, but I finally realized that this was a whale, traveling South from the Baring Sea in Alaska to, probably, Baja, California for the winter. This gave me inspiration and I told myself, 'If that whale can swim all the way from Alaska to southern California, you certainly can get up off your ass and get back home.' So, I got up and found my way to the beach and a small pathway back toward the now city lights of Seaside. Dusk was turning into darkness. I made it back to the road that went up a hill to where my car was parked, about 1.5 miles away. I was filthy, tired, thirsty, hungry, and I stuck out my thumb to try and hitch a ride should anyone pass. There are few people who live on the road, but it was worth a try. Two cars did pass me. They probably saw what a mess I was and decided not to stop. I was covered in mud and gunk from my ordeal, and I probably stank. Hell. I wouldn't have picked me up!

When I finally arrived at my vehicle, it was all I could do to lay on the hood and rest, just to muster the strength to open the car door and get in. The trip back to the cottage was slow and deliberate. Upon arrival, there was a trail of boots, pants, shirts, socks, and underwear all the way into the shower. The shower felt as if I died and gone to heaven; soothing warmth and relaxation. I stayed in there for as long as I could. Then I went to the kitchen and made a triple decked turkey sandwich which I washed down with a big glass of milk. I don't remember chewing. Then, bed.

I slept until noon the next day, and then went out for a big breakfast. I had "almost" conquered the mountain. I grew to respect the prowess of elk, and I felt very lucky that I didn't suffer a catastrophe like a serious fall or worse. I knew my cell phone would have reached the local Coast Guard who do fantastic rescues all the time on this beautiful, but dangerous coastline; but, all the same, I probably should have talked a buddy into going along. It's usually wiser not to go it alone.

I'm sure there were other times, I may have been unaware of, that I may have "met my maker" (so to speak), but I'd just as soon NOT know about such instances. I now see life as being way too precious to play "chicken with the devil." I relate the above stories to you, dear reader, so that you make have some idea of how thankful we all should be to be alive in this wonderful, crazy world we live in. I am thankful for every day, come rain, sleet, snow, or shine.

As far back as I can remember, I've had "high energy" and, it has only been since I was hospitalized with Major Depression, at age 63, that my energy level has waned. As a child, and a young adult, I was always thinking, always trying to figure stuff out, taking things apart and putting them back together (some of the time), and playing "hard and fast" with anything I did. My thoughts did not "race" or come so fast and furious that I was in a constant state of manic confusion and doubt. This behavior has been described to me by many of my cohorts in my local Depression and Bi-polar Support Alliance participants. I don't believe I was Bi-polar in my younger years; ADHD? Maybe. But psychology wasn't even calling it that in the early 1950s and 60s.

Psychiatric medicine is a relatively new science when compared to, say, Internal Medicine; what fewer General Practitioners now practice. My personal doctor recently told me that most new medical school trainees are specializing and, they will be on Advanced Medical Teams. We soon will not be seeing just one "family doctor," but many doctors, depending upon what ails us. I had a doctor tell me once," Medicine is the practice of what 'it's' not John."{"it" being the ailment or disease}. It's a process of elimination, one step or process at a time. If all the symptoms and indices, testing, and statistical models line up, then there's a good chance that the diagnosis will be correct. But, not always. Physicians and therapists do make mistakes. There are volumes of medical and psychiatric journals attesting to what I've just written. It's always best to get a second and third opinion in many cases; especially, when an invasive surgical process is being considered. It's YOUR body, it's YOUR right not to have someone cut it open, put some foreign substance into it, and take you down a pathway of "medication roulette" (remember?: "Which pill works Doc?!!") after being given a plethora of pills, some of which can cause extremely uncomfortable side-effects (vomiting, diarrhea, headaches, stiff muscles, heart palpitations, low libido {no or great disinterest in having sexual relations with your loved one, which can bring about a whole other set of issues}, confusion, insomnia, anxiety, low or high blood pressure, low or high blood sugar {really not good if you are diabetic!}, feelings of anger and extreme displeasure with life and those around you, agitation and general discomfort, general lack of energy or motivation, thoughts of suicide, and others).

My childhood and early adult life was filled with much activity. I swam, boated, fished, skied, played sports, played my violin and guitar, drove a car on trips, went on dates, went to work at many summer jobs while I was attending both undergraduate and graduate school, hiking, camping, writing, reading, and just enjoying being active and alive. I was a very "curious" person...I had to find out how things worked...what made them "tick." That also included people. Sometimes I think I was a little too curious. Like the time I wanted to find out how babies were made...literally, and walked in on my cousin and her boyfriend, when I was about 12 years old, and saw them "doing the horizontal mambo" (as my uncle Bob called it... he would have known, they had five kids). I was told to "Scram!!." Rather embarrassing for all of us I'm sure. I went to the library after that and found books on sex and sexual intercourse. Of course, the selections weren't as varied or illustrative in the late 1950s and early 1960s as they are in today's world. And, we did not have the Internet, I-phones, X-rated movies, "sexting" (what the f... is that?), and videos yet. There were some "girlie" magazines my friends shared, but they were not very instructional. I wanted to learn the "real stuff." Mostly, what I gleaned from my poor sources was very little and, what talk there was, I found out later, was mostly bullshit, poppycock, and drivel. Boys make up stories to brag to their friends about. Especially, when it comes to the girls they've been with. I now know that women, in my youth, did the same thing, but they were, usually, more subtle/discreet about it. But, today, women let "it all hang out." No pulling the punches...full steam ahead. I guess the good part is that you'll know, almost immediately, whether you are an acceptable mating partner or not. I'm so thankful not to be in the current "dating" world. It's got to be tough to establish a "true" relationship. Too many distractions, head games, and false moves.

I excelled in football and baseball in high school. I guess I could have been considered to be a "jock" by my classmates; but I never lowered myself to be crude or disrespectful of others. My parents had taught me to respect people and their feelings; even if I disagreed. I was part of the usual funny prank and jokes stuff, but I never lowered myself to bullying or "put downs." I even got into a fist fight, once, with a local bully for standing up for a mutual friend of mine who was not as fortunate as I in having an athletic build and the "chutzpah" to back it up. I won and the "bully" never bothered my friend again. It was the only time in my life that I got mad enough to go to fists. Later in life, I prided myself in my ability to talk people down and, I practiced being a good listener (a hard thing for an active, vocal kid to do). It parlayed itself into a career as a counselor and, eventually, a probation/parole officer. One must have very good listening skills to work with people who, in many cases, are "damaged goods," who did not have good role models growing up, who have mental health and/or substance abuse issues, and who commit crimes.

To this day, I remember my father having a sign that hung in his office. My dad was a very good listener, and most people knew this; especially those with whom he worked in the Juvenile Court System. The sign read: "The best part of a good conversation is when you are listening; except in my case, where verbal skills happen to be genetic." Everyone who saw this sign chuckled, because, unlike me and my mom (verbiage mongrels) dad would always take time to have you sit and talk while he listened. When he did, finally, comment, it was usually something heartfelt, understanding, filled with compassion, and reasoned out to "fit like a glove" for the talking person who left his office feeling and wanting to act more responsibly. He just had a knack for doing this. I always thought of it as a gift that I was fortunate enough to witness and use on occasion.

My dad's life reminded me of a paraphrase I once heard that was written by Pericles, a famous Greek philosopher: "What you leave when you die is not what is written in stone, carved into monuments, nor put into wealth, property, nor possessions. What is important and remembered is what is woven into and carried in the character of those you leave behind." My dad was like that, he helped people build character, courage, and wisdom for themselves to "play it forward" in their lives. He was a very, very wise man, and I miss him greatly.

In football, I played both offense and defense. We did not have "special" teams as most sports venues now have; with specialized talent for kickoffs, returns, defense and separate squads for offense. We did it all. A player would go onto the field of play and play his heart out at offense. Then, when the time came to be on defense, he'd do that too. Most players were totally exhausted by the end of the game, but not me. I was still "hyped up" for more; a real "Action Jackson" junkie. My endorphins were "maxed" in those days. I didn't have any problems "bringin' it" to use today's jargon.

In 1959, I won my high school's trophy for "Best Tackler" on defense. It was my Sophomore year. I played middle linebacker, a position in the middle of all the action on the field, usually about 7 to 10 feet behind the defensive center's position. A defensive linebacker is constantly on the move, even before the ball is snapped by the opposing team. One must be alert, fast, hyper-vigilant, and smart. In many cases, the middle linebacker is "calling defense" or, how the rest of his fellow players are going to "cover" the opposition in order to prevent them from moving the ball down field. In my case, I usually turned my back to the opposing team, between plays, and gave finger/hand signals in front of my chest so the other team couldn't see what "cover call" I was making.

During football practice, I recall, we had a "blocking sled." This was a solid steel contraption that was, in fact, on a concave sled. It had an overhanging frame, upon which was a canvas "dummy", filled with cotton and sawdust, to resemble a human body. The object of blocking and tackling practice was to run at this "dummy" and hit it with one's shoulder and body and force the sled backward. To make it even more challenging, our Italian coach, Mr Bongorni, a feisty, gruff, hard nosed "hit 'em again, harder, harder!" kind of guy, would ride atop the sled, standing behind the "dummy", holding the frame, and yelling at us (not encouraging us like most coaches of today do), literally screaming at us to,"Hit this thing so hard it'll make your grandmother's false teeth rattle!" We (myself included) got to a point, about a third of the way through practice to where we hated that "dummy" so much that we wanted to kill it. At some point some of the players, I think, confused the real "dummy" with Bongorni, and wanted to drive their torsos right through the "dummy" into Bongorni. I know, at one point, I did. I cracked three Rawlings football helmets to prove it; cracking them at the apex where the face opening and the forehead brace meet on each side of the helmet. Of course, I payed for this by suffering nerve "stingers"; pinched stinging sensations that run from the upper neck down the upper shoulder. Bongorni's voice was all I heard, above me, as I lay on the ground, in front of the sled: "That's how you hit this goddamn thing...good one Crawley...just rub it out...you'll be fine!"

During the real games, I'm sure there were players who suffered minor concussions. We called it "getting your bell rung." If you were able to get up after a devastating hit, recipient of deliverer, you were "good to go." "We ain't got no pussies on this squad...now get the hell out there and hit that sonofabitch....put HIM on the ground Carlson!"

I've done some research on concussions for this book. In professional sports, especially sports where head to head or head to surface contact is frequent (football, hockey, soccer, professional wrestling, rugby, NAS Car drivers, and the like). {I've written about this before in this book, however, I'm now including some of the history necessary for this chapter}. I've found that a Forensic Pathologist by the name of Dr. Bennet Omalu, originally from Nigeria, in 2010, was able to isolate and correctly diagnose Chronic Traumatic Encephalopathy (CTE), a brain disorder where *tau proteins* were collecting in a player's brain to the extent, after successive concussive "hits," to where the player's cognitive processes were greatly affected. In actuality, CTE was first diagnosed in professional boxers, in the 1920s, when boxers who had taken successive blows to the head, over time, exhibited a "punch drunk" type of behavior. But it was thought that CTE was only specific to boxers. Now, we know better. CTE has been found in football players, ice hockey players, professional wrestlers, mixed martial arts fighters, rugby players, soccer players, and even baseball players. What happens with CTE is the *tau proteins* act like a spider web, encircling and weaving in and around the brain synaptic cellular structures, causing the brain to malfunction, "shot-out" if you will, and bring on a whole series of mall-adaptive behaviors. The symptoms of CTE are manifested in a progressive deterioration of brain functions; including memory loss, social instability, erratic behavior, poor judgment, progressive dementia, slowing of muscular movement, hypomimia, impaired speech, tremors, vertigo, deafness, and extreme Depression to the point of wanting to commit suicide. The synaptic contacts were not working properly or not working at all. Some very famous professional football players suffered from and are now suffering from CTE: Mike Webster, Terry Long, Andre Waters, Justin Strzelczyk, and Tom McHale, just to name a few. Other NFL players who have died by their own hand or from complications of CTE are: Detroit Lions' Lou Creekmore, Huston Oilers and Miami Dolphins' linebacker, John Grimsley; Tampa Bay Buccaneers' guard Tom McHale; New England Patriots' and Philadelphia Eagles' running back Kevin Turner. And, a name everyone who's ever watched professional football recognizes: Ken Stabler was a victim of CTE and he committed suicide as a result. Some players virtually went "crazy."

The recent movie "Concussion" so well produced and acted by Will Smith, tells the story of Dr. Omalu, and his struggle with the NFL, the owner's association, Congress, fans, and other medical professionals to bring CTE into the light of day. (excerpts, above paragraph, are from Wikipedia source find 1-16 pages of description and data). It's through this man's dedicated persistence, conscience, and will to do something pro-active that we have the "concussion protocol" that is now required in most professional sports. We need it in pee-wee leagues and, high schools throughout the world. A young brain is still developing and to suffer repetitive strikes to the head is not a good thing. Many players have actually committed suicide over their discomfort and pain. We should all be thankful for this man bringing CTE into the light so we can prevent serious injury and death. But the struggle isn't over yet. Some organizations, some in the Big Medicine field who have very lucrative contracts with the professional sports organizations, are now demanding more studies and doubting Dr. Omalu's data. His research is factual. It has been replicated over and over by qualified medical personnel, and his reputation, which was first questioned, has not been besmirched.

I find it particularly annoying that a man who is trying to honor the Hippocratic Oath... "do no harm...." is being questioned in the same manner as Dr. Harch with his HBOT therapy, all for the sake of protecting the "status quo" and the wealth of these mammoth enterprises. Where is their sense of priority? Is the "bottom line" their only god? Do they have to be so rich that they will sacrifice the health and welfare of others just to make another billion dollars? Someone needs to draw the line here. I like football. My father and I watched football together both when I played and, as adults, as spectators. Dr. Omalu, in his presentations, has said, over and over, that he is not trying to crush the life out of professional sports; but, there needs to be some distinct prioritization here. We need to protect and save lives BEFORE we send them into harms way. This is as true for professional sports as it is for police and fire personnel, soldiers, or anyone whose life may be put in danger. "Be prepared," isn't that the boy scout and girl scout's motto? So, what's the problem? Perhaps, in this new age of technological speed memos and Instagram tweet's, we've lost some of our "humanity" and common sense. More on this later.

I was injured at a football game my Senior year in High School. The only good part about this is that it was toward the end of our season and we only had a couple more games to go. I was hit from the rear and front at the same time. I guess the other team wanted to "take me out." I must have been making too many tackles. This type of "blocking" is illegal now because of the potential for serious injury. Players have suffered broken necks from "crack" blocks as they were called in my day. Anyway, on this particular evening in the cold of December, I was jack-knifed the wrong way (bent backward from the top and had my legs cut out from under me from the bottom by two opponents). The ground, not "Astro Turf" (wasn't invented yet), was frozen and it was like hitting a block of ice. My head made contact with the ground first. I think I was knocked out because, when I woke up, I saw all my teammates, the trainer, and the team physician peering down at me and asking me where it hurt. I was really "groggy", and unstable. I probably had a concussion. At least that's what a doctor let onto when I arrived at the Everett General Hospital ER where I arrived, by ambulance, in my football uniform, to be checked out. Final diagnosis after a weekend in a hospital bed: Multiple contusions of the torso and lower legs, and concussion. I was given a prescription for aspirin with codeine for pain. I don't think I took any. And, I was told to do bed rest for the remainder of the weekend, being a Sunday, the day I was released.

The game had been on a Friday night, and I was told all the cheer leading squad and some of the players and booster club wanted to come visit but, the medical staff told everyone I was to rest and be quiet without any stimulation. So, the only people I saw while I was in hospital were my parents and the medical staff.

The following Monday, though, was a hero's welcome. Apparently, my being "hit so viciously" as one of my teammates put it, roused the ire of the squad and they went on to win the game! So, something good came out of a tragic situation. I was pleased, but very sore, physically. I also had a lot of really cool dates, with some of our school's most attractive girls, after that. The later part of my Senior year was very, let's just say, "social."

Unfortunately, I think, my fame and good fortune led to a lot of partying and goofing off. My grades suffered a bit, but not to where I couldn't qualify for entrance into the local Junior College in Everett (now Everett Community College) the following Fall, after a summer of work on a purse seiner fishing boat in the inside passage, off the coast of Alaska. Beautiful country, hard work; fishing that is. I made good money, but the "after hours" down time (offloading our catch and refueling for the next foray out to sea) in ports like Ketchikan, Sitka, Wrangle, and others is nothing but "party on." There's not much else to do but play poker, drink, and "raise a little hell." Most of the women in these towns are "spoken for" so to speak. You don't mess with Jane, or "Dolly", or Candice, or Flo. They have their "regular" fishermen friends who are usually not willing to share. Sure, you can dance with them, but you don't dare try to "date" them, if you know what I mean. I saw one crew member from another boat try to kiss one of these "ladies" and, the next thing I knew, he had a chair busted across his head, The chair didn't break….his head did...split wide open. There was blood all over the place and a medical EMT team took him to a local clinic for the stitches. This was 1961-1962. I don't know if things have changed any, I doubt it because I've been up north to Alaska a couple times and the thing I know about "natives" (people who've lived and worked there most of their lives) is that they are a flag waving, gun toting, "chaw-chewin" bunch of independent folk. If you are in trouble and need help, they'll come running and pitch in, no questions asked or enumeration necessary; but, never cheat them or theirs, nor try to take what isn't yours. You may get "disappeared."

This is also the time in my life when I was really "introduced" to al-co-hol. The hard stuff. Beer is okay, but a "real man" drinks Jack Daniels or Old Granddad, 100 proof...straight or, as an acquired taste gentleman would put it, "neat" (straight, in a glass, without ice). Some of the crew didn't even bother with glasses...right out of the bottle was their choice. I actually don't remember much of those days other than the fact we worked hard and played hard. I don't remember ever having a hangover....not a good thing. It may have been a deterrent to me (to have a bad hangover). So, I became alcoholic but, I never drank on the job. That was the rule I learned on our boat (it stuck with me throughout my career in Adult Corrections). "There's a time to work and there's a time to play," old Captain Len would say. He meant it too. If you got caught with booze on you, in you, or in your gear, the next stopover in the next port would find yourself alone, without a way back to the States and without a job. Only one crew member violated that rule that summer...it wasn't me. Crew replacements are easy to find. There are always a few bumming around in each port and, the captains know who they are; who's reliable and who's not.

I had consumed some beer at socials in high school, but I was never a binge drinker like some of my fellow classmates who "practiced at it" for college. Allot of them flunked out of college because of their drinking behavior. My drinking was usually confined to social gatherings on the weekend at various campus parties and "keggers." I tried to avoid the people who were "lushes" and didn't have much control over their behavior. My grades didn't suffer, and I never drank during the weekdays when I knew I had early morning classes. But, all the while, I was verging toward the precipice of "self-medicating" for Major Depression. I did notice that I felt more "down" after I'd consumed. I thought my Depression was a "minor" thing. Everyone "gets the blues now and then" (like the old Neil Diamond song goes). Right? At the time, I had not learned enough to know the difference between feeling "down" and feeling so depressed that nothing was ever going to pull me out of it. It hadn't become that bad, yet (1962-64). Besides, I thought really depressed people were mentally unstable (here's the "stigma" again, even I believed it then). So, why tell my friends or parents anything; they wouldn't understand anyway, right? Wrong again John! A couple things I have learned about many folks who suffer from mental illness:

1. We're experts at beating ourselves over the head with guilt sticks. We do it over and over, just to make sure we are feeling guilty; even if there's nothing to be guilty about. We just do it.

2. We have great difficulty conforming to "normal" patterns of behavior. Some of us wear our illness like a cop wears a badge. So everyone can see (but we really don't want to be seen by most people because they may judge us…...and then we'll feel…you guessed it…...guilty!)

But the fear of being "stigmatized" IS very real….because stigma is a reality for the mentally ill and substance addled folks. Especially, the homeless. I have spoken with a lot of homeless folks, both professionally, when I was working as a parole/probation officer and, for the research on this book. Homeless folks ARE you and me. The only difference is, they may have fallen on some bad luck, suffered a disease and lost their medical insurance, lost their job, and it just escalates from there. They may have lost a loved one in a tragic accident. Their main breadwinner may have decided to run off to Mexico with the young blonde secretary at his office, cleaned out your savings account, and left you "high (literally, because you had to smoke a joint to calm down) and dry (no money for booze)." There are many, many stories; most of them sad; so, I won't relay many of them here.

I WILL tell you about a young man, slight of build, average height, with sandy colored hair, about 32 years of age, who I met on the sidewalks of Seaside, Oregon last summer (2016). His name was Jason. He was a nice looking man, and he still seemed to care about his appearance because his clothing, although worn, was clean and, he appeared fairly well groomed and bathed (he didn't smell bad). He was busking for money with his open guitar case at his feet, while playing a variety of songs. He was also singing. He had a very melodic soft tenor voice that blended well with his old Gibson flat top guitar.

During a break from his street entertainment, I placed a $5.00 bill into his guitar case and complemented him on his artistry. He thanked me profusely and told me not many people comment on his talent as I did. I told him I'd been a musician in a band in one of my former lives (which is true, we'll come to that later) and, I appreciated what he was trying to do by still using his talents to survive. He laughed at this juncture and told me, "This wasn't all I did for the past couple of years." I then said, "Really? What did you do?" Jason then revealed to me that he had worked as a software engineer at a high-tech company in silicon valley California. He told me he was diagnosed Bi-polar 2 in August, a couple years prior. He told his immediate supervisor and, he had his "pink slip" a week later with the reason for termination being that he could no longer work in an area where "sensitive data" were being processed; as if he was some sort of "Snowden" (the alleged American "spy" who gave compromising data to the Russians, as Jason put it) or something. He felt as though he was perceived as a threat to the company; even though he'd worked there since graduation from Cal-Tech, in 2006.

I was aghast at this disclosure. I said something to the effect, "You mean they thought you could be "turned" as a spy or, intellectual property salesman to the highest bidder?" He just shook his head affirmatively. I then remember asking him if he tried to contact the EEOC (Equal Employment Opportunity Council) or, an attorney to see if he had recourse in a discrimination action. He told me it would have cost him a fortune and still, no guarantee of a satisfactory outcome. So, he got all his savings together, moved out of his apartment, got into his car and traveled North. Of course, the money ran short. He had no references to find a new position, so he hit the streets to "make ends meet." I thought, surely this guy has a good education, he appears relatively healthy, intelligent, and he probably can work; but, he apparently has chosen, because of being "stigmatized," to say "fuck it." I kind of felt sorry for Jason. I encouraged him to get "back in the race" because all employers are not jerks. There are some who do understand, have people in their own families who suffer from mental illness, and are willing to work with people as long as they are "balanced out" through medications, therapy, or a combination of each. That was another issue with him, he was out of medications and worried he'd have a manic episode. I gave him the name of a local resource person I knew at Clatsop County Behavioral Health in town, directions (about 3 blocks away), and told him to tell her I'd sent him over to get "hooked up." I knew, if Jason went, he'd get some help. A week later, I had to leave to come back to Marysville, so I didn't have a chance to talk to Renee'(a counselor I know at Clatsop Behavioral Health) to see if Jason showed up. I still regret not following up on this, but I did give it my best shot.

So, Jason is just one example of the "potential" that's on the street folks. Remember? "...ask not for whom the bell tolls"......They are us and we are them. A little help goes a long way with these folks. If they are offering a "street talent", by all means give them a few bucks; but if they're panhandling, instead of money, I would suggest handing them a food bank voucher, a meal ticket to the local mission, a voucher for the Good Will store or Volunteers of America, addresses of local VFW (if they are a vet), local church that helps the homeless find resources, some warm socks or clothing, a bottle or two of good drinking water (homeless folks, by the time they get to a hospital ER when they're sick, are usually very dehydrated—I was told this by two separate ER nurses at two separate locations, one in Oregon and one in Washington State). There are so many simple ways you can "play it forward" to help folks who, mostly, I've found, are very appreciative.

If you are really ambitious, volunteer at your local church that has a program to help the homeless. Your local missions, Good Will, Volunteers of America, Synagogue, Mosque, and First Aid/Red Cross organizations often have resource providers who can use some help. Donated clothing and underused backpacks offer these folks some sense of dignity. In the final analyses, of all those 53 (or so) homeless folks I've spoken with over the past 4 years, all they want is to be acknowledged and know that someone, as one fellow put it, "...gives a shit. We're not lookin' to rob you or take anything from you that you're unwilling to give, but you will get our heartfelt thanks when you do."

Sure, some of these folks are not well versed in manners or the finer elements of conversational English; and some may have a tendency to be aggressive with their panhandling (in most states a law violation), but most are not. I've given out 3 by 5 cards, with resource names and addresses on them (if you do this, make sure to wrap the cards with cellophane packing tape to waterproof them), so these folks can make contact, and they thank me for caring. So most are appreciative and thankful that someone cared enough to stop and lend a kind word, a pair of socks, and a bottle of drinking water. How much does that cost? The value is in your character and woven into the fabric of your soul….the price? Who cares. The reward?........PRICELESS! You will be a genuine "fire fighter" when you do these things. You will be doing "for", instead of "griping about." I like what the now deceased, famous African American poet, Maya Angelou said: "If you learn...teach," and, "If you get...give." Always "play it forward." It will come back; sometimes, when you least expect it. This homeless/ substance-addled population isn't getting smaller. It's growing every day and, it IS part of the "fire" of which I write.

During my formative years, when my parents and I were traveling, and staying at our "home base" on Tulalip Tyee, I recall that I became interested in psychology. Part of my curiosity stemmed from a certain "fear." My mother's brother, Bill, suffered from some sort of mental illness in the 1950s. I believe he was diagnosed as being schizophrenic. He had severe mood swings and uncontrollable fits of rage. On occasion, he had auditory and visual hallucinations. Bill was a stocky, barrel-chested man, who exhibited great physical strength. I once saw him lift a log, about 40 inches in diameter and 20 feet long, pick it up and carry it to a location where he could cut it up for firewood. When he worked for the Wyerhauser lumber mill in Everett, Washington he once put another co-worker into the hospital after striking the man with his fists. I don't recall the circumstances, but he was fired for his angry tirades. Of course, in those days, no employer made any concessions if an employee had mental health issues. Many employers do not in today's world, either. The "stigma" is very much alive and thriving in many arenas of our society.

Following formal diagnosis, Bill was hospitalized at Northern State Hospital (no longer a mental health facility), in Sedro Wooley, Washington. He was hospitalized at this location on numerous occasions. I remember mom and dad going up to the hospital to bring my Uncle Bill home, for weekend visits. At the time, I didn't know that the medical staff at the hospital were "stabilizing" Bill with medications. They were also giving him electro-shock "treatments" (where two paddles are affixed to the sides of the patients head, after strapping him/her down on a hospital gernny, and electric current is passed from paddle to paddle, through the frontal lobes {where "emotions" and basic libido and other sensorium functions are located, making us "human," are located}of the brain. (You have my permission to, again, think "One Flew Over The Coo-coo's Nest" on this). I found out, some years later, that Bill was given Thorazine, a heavy tranquilizer which puts a patient into a sort of "trance-like" state (from Physician's PDR, DSM-IV). When I worked with and around mentally ill inmates, later in my career, we used to call the folks who took this drug, "dancers doin' the Thorazine shuffle." It was very obvious that they'd been drugged because their gait was a shuffle exhibited by short, little steps and drool coming out of their mouths. They were extremely "manageable." Even those with Manic or Psychotic issues.

Bill would be very docile and compliant during his weekend visits with the family. He was also devoid of emotions. It was like he was "dead wood," no feelings or "humanity." He would respond with short, monotone speech when asked a question or spoken to. He often just stared out into space. There was "no life' to him. It bothered all of us, but the psychiatric staff at the hospital stated that it was for his and our safety that these "procedures" were done. The reason I know these things, is because I overheard my parents discuss them on numerous occasions. My father's concern for Bill was that he was showing NO SIGNS of getting better. In fact, according to my father's comments, he felt Bill was getting worse at the hands of these "draconian, butchers" as he referred to the psychiatric staff. It hasn't changed much from those days. I saw it, first hand, when I was hospitalized in 2008-2009.

Bill had a wife and three children, but his marriage was also strained and his children, although they loved him, feared him. As far as I know, he was not physically or sexually abusive toward any of his own family members. He did visit with them, while "supervised" by my parents who had "signed on" as guardians. I guess there was a legal requirement to do so.

Now that I've been educated, and spoken at length, with Bill's oldest daughter, Carol, about those days, when she and her father had communication, I'm almost sure he was miss-diagnosed. I'm almost sure he was Bi-polar 1 (there have only, recently, been greater clinical studies and information about Bi-polar 1, 2, and 3. In fact, Bi-polar 3 has only been in existence, as a diagnosis, for about 2 years), with Schizo-affective manifestations. This would mean he had extreme mood swings, which I remember, before Bill was hospitalized; where he would be almost euphoric, happy, elated and exited about something; two hours or so later, he's be in an extreme depression, almost ready to kill himself. He was "successful" in the later statement. Bill "escaped" from Northern State and, he committed suicide by running under a locomotive traveling at high speed. (Something about my family and the trains...go figure). It was a tragic and sorrowful event. I always faulted the treatment he received, my having (in later years) received similar, minus the electroshock and Thorazine. Our mental health treatment delivery systems haven't come very far in today's world. I was age 15 when Bill killed himself. I was devastated because, in earlier years, we'd gone deer hunting, fishing and camping, and played baseball together. He could "powder" a ball over the fence line just like Babe Ruth. I liked him and I always saw him as a kind soul who had some issues with anger control. I knew he loved and cherished his kids. Carol, the eldest daughter (Bill's wife was also named Carol), told me so and, I saw it up close and personal when I visited them in their home. Unfortunately, Bill's wife divorced him due to his illness and, she left with another man and pretty much abandoned her family. My younger cousin, Billy, the younger son, was raised by my Aunt Dorothy and Uncle Steve Philipp. Beverly, the 'middle' sibling and a person who my mother dearly loved, passed away early in life from cancer. She was married to a great guy who I used to hang out with at a local drive-in in Everett (The Totem Drive-in, still operating all these years and a landmark). I always was envious of the "hot-rods" Bev's husband, George Atterson, and his friends drove. They were "classics" (1955/56 Chevy Bel-Aire hardtops {no post}, 1954 Mercury {no post}, El Camenos, Impalas, roadsters (39s and 40s, all customized, some with really "cool" candy apple red lacquer paint jobs, and so forth). My "fear" was that mental illness may run in the family. It doesn't, but when one is an impressionable teen, the mind works a lot of fantasies, at least mine did.

There were other instances of "hyper" activity exhibited by relatives on my mom's side of the family. I've already written about Aunt Jean, who's rage and rail against her passive husband was a common, almost daily event; until he couldn't take it. Bob Morgan would either get up and leave the house or go to visit some friends in order to avoid Jean's rages. Their children, as teenagers, were often gone from their home; I think, to avoid their mother's fits.

My own mother often got very upset over what I considered to be "small stuff." She would cry at the drop of a hat if something she saw or heard was displeasing or, what she determined to be cruel. I remember, once, her crying over the way a man was treating his dog, scolding the animal for peeing in the house. In this particular instance, she, in tears, got angry and told the man that his dog would probably not relieve itself if he took the dog outside more often. The man told her to mind her own business. Of course, this made her cry even more.

Uncle Steve, mom's other older brother, would sometimes exhibit anxiety over the way some of our political leaders did not serve all the people. It wasn't just a comment or two; it was a dissertation. Steve would sometimes go on and on about this or that. As a budding teenager who spent a lot of time with my Uncle, I wasn't into politics that much, so I found his tirades rather boring; but, sometimes they were funny. I remember him going on about how much a toilet seat cost to produce for military aircraft, "$500.00 for a toilet seat....I could buy 100 of them, the whole toilet, for what this guy voted through...they need to throw him out...he's a no-good-nik!" Steve also loved the comic strip "Pogo," in its heyday, a great satirical look, using cartoon animals, who exhibited and characterized some of the political hacks and shenanigans of the day. I learned, as I grew older, to love this comic strip too. I wish we could bring it back. It would be so apropos for today's political climate (2017).

My unfounded fear was predicated on what I saw and heard. There is an old saying, from Mark Twain, which I've since incorporated into my thinking, as a reminder: "It ain't what ya know that'll hurt ya. It's what ya think ya know, for sure, that ain't necessarily so." (from Mark Twain, The

Life and Times of Samuel Clemons). So true. As we get older we, hopefully, "wise up." My grandfather, God rest his soul, once said," Too soon ve git oldt and too late schmardt." He was a very wise man.

Growing up, I went out of my way to NOT be derisive, violent, or unkind to people. I knew, at a very young age, that violence breeds violence, war breeds war, and why make an enemy, when a friend has more "staying power." I still had plenty of energy to burn off and, I made a lot of friends along the way. Playing sports and music, being active, traveling, sharing stories with family and loved ones; these activities are the kind of stuff where great joy, passion, and satisfaction incubate and blossom. To this day, now that I'm on the road to recovery, I firmly believe that.

At one point, following graduation from high school, I had the opportunity to play collegiate football for the University of Washington. This was in the early 1960s; the years that the U. of W. went to the Rose Bowl, not only once but twice. I turned the chance down and now, looking back, and knowing what I now know about CTE, players having their careers cut short by injury and other issues, I think I made the right decision. Having recently suffered an injury, in my high school senior year, added to this decision. I wanted to focus on my education. And, besides, I was beginning to experience periods of extreme depression. I hid this from others, including my own family members, successfully, by immersing myself into all that I did, with great "penasche" (in the "exhibitionist" sense), verve, spirit, and dedication. I never undertook anything, during my youth, that I did not feel confident in accomplishing; be it a high school play ("Harvey") or something as mundane as a fund raiser for the prom. I wasn't a "quitter." Loyal to the end, no matter what.

Sometimes, my over exuberance cost me dearly; especially with women. I was a horny man; and, sometimes, things got the best of me. I never forced myself on a woman; that was "drilled" into my psyche by my parents ("always treat a lady with respect and don't hurt her," were my father's very words). But it sure didn't stop me from trying to "score". Some women liked the confidence and energy I exhibited; some did not. So be it, I thought, there's "a lot of fish in the ocean and I'm a pretty good fisherman."

Or, so I thought at the time. I still needed some more "education," if you know what I mean (about the finer points of opposite sex relationships).

The time I write of, was during my subsequent military stint in the United States Air Force and during the remainder of my college years. I took a "break" between my sophomore and junior years in college. I remember the event that initiated my decision to go and "fight for my country." It was in November, 1963 when I went to a morning chemistry class at the (now) Western Washington University in Bellingham, Washington (near the Canadian border). My chemistry professor came into the class, walked to the lectern and made this announcement: "President John F. Kennedy has been assassinated. Classes have been suspended until further notice." He then left the lecture hall. You could hear a pin drop. Dead silence from a group who had been chatting away a few moments earlier. I recall walking from the classroom out onto "Red Square," a large bricked yard area, and looking at the shocked, crying, stunned facial expressions of students and faculty. Classes, of course, were canceled for the remainder of the day as most of us huddled around television sets in the student lounges, dorms, and other places to try and find out what the hell had happened and, to confirm our greatest fears: that our President, the Leader of the Free World, had been murdered. With each news release, on every channel, our fears were confirmed. Anyone who has studied history knows the rest of this story, so I won't belabor the point by going into a recap. I was somewhat depressed, but more angry; especially when I learned that Lee Harvey Oswald, the shooter, had Russian ties and, allegedly, had sworn fidelity to the Communist Party in this country, the United States of America!

I left college to work for awhile and, to make up my mind about what I was going to do. I knew that the chances of winding up face down, in a rice paddy in Viet Nam, was about 1 in 3, in those days (1964-1967), if one joined the infantry (Army, Marines mainly). We still had the "Draft," and there was no "lotto" draw (a low number meant you were going to be drafted to serve; a high number, maybe not). The "lotto" drawings came much later.

I chose to work through what would have been one quarter of college, earn enough money to return to school, and finish my college education. I lived with my folks, at the Tulalip Tyee homestead, telling my folks I would "learn more if I pay for it myself"(true). Well, I soon received a notice from the U.S, Government that informed me, since I'd dropped out of college, I was now eligible for the "Draft." This scared the shit out of me because I had friends who had died in Viet Nam; killed in action. There were "war protests" fomenting all over the country. People were saying that it was only a war for the rich to make more money and the corrupt politicians to do the same (by the end of the war, one could deduce that the preceding statement was partially true; only worse!)

So, I went shopping. Not for clothing or food; shopping for which branch of the military would give me the best "deal." I had no desire to actually "fight." I'd serve, if I had to; remembering that I'd been a "service brat" in my youth. I knew about the military, I'd seen what these people do. Or, so I thought. The one good thing about television in those days was that, for the first time in the history of the United States of America, the war was brought home, up close and personal, by cameramen and women, correspondents, and reporters whose excellent coverage helped to shape what was about to come. We all watched David Brinkley and Chet Huntley's News Hour and Walter Cronkite's outstanding broadcasts of the war. It became VERY personal. Our friends and family members were dying and being maimed over there...with no end in sight. Each year, more casualties and injured….10.000….27,000…...29,500.

I, on the other hand, didn't have the time. The start of the next quarter was over 60 days away and an Army Sargent Recruiter told me, "Well son, you may make it (avoid the draft), but my bet's on the United States Army... we're going to getcha." He said, once a person got "The Letter," as I had, it was usually about 30 days later that they would receive their Draft Notice to report for induction. That, I wanted to avoid.

So, I enlisted in the United States Air Force, with a "guarantee" of "non-combatant" (NC) status. They also told me I could pick my career. So, I chose "Personnel Specialist." I figured: this was working with people helping them keep their service records and activities in line. It was a worthy position and I'd still be serving my country.

Basic training, at Lackland Air Force Base in Texas, near San Antonio, was hot in October, 1964 (during the daily marches in our civilian clothing, for the first three days of basic training; they did this on purpose so your clothing stunk so bad from sweaty exercise that a new, clean, "green fatigue" uniform would be a welcome sight, and it was a "rite of passage," acknowledging you made it thus far. After two days, I didn't have to hang my clothing up, it was so "stiff" from sweat soaking that all I had to do was prop it next to my bed), …..and cold. There was snow in Texas, in November, only, by the time I got to Tech training, in Amirillo, we marched, again, in something the airmen called "snust," a mix of dirty snow and dust. So much fun, re-polishing the mirror shine on our "brogans" (military marching boots), EVERY MORNING, before muster. I got lucky though. Being older and having two years of college under my belt, the First Sargent made me a squad leader and, with that, came the "perks." I didn't have to march, as much. I was first in line at the chow hall, and I could miss "muster," on occasion, because there were two of us who would rotate weeks, one "on" and one "off." I also was made "runner." In other words, I worked in the HQ in the mornings, getting coffee ready, running to the PX for fresh donuts, and actually running messages and documents to the various locations the command wanted me to. There were no Fax machines in 1965; at least, if there were, I never saw one. We did have "teletype," but that was what would be considered to be an old version of "e-mail" in today's world. Considering what the rest of the "grunts" had to do (march, march, march, peel potatoes at the mess {aka KP duty}, stand guard for hours in the "snust", march, march some more, etc.), I had a pretty "cushy" job. As a contrast, I remember some poor airmen who were singled out to stand guard, in the "snust," fully outfitted in combat gear (unloaded AR-15 included), at the "Squirrel Cage HQ." The "squirrel cage" was a rectangular set of cyclone fencing wire, top to bottom, that surrounded the local garbage bins. The reason for the fencing was so the garbage or papers wouldn't fly off, in the strong winds that are common to the area, and clutter the base. The "Cage" as it was called was said to be tornado proof. That doesn't say much for anyone standing outside the cage in a severe wind storm. We were, after all, right smack dab in the middle of "tornado alley." The Texas panhandle. The unwitting airman might go "AWOL" (Airborne Without Leave). This "duty," which I was fortunate never to have had, I think, was for a minor insubordination (not quite rising to Courts Martial level) or something; to teach the novice airman discipline and decorum, no doubt. I'm sure those airmen who had to do this never repeated their "transgression" again.

As I've written, I kept myself busy. I never let my depressive moods get the best of me. I knew they were always there, in the background of my psyche, but I fought them off; sometimes, with alcohol. Yep, I self-medicated, as many who suffer, and don't suffer, do. I am an alcoholic. But, at the time, I wouldn't have admitted it (mid to late 1960s and from there on into my career as a Parole/Probation Officer.) I was once told, by a certified psychiatric social worker, that I was a "high functioning" alcoholic. She said there are many people, around the world, who put in a hard day's work, successfully raise and support families, have friends, are beloved in their churches and, the community organizations in which they participate; but, at the end of the day, they drink like fish. She said this to me, she said, because, after reviewing my career (s), and interviewing my friends, spouse, and co-workers in probation and parole, she deduced that I never drank on the job. That's true. I told her that I had the opportunity, and permission (during our hour off for lunch, it was our time) to consume. Some of my co-workers did. I always felt it would be hypocritical, as a probation officer, to consume at lunch and then, go back to my office where clients, many of whom had drug and/or alcohol issues, would smell it on my breath. Not a good way to establish credibility and rapport with those you supervise. I waited until I got home to be a hypocrite. By the way, there are no such "animals" as "high functioning" alcoholics. Alcohol messes up your brain. It actually changes the brain's cognition and receptors to where it takes years of sobriety to come back to a semblance of normality or "stasis" (balance) as some therapists like to call it. The damage is usually pretty permanent. If you don't believe me I'd suggest you read a few books regarding alcoholism and what it does to the human brain. The evidence is overwhelming. Pick any book, the evidence is all the same. I, too, was in "denial." That's one of the first signs of alcoholism.

Anyway, I'm getting ahead of myself with my story here. Back to the Air Force. Once I'd finished Personnel Tech School in Amarillo, I had the opportunity to "select" a potential "duty station." No guarantees, but one had an outside chance of getting to go to where one wanted to go in the world. I put in for Germany, thinking it would be a great way to see Europe. We had a lot of bases in Germany.

They sent me half-way in between, on the Northern Hemisphere: Alaska. Elmendorf Air Force Base to be exact. I didn't mind, but everyone still spoke English there, unless you were Inuit or something. I wanted to learn another language, see a different culture; what's with this Alaska stuff? I was stationed with the United States Air Force Security Service; having been thoroughly vetted as to my loyalty to God and country, my parents vetted (I later found out), my teachers (both from high school and college), my employers, my closest friends, and (I think) former lovers (one of them told me she'd received a phone call "from some guy in 'intelligence' asking a lot of personal questions about you John, I told him nothing." {right, knowing her, she probably told him everything; that's why I dumped her}).

I held a Top Secret Script Clearance, as far as I know, about the highest clearance one can get in the U.S. Military. We had access to Top Secret documents and procedures. There were no computers in those days. We typed on regular typewriters. We had a burn bag and a furnace at the instillation I was at. Each day, we'd have to burn our used carbon paper. When we replaced a typewriter ribbon, we'd have to burn that too (I always thought this was dumb because, you overwrite on a ribbon so many times, that, by the time the ribbon's been used up, it has thousands of written over letters on it and, no one could decipher what's on it.) Anyway, it was a Courts Martial offense not to burn one's carbon paper; or, anything that was combustible and no longer in use. We burned a lot of stuff at that place. We also had "suits" walking around (men and women in civilian dress) who, I was told, worked for the Central Intelligence Agency (C.I.A.). They were "invisible" my Section Leader told me. In other words, 'they weren't here and you didn't see them.' Pretty spooky I thought. I didn't have much interest in what they were doing, anyway, out in the middle of no where. We worked on a "need to know" basis. If you didn't need to know the information to do your job, then it didn't exist. Pretty simple.

I gave airmen and officers their record's checks on an annual basis. We had over 1,300 personnel attached (the actual number probably has changed and it was classified at the time) to our command, the 6981ˢᵗ Security Group, so I kept busy. Records checks consisted of interpreting a "coded" spread sheet and correcting any erroneous information. I did this, in groups of twenty personnel, twice a day, among other duties, on a daily basis.

I also gave personnel their "orientation" seminars. These young troops were going for a one year "remote" tour into the upper regions of the State, running, mostly, along the Pacific Corridor to the Baring Sea and beyond. I told them "there's a woman behind every tree." It was in jest to try and cheer them up; because most of them did not "choose" to go "remote," but that was part of their duty as Security Personnel. They were part of what was then called the "White Alice Security Perimeter" that ran the whole west coast of Alaska. You may have seen pictures of these big, white-domed, hexagonal (like a big round egg-crate), structures in the arctic back in the day (1960s through 1980s). That's what I'm describing. They were Aircraft/ Warning Air Control Stations (AWACS). We listened to the Russians, Chinese, Vietnamese, Cambodians, and North Koreans; and, they, in turn, listen to us. Any inkling of an attack or out of the ordinary movement and F-16 Fighter Jets, fully armed with nuclear warheads, would be scrambled to the site. We were at war, so a "no tolerance, high alert" status was maintained at all times. Most of the time, the job was extremely boring, with little to do. Winter lasts 8 months (at least) in Alaska, and the chill factor usually prevents much outdoor activities; especially in the arctic north. Most of this system has now been upgraded through digital/ satellite technology. By the way, there are no trees in the tundra of Alaska. Hence…..you guessed it. These guys (mostly men) were some really horny men when they returned to "civilization."

At one point, during my duty in Alaska, we acquired a new Section Commanding Officer. He was from Alabama, a red head, and fresh out of R.O.T.C. (Reserve Officers Training Corps). He thought his shit didn't stink. He was a certified asshole. No one in our unit liked or respected him as a person, but we had to respect the rank. He was a Second Lieutenant. One of the irritating "duties" he foisted upon the enlisted personnel was the requirement to clean and polish the tiles of the office floor, EVERY Friday afternoon. He would require us to use old tooth brushes to whisk dirt from the tile crevasses and use steel wool on scuffs so there would be "no marks or mars" when the floor wax was applied. This wasn't self polishing wax folks. We had to put it down, on our hands and knees, wait for it to dry, and then "buff" it with an electric polisher. Then, often after duty station hours, he would have us wait, stand at attention, while he inspected our work. He was a real JERK. This, in our opinion, was particularly irksome because we had better things to do and, we wanted to get out of the office for the weekend. He did this on purpose just to show us who was "boss."

Well, the time came up for "rotations" (reassignment orders to another location) and, somehow, our red head came up on the list. One of the fast rules one learns is that you NEVER give anyone "shit" who works in HR (Personnel in our case). We had IBM 836 punch card machines that coded everything from housing allowances, pay, promotions, job description, to reassignments...yep, RE-ASSIGNMENT. So, our sorry-assed Lieutenant put in for Hawaii. Our Section Tech Sergeant knew that there was one digit that separated the code for Hawaii from Karamursel A.F.B., where he would deploy to a "remote" site in northern Turkey, a tour lasting 12 months. The "remote" site (I don't remember the name of it) was a godforsaken place that I learned from other airmen, who'd been there, was cold, isolated, and barren. They told me that the native tribesmen used camel dung for firewood (there were no trees), and one smelled this burning dung from morning through the night. It was constant. Guess whose orders for reassignment came in for Karamursel?

He was livid. His face was the color of his hair with rage. It was said he marched his ass down to the 6981st Commander's Office and demanded a change of orders. He failed in this regard. I think the "word" of his previous insensitive actions did not fall far from the Commander's ears. 'What goes around comes around.' So, the reason I tell this story is to remind people that we are all trying to be good people; but, sometimes, we forget and think we're "entitled" to be better than others. Obviously, we're not.

One of the things I did love about Alaska is the outdoors. One could drive out of Anchorage (Elmendorf A.F.B. is three blocks from town), and in fifteen minutes you are in wilderness, communing with Mother Nature. The fishing, and I'm told, hunting, are fabulous. I know the fishing was; I caught my fair share of salmon, sea-run Cutthroat trout, Steel-head, Arctic char, and Greyling during my 3 years, 8 months, and 28-day stay in the great Northland. I also played music, in a rock-n-roll band.

One day, I met our lead guitar player, Eric, while practicing my Gibson LTD 330, cherry red, double cut-away, the second guitar I bought with money earned when I worked summers at the Everett Scott Paper Company(well before joining the Air Force). Eric came up to my room in the barracks and introduced himself and said I sounded good. I found out that this red headed guy was also a musician and he'd had a band in South Dakota, where he hailed from. In fact, he told me many of his family members were professional musicians. We decided to "jam" together, sharing songs we mutually knew and teaching each other songs we wanted to learn. We soon had a pretty good repertoire. We found another airman, Tom, who played drums; and, a bassist, another Eric, who worked on base as an ambulance driver. The band was rounded out by Tim, another airman, who had a great tenor voice and a good memory for many song's lyrics. Unfortunately, he was a drunk; but, that's a separate story wherein I honed my budding "counseling" skills.

Initially, we were hired to play at the Enlisted Men's Club (women Air Force personnel were there too) on weekends. The club paid us $125.00 per weekend stint, each night, (for all five of us, not a lot of money in 1965-67), but it was exposure and, we figured we'd have the opportunity to move on. And move on we did, in grand fashion. While playing at the Officer's Club on base one night, a fellow we knew brought and introduced me (as band manager) to a friend who owned a nightclub in Anchorage. This friend of a friend asked if we were interested in playing at his club: Johnny Penguin's

Club. I asked him how much he was willing to pay us. I recall him saying, "How about $800.00?" I told him there were 5 of us and I didn't think the rest of the band members would want to work the long hours, I knew most clubs in town wanted, for $800.00 a night (about $160.00 apiece for over 8 hours of being on site and, playing, about, 6.5 hours of that on stage.). This man, the owner, Johnny, then said one word, "apiece?" I cleared the lump in my throat, and replied, "For real?" He affirmed his offer and, after a rather quick "conference" with my fellow band members, a contract was signed. I had, from my one college class of Business Law, learned what the basic performance contract should look like and, I had a briefcase I carried around with my "wish list" for "gigs" in town. It worked.

It may be an exaggeration on my part, but I recall Anchorage having a bar, a nightclub, a restaurant with nightly lounge entertainment, or a liquor store every three blocks. I'm sure it hasn't changed, only bigger and more of them in today's world. Anchorage is a "boom or bust" kind of town. We were there prior to the big oil finds on the North Slope, but that didn't mean there weren't times when money wasn't abundant (crabbers coming in off the Baring Sea with big rolls of $100.00 bills, Construction Camps and some mining consortium letting their crews have a week in town, oil platform workers in for a shift change {ten days out, ten days in}, and so forth.) All looking to "party down." One night, I remember some crabbers who'd had a really good season, coming up to stage where we were playing, and tossing $100.00 bills onto the stage and asking if we knew: "Shake It Up Baby (Twist and Shout)." I looked at Eric, lead guitar, Tim just winked at me, and I said, "Hell, it's a three-chord change-up...sure we know it!" That was the easiest $1,000.00 I think we all ever made in a night. The crabbers went back to their boat a little lighter in the wallet, drunk, but very, very happy.

So the stress of doing the "security job" on base and, the time I spent playing and negotiating contracts for our band, plus trying to keep all the "newly rich" band members in line, was taxing. $800.00 per night, apiece, was really good money in those days, even if we had to play 8-9 hours a night. The usual club hours in Anchorage are much like Las Vegas, "open" almost 24 hours a day, except Sundays (in those days). The night clubs would close for about an hour, around 5:00 A.M., to clean up and sweep the drunks out the door, and reopen for business by 6:00 or 7:00 A.M. We'd work, as in my case, from 7:30 A.M. until 4:30 P.M. on base and then, go to get a bite to eat. The 6981st had its own chow hall, where the officers and airmen ate at the same "mess." The quality and choices of menu selections were better and they were more flavorful than those on the main base. I think the Command recruited for the best chefs (and I mean "chefs"; these folks were good, really good!) they could find. And, with the high quality of "specialists" (Morse Intercept Operators, Language Technicians, Electronics Specialists, etc.) they had, they wanted a high rate of reenlistment. These fellows received REALLY nice reenlistment bonuses, some as high as $10,000,00. I know this because I typed the documents.

Of course, as has been said many times 'money is the root of all evil.' And "evil" did creep into our lives. We were playing clubs where topless acts were brought in from the "lower 48" and these girls, of course, would flirt with the band members. Some band members got "hooked" on "free pussy." Their playing and showing up late got worse. So, I had to corral a couple, who shall go nameless, and tell them I was going to dock their pay for each minute they were late; and, it would be a "progressive" fine: $10.00 for 1 minute, $20.00 for 2 minutes late, and so forth. They weren't happy, but I told them, by that time, there were 6 other people who were great musicians and singers who would give their left nut to play in our group. It's either 'shape up or ship out' as they say in the Navy. They 'shaped up' and we went on to have a very lucrative and successful second jobs in Alaska.

I didn't shy away from the women. I wasn't a "prude." I did date a waitress for a period of time, but she had a "ready-made" family, two little boys who I liked very much, but it was complicated; the ex was still "coming around." She wanted to get married; I bowed out because I knew her ex was still involved...tooo messy for me.

We once were offered a job, in 1967, at the combined officers/airman venue in Fairbanks. I remember driving the band equipment, in my 1964

Pontiac Bonneville (lots of room), with the rest of the band members in a second vehicle behind, on the Al-Can highway, some 360+ miles North to our destination. It was in late August, with the blush of Fall color just beginning to change the tundra brush and the few trees, with leaves, that we saw. At one point, after dark, we saw this beautiful, rainbow colored shimmering ahead of us in the night sky. We stopped and got out of the cars. We witnessed, probably, one of the most spectacular displays of the Northern Lights I've every seen. I'd seen them stateside, but this was beyond awesome. These veiled curtains of constantly waving, rainbow color, changing, shimmering light looked as if they would touch the ground at any second. They went on for miles. Had it not been for that "gig" we wouldn't have seen such a beautiful sight.

We also were invited to "sit-in" with a band (The Hiway Men) who we knew from the states and who often "made the circuit."(Los Angeles, Nevada, Portland, Seattle, Anchorage, etc.) They just happened to be playing in Fairbanks at a local nightclub when our band, The Nickle Bag (not named for what you may be thinking, we had FIVE members, remember?), was playing on base. I distinctly remember when we took the stage and began playing "Stormy Monday," a song Tim particularly excelled at. As he reached a high point in his vocal, I heard a loud "Bang!" and a crash. I looked at the back of the house and, as best I could see, people were in a melee', a big fight. I saw the barkeep leap over the bar with a baseball bat in his hand. It looked like a Louisville Slugger, you know, the biggest, baddest baseball bat that was ever made. I saw him begin to swing the bat at people. There was no security or "bouncer." Apparently the barkeep was it. What a job! Especially, if he had to do this on a regular basis. Not the kind of job I'd want. 'No sirree'. Well, this went on for a few minutes and we were told by the owner to, "Just keep on playin'." So, we did. It was over just like that and, the brawlers and drunks were pushed out the back door which, I saw later, was made out of steel plate and had two deadlocks on it. So, I guessed that this event was a deja' vu on many occasions. The other band got a kick out of our reactions, because they'd seen this many times before. The owner just wanted the music to go on, without drawing attention to what he called, "a minor disturbance." If that was "minor," I wondered what "major" was. I noticed that some "patrons" had "open carry" (firearms) strapped to their sides. So, one could only guess what "major" would be. If the lead was flyin' I wouldn't be playin.' And that's a fact, Jack! I'd be outta there! So much for the "wild northwest" in Fairbanks.

I didn't "miss out" on Vietnam though. Remember? I thought I was guaranteed "non-combatant"(N-C) status as part of my Air Force contract. Well, I was in N-C status but that didn't mean I wouldn't be sent into a war zone. So, we had a records inspection team that was called upon to go to the 6994th Security Group at Tan Son Nhut A.F.B., and then, to the 6924th Security Squadron at Da Nang, right on the DMZ (demilitarized zone), with bombs and actual combat going on about 2 miles away. I remember flying into the 6924th base, past Monkey Mountain, and coming through the mist, landing on what someone wanted to call a runway, but really felt more like a washboard when we landed. The aircraft, a KC-135 tanker/cargo carrier, a real "workhorse" of the Vietnam Conflict (it was never declared a War by Congress), dropped us off, unloaded cargo, and took off in a very short period of time. I found out later that the Viet Cong "spotters" watched for these aircraft so they could "zero in" their howitzers and drop bombs on the tarmac, trying to destroy the aircraft and anybody nearby. Hence, why the runway was "rough." A really "fun" place to be.

We, all eight of us, were housed at the 6924th in the "temporary barracks." There was no running water. One had to go out of the "shack" and go to a latrine/shower/sink field unit to do one's business. We nicknamed the place the "Hanoi Hilton" after the infamous prison camp where the, now, Senator McCain was kept at the time. He'd been a pilot who was shot down and subsequently captured by the enemy. His stay was, I'm sure, much more unbearable than ours. At night, as I looked northward, I could see the flashes and hear the muffled sounds of carpet bombing that was being done by Air Force B-52s. There were, probably, literally thousands of bombs dropped each night I was there. It got to be "old" real fast, but scary to know we were within striking distance of the Viet Cong and they could come surging over the DMZ at any time (as they did during the Tet Offensive in 1968, a surge that, eventually, caused the end of the conflict). I also knew, from some of my fellow security personnel, that the Chinese were aiding the Viet Cong and, there were battalions of Chinese soldiers, embedded with the Viet Cong regiments, within a few miles of us.

Our duty was to inspect records. The records were being kept in an underground "vaults." The vaults had been poorly constructed and water had seeped in. Something called "jungle rot" (a blackish, gelatinous, ooze) was seeping out of the records bins. Our Captain was pissed. He felt that someone should have noticed and, "...remedied the situation a long time ago!" Those were the very words I recall hearing (there were some pretty choice expletives in there too, but I won't repeat them out of respect for his rank). So we had to wait for "master file copies," which were recorded on tape (by large computers as big as refrigerators) and kept in Washington D.C. at the Pentagon. These would take around half of our 120-day TDY (temporary duty station) stay in Da Nang.

So, we couldn't go to town due to our Top Secret status (someone might kidnap us and put bamboo shards under our fingernails and, torture us into revealing to how much we didn't like the warm 3.2% local beer, nor the hot, sticky humid climate, the old B-rated movies, the old newspapers and magazines, and the war.) Needless to say, if boredom was a matchstick, it would have lit all by itself, without our help! This was a godforsaken place. As far as I was concerned, hell on earth. The sooner we left this place, the better. We finally did, once the record copies were annotated and put in an "above ground" vault. Our Captain insisted, and he told the C.O. of the bases he didn't "give a damn" if the regulations required the records be placed underground for security reasons; he wasn't coming back to waste his "goddamn time" doing the work the C.O.'s people should have done in the first place. And, on that note, we were off the ground, back to Elmendorf. I was really happy to be back in a safe place.

One of the things that bothered me greatly, while I was in the military, was how this Conflict seemed to drag on and on. There seemed to be no end in sight. Eric, the bassist in our band, was an ambulance driver who had a big blue bus, outfitted with stretcher barer racks, that he drove out to the airfield a number of times a day. He picked up the wounded, ambulatory and not, to take to the big hospital complex on base. We were co-located with Fort Richardson, an Army instillation and troop deployment venue. How do I know this? I went with Eric one day, at my request, to see what he did. I was visibly shaken when I saw the sheer numbers of men, and women, who were being brought back, from Vietnam, for medical care. Eric told me, "Sometimes we're going night and day John...200 flights a week."(Eric was able to trade shifts with other drivers when he worked in our band). I was shocked at hearing this number. I knew these KC -141 "Starlifter" troop transports could carry a lot of people, but the number he said, and what I saw in one day, blew me away. It really "soured" me on what my country was doing. By 1968, I'd had it and wanted out. I put in for an early discharge to go back to college and, it was approved. Thankfully, I was able to be released from "active duty," with a 2 year Reserve obligation. Apparently, I didn't read the "fine print" on the enlistment paperwork. My "guaranteed" NC status did not exempt me from an additional 2-year Reservist obligation. My Section Sargent told me. "Don't worry son, the chance of gettin' recalled is really small." I'd learned, by then, not to believe everything one is told; especially by military higher ups when there's a war going on.

After leaving the military, I tried keeping up correspondence with my former band members. We'd grown close over the years, and they "covered" for me when I was in "Nam." I'd written Eric's sister (bassist Eric), because that's the address he gave me. She wrote me back a couple weeks later saying that her brother had been hospitalized. They thought it was PTSD. Since Eric had not been in combat, to my knowledge, I wondered how he could get such a diagnosis. I've since found out that one does not need to be a direct recipient of a traumatic event to suffer from PTSD. If one sees enough of the aftermath of such events, in this case, thousands of wounded and possibly dying soldiers coming back to the States from harm's way, one could easily be affected. One day of seeing this carnage did it for me. Eric's sister wrote me that he was experiencing nightmares, night sweats, was agitated a lot of the time, was drinking way too much, and smoking as if there were never going to be any more cigarettes. These, among other symptoms, are indicative of PTSD. I lost contact after a couple of years and never heard from them again. I've often wondered what cards they were dealt in life, after my correspondence with them.

Our band was good. We had a repertoire of over 250 songs, from all genres, many decades, beginning with the 40s ("Star Dust", "Melancholy Baby"), 50s ("Jail House Rock", "Rock Around The Clock"), and 60s ("Walk Don't Run" Medley, "Only the Lonely", "Runaway", "Night Life", "She Loves You", "Hold On, I'm Commin', "The House of The Rising Sun") and many others, just to name a few. At one time we played at a bandstand rally for Vice President Hubert Humphrey in Anchorage. We were asked to play and paid for party "gigs", grand openings, and wedding receptions. I'd hired a Band Manager, Rich Moreno, and he was talking to people from Northwest Shows. Inc. a talent agent group in the "lower 48" who booked acts all up and down the West Coast. At one point, a recording contract was being discussed. We all planned to, originally, stay together, as a band, after our military stints. But, as fate would have it, different "Separation from Service" dates, family issues (Eric the bassist who was released before I was and got sick), marriage and divorce (the other Eric), and alcohol abuse (Tim) got in the way. Our "star struck" ambitions fell like a brick. So, we all went our separate directions. Our home towns were just as diverse as our personalities were: Boston to Shreveport, Los Angeles to Seattle, and some small town in South Dakota that had a French name that I forgot. I can say, for the most part, it was good while it lasted and, we made some people laugh and sing, we all made some money, and we all got laid (more than once).

After my release in August, 1968, I was able to buy a nice used vehicle (1967 Buick Skylark with low mileage), so I didn't have a piece of junk in which to travel around. The ant-war demonstrations had really heated up. Richard Nixon was in the White-house, Watergate was mushrooming the political scene, Hippies were flocking to Height-Asberry in San Francisco, "tune in, drop out" was one of the mantras of the day, Timothy Leary, Psychedelic music, The Beatles were in their full transcendental mode, and I was going to "keggers" where there were none. I'd go to a campus party and be met with a "purple haze" (marijuana smoke through strobe lighting) quaffing out the doorway. At one point, in 1969, I remember just about everyone, faculty and staff included, marching to shut down the Interstate 5, for over 2 hours, backing up traffic, in protest of what was going on in Vietnam. Citizens from the city joined us. In all, maybe

13,000 people that day. There was a guy in an old Air Force jacket, waiving an American flag, right in the middle of it. My picture was on the front page of the Seattle Post-Intelligencer. No one was arrested. The police just stood on the sidelines and watched. Somehow, I think they were with us on this one. I know, for a fact, that some officers had their children over in "Nam" and they wanted them home. One of them even told me about his 20-year-old son and how worried for his safety he was. It was tumultuous times, but it felt so ALIVE! It was alive, every day, and when the war finally wound down, the "party" ended. We all seemed to go back to our own, little mundane worlds, yours truly, included. I graduated, in 1971, with a degree in Psychology, 2 credits shy of another degree in Sociology, and took a job as a Youth Camp Counselor at a State-run camp: Indian Ridge Youth Camp. We counseled youth who were sent to us by the Court system. These kids were "light weights": Burglary, Car Theft or Prowl, Possession of a Controlled Substance, Theft, etc. Nothing so serious that they weren't "redeemable."

I remember a few incidents at the camp that stood out in my memory bank. One involved a co-counselor named "Rich" (I will not use last names here to protect their identities). Rich was of slight build. By that, I mean he was about 5 foot six and weighed all of 150 pounds, dripping wet. He had very thick glass lenses he wore and, he was often the brunt of jokes by the residents of the camp. He had a "thick skin" though and, he had a great sense of humor. One night, I was on call for "runaway" watch and, I was called in to work to help with finding and catching a boy who had run from camp. One of the disadvantages of living so close to camp, about 2.5 miles away, was that you'd get called in on emergencies. The overtime pay was good though. We were in a fairly remote location and boys usually found their way back, either by walking back into camp, tired, hungry and worse for wear from trudging through the woods all night or, by being picked up by neighbors who brought them back. They usually had to go to the "hole," as punishment, for a week. These were six isolation cells behind the "Duty Staff" office, a central hub where assignments for the day, medications, and roll call emanated from. The runaway's counselor would then be tasked with "working the boy back into program mode."

It was a "motivation" challenge for the counselor and, most of the time, they were successful.

Rich, as a fairly new employee, met me at the junction of where two roads met; one going to the camp. He was very visible to me and to anything within 300 yards of him. He had one of the Department of Natural Resources (DNR) hard hats on and a miners lamp attached. The lamp was on. I told him to shut it off so we couldn't be seen. He then asked me how we were going to see in the dark. I told him it was a clear night and there was a half moon providing just enough light for us. He grumbled something I didn't hear and off we went, climbing up the hills and down the vales near the camp. I told him to stay close and I'd shine my flashlight at right angles so he could see where I was at and no one ahead of us could see.

There was a local farmer who lived just down the road. This farmer had a German Shepard dog named "Butch." Rich had not met this dog. The kids in the camp knew "Butch" and loved him. Butch was very gentle and sweet for a German Shepard; and, he belied the reputation of these dogs being great protectors and vicious when their territory is challenged.

As we were about to crest a hill, Rich came eyeball to eyeball with "Butch." All I heard was a loud scream and the sound of brush and breaking twigs going the opposite direction from where we'd come. I also had heard what sounded like a muffled bark, and something moving the opposite way down the other side of the hill. I went to see what all the commotion was about. I found Rich, huddled in a fetal position, whimpering something about a "big bad wolf coming after me." I told Rich to calm down and that what he saw was, most likely, "Butch," and he'd probably scared "Butch" more than himself. I saved Rich the embarrassment of telling this story so he wouldn't be the laughing stock of everyone in camp. The lost boy was brought in by a neighbor down the road who had picked him up hitch-hiking on the main road.

The other event I remember so well was on a fire crew call out in Eastern Washington. The boys in camp were responsible for working on trails, clearing brush, and for the more mechanically inclined, a construction job was in the offering, building culverts and digging ditches, operating heavy equipment, on the DNR forest service roads in the area. They learned proficiency skills in the safe use of a chain saw, a "hoedag" (a double-bladed tool, one side an ax, the other a hoe; used in brush clearing and digging out "hot spots" in a forest fire so water could be applied), and other tools used in the forest management business.

Fire season was something the boys really relished; for a number of reasons. First, they got paid $.50 cents/hour; a really good deal for the State, because regular professional fire fighters, at the time (1970s) made about $20-25.00 an hour, depending on what their skill level was. Smoke jumpers made much more. Probably, due to the fact that they were risking their lives to go into the heart of the fire. Some of our boys wanted to work for the DNR when they completed their Court sentences, and some did, because they took to heart the skills they were taught.

The fire I remember the most was in Omak, Washington, all the way across the State, in the upper eastern region, a few miles from Canada. We had two counselors to go and make sure the boys were NOT placed into harm's way. Some DNR bosses treated the boys as if they were chattel. We didn't go for that. The kids were trained yes, but they were far from being professionals. We traveled to our destination by "crummies",(nick-named, I think, because they were, usually, pretty "crummy" inside and no fun to ride in...no seat belts), older GMC truck vans with doors that swung open in the rear. The panel seats were bench-style so more people would fit into the van-truck. They were 8-cylinder vehicles, plenty of power for a large load, gear included.

The kids were up and eating breakfast at the crack of dawn. Now, these fire camps were major operations. There were refrigeration semi trucks circling the "mess tent" and a full service portable, gas operated kitchen. The cooking crew worked 24/7 putting out meals for the fire fighters. These meals were "state of the art." For example, breakfast consisted of eggs any style, potatoes, any style, bacon, sausages, toast, cereal (dry and wet), all the condiments, fruits, juices, milk, coffee, water (lots of water) and if you wanted to help the cook, you could cook your own (most opted for steak and eggs).

At the end of the day, usually sunset, a bedraggled crew returned from the fire line. They were tired, filthy with soot and dirt, sweaty, and hungry. And they stank….bad. A communal shower/latrine/sink set up was available and, after a hot shower it was chow time. You were not allowed to sit at the mess table if you had not showered and cleaned up. Dinner was usually steaks, seafood when available (salmon, prawns, scallops), potatoes any way you like 'em (mashed, fries, scalloped), salads, breads, jello, cooked vegetable medley, salami, pizza, Tex-Mex dishes, mac and cheese, and a variety of deserts, including ice cream. You could eat your fill, there was no portion control. These kids usually cleaned their plates. We were supposed to counsel with them before bedtime. Their beds consisted of a cot and a sleeping bag in a large bivouac Army surplus tent. Foam roll-up mattresses were available, but most kids were too tired to get one. Counseling was made "available" if someone really needed to talk; but most were too tired to say anything but, "Good night Mr. Crawley" or "Good night Mr. Sam." Next morning, deja' vu.

The only part I didn't like about these trips was that the counselors had to do crew laundry while the crew was on the fire line. We had three day's-worth of clothing changes right down to socks and underwear. The closest laundry mat to this fire line was about 30 miles away in Omak. If you ever have tried to find a place to wash clothes in a small town such as Omak, where you have to find directions to an unmarked building and old equipment, the task is foreboding. I did it and it took me all day because I only had two washers and two dryers. The other working washer and dryer were in use by one of the local tribal members, and I wasn't about to ask her to relinquish her machines. This went on for a whole week. It was a drag, but we did it, switching off each day because one counselor had to stay in camp in case one of the kids got hurt, fell sick, or had something else that needed attention. We also were expected to make surprise visits to the fire line to see if the kid's safety was being adhered to.

Of the many fire operations I went to, not once did we have a disciplinary problem or a runaway. One, I think the kids were too tired to do much of anything but sleep, and (2) they really appreciated the letters of commendation that went into their files on a "job well done" in fighting each fire. I made sure these letters were written by the DNR HQ staff in charge of each operation. These letters made a great impression when it came time for a boy's parole review. They also held merit accompanying job applications.

I also remember one boy named "Jack" (not his real name). Jack had hemorrhoids and the camp doctor had given us suppositories to give to Jack. Unfortunately, no one apparently gave Jack instructions on how to use the suppositories. So, here comes Jack, up to the medications dispensary window (a dutch door contraption). He says, "I need my medication". I gave Jack a suppository and told him to go into the camp restroom and do his thing. He looked at me kind of oddly, but went into the can. A little while later, I saw him and asked if everything was okay. Jack just looked at me with this blank look on his face and said, "I guess so Mr. Crawley, but that big pill you gave me didn't taste worth a shit." So, we instructed Jack on how to use a suppository. Just goes to show ya, never take things for granted or ass-u-me. Right?

The kids weren't the only ones who needed to learn. We had one staff member, who shall go nameless here, who wanted to help one of our newer staff re-roof his house. I guess it was his way of welcoming the "newbie" into the flock. So, I'll call him "R.", left his shift early to start on "G.'s" roof. The next day, we learned, when "G." arrived at home he found "R." on the neighbors roof, finishing up on ½ of the tear offs. The neighbor was not home. Fortunately, the man was out of the country and not expected back for about a month. So, when "R" became befuddled or confused about something, staff would ask him, "Which roof are you on today R.?" He never could live that one down and, it cost him most of his next paycheck to fix the neighbor's roof.

One of the reasons I relate these funny stories to the reader is to demonstrate that we are all subject to foible and mistakes. Life is too short to take things too seriously. I lost my sense of humor when I was ill, in hospital, and for about 6 years in recovery. I will never lose it again. Why? Because, I know now that it's a life saver. It helped me regain a sense of perspective and joy. To find "joy" in one's life is a true blessing. So many folks are without "joy." The funny thing is that it doesn't take much to find it. I'll give you a few examples. Look into a child's eyes. If you cannot find "joy" there, then look elsewhere. Look into someone's eyes who you love. Gaze at a beautiful sunset, take a walk along a beach, eat your favorite ice cream or food. Make love; not just the "mechanical" kind of love...true and deep, "tantric" (magical) love; the kind of love that is almost spiritual and transcending. Give someone something you know they will cherish. It doesn't have to be very valuable in terms of monetary value. It can be a verse, a song (if you play an instrument), and if you can't find "joy" in music or meditation, maybe you need to see a therapist. Read a book you've always wanted to read. Joy can be found in the most simple things…....

I met Susan on a "blind date" in 1972. We were introduced by a mutual, married female friend. Coincidentally, I had dated this friend in high school. We went bowling at the Strawberry Lanes in Marysville; another place that still exists. Some places seem to have their own immortality. I had not bowled since graduation from high school in 1961. I felt I might be pretty "rusty." One of the games I bowled was over 230 points. I surprised even myself. Had to impress the lady, right? I was just very lucky that night. We had a good time and I asked Sue for another date. She accepted and I was the "perfect gentleman," taking her back to her residence and saying goodnight. We seemed to "hit it off" rather well. The second date was filled with lots of passion and physical romance. Sue told me later that she knew who I was the minute I walked into the bowling alley. We felt it was "love at first sight." We also felt as if we'd known each other all our lives. We held a lot of the same beliefs and interests, and we had common goals in life.

We became "best friends" before we became lovers. We were married on June 4, 1972 after a rather short courtship; but, as I said, we seemed to "know" one another, as if we'd had a past life together. It was odd, but wonderful. Susan was the only woman I've ever really loved, deeply and spiritually. There were other "loves," but none so pure and strong.

It remained that way until my illness in 2008, shortly after I retired. I've already written about our two beautiful and successful daughters, Kimberly and Christine, both grown women now with their own lives ahead of them. Unfortunately, we're all going to be in that group of divorced people, soon. Kim and Chris' marriages didn't work out, and I won't go into detail as to why, it's personal and private. I would never violate my children's confidence. It would be so wrong.

With the exception of the past 9 years, I believe our marriage was good, passionate, strong, dedicated, hard working, and successful. We successfully balanced three careers while raising a family. We bought and remodeled a min-farm house before trading the land (2.5 acres) for a larger home in 1997, in Marysville, on a large lot. We grew our own gardens in Arlington Heights (the mini-farm), had horses, chickens, made grape juice and wine from the old grape vines on the property, cut firewood for the fireplace, hunted wild mushrooms in the back woods, went on trips and vacations, camped, fished, had three pet dogs and four cats, and we shared family times and holidays with the extended family.

I will dedicate a few paragraphs to Christmases at the Crawley house. Each year, we would put out a "full spread" meal for family members. Actually, we did this twice; once for my side of the family and once for Susan's side. I don't remember how this came about, it may have had to do with sheer numbers of people. Our house has 3,000 square feet of space, but it's equally divided between upstairs and downstairs. We could fit only so many people into the big main room that was converted into a dining area. We all pitched in to make the area festive and, we always had a big Christmas tree, usually over 9 feet tall. We have cathedral ceilings in the big room.

I would help with decorations, inside and out, and setting up large tables in a row, put out the linen and lace tablecloths and arrange silverware, napkins, plates, glassware, etc. Susan and the girls would busy themselves in the adjacent kitchen creating a feast for about 15 to 20 people, Sue's relatives being the larger of the two groups. We'd do my relatives first. They were older, didn't eat as much, and went home early after gifts were opened. We had one rule about the gifts that were opened after the meal: One person opens one gift at a time. No rushing and tearing into all the presents at once, which, we know can be chaos. And things get lost and, someone invariably goes home with another person's gift. It happens, trust me on this one. So we'd all help pick up the wrapping paper after each gift was opened, put it in a large bag for recycling, and everyone was happy. No loses, no "missings", and no errors.

I, unfortunately, was usually in my cups during all of this. I'm not proud of this. I was a happy drunk. I wasn't too loud or boisterous, I was just happy to have family together, celebrating the holiday. Cleanup, after the first meal, was a busy event. We'd have to get ready for the next "shift" of family; usually, expected the next day. Sue's family was larger in that she had one younger brother and two younger sisters. Unfortunately, Sherry, the baby of the family was tragically killed in a pedestrian accident in Redmond, Washington during the mid Nineties. Sherry was the Redmond City Waterworks Manager. She was a very bright and funny woman with a great smile. She left a bereaved husband, John, and two young children, Alex and Ann, both now young adults with careers ahead of them.

The meals were pre-prepaired, mostly. We have two large refrigerators and one large upright freezer. So, with the exception of the Chateau Briand meat and ham, which had to "slow cook," most everything else just needed warming in the oven or on top of the stove. As an example of a Christmas meal: we had a heart-shaped jello mold with infused fresh raspberries, cooked vegetables, Brussels sprouts with bacon crisps, fresh-made rolls, garlic mash potatoes with the butter already "spun" in, asparagus spears with a balsamic dressing drizzled on top, assorted home-made cookies for desert and a "gift plate" of same for each guest. Some years, there was a Bouillabaisse and seafood theme to the meals, with steamed clams and fresh crab meat, soups, various Christmas breads made by Susan (she taught baking and culinary arts), and scallops. Cookie making in our house was a "factory" production that started weeks before the guests arrived. The fortunate part of all of this is that no relatives had to come great distances and stay the night; although, we did have the space and beds.

No one, except yours truly, consumed enough alcohol the be "in their cups." Although I did see a few in a very happy state before they went home. They weren't driving. I was usually very depressed following these events. Not because I'd consumed, but because I knew that many of these people would be gone some day, especially on my side of the family. I know, it's a stupid thing to do, to use as an excuse to drink at one's Christmas celebration, but that's what I did. Year in and year out, for well over 20 years.

Now, our Christmases and other holidays are celebrated separately. Susan and the girls go to her mom's place in Issaquah and, I usually spend my time with close friends in Bellingham, Washington. Our house, once filled with music and merriment is a very lonely place. We "exist" in this house. We certainly don't "live" in it, at least I don't. Susan requested I move into the basement not long after my last release from hospital, in 2009. I've been sleeping there for over eight years. I get one cooked meal a day: dinner. The rest of the time, I'm on my own for meals. I have a small music studio in the basement and there are windows so I can see the outdoors. Not so much by Kim, who moved back in to help with my situation and my aging parents (she was a God-send in helping with both of my parents; especially following my mother's second stroke that disabled her and made her bed-ridden. Following mom's passing in 2014, Kim was like an angel from heaven, helping an aging widower in his last days, almost daily, and daily during the last two years of John L.'s life.). Kim has been supportive of both her parents and has, rightly, chosen to stay out of the dissolution of our marriage. As to what the future holds, I know not. As I write these words, everything is in... limbo. Maybe, if I choose to write it, the next book will shed light on the progress we "fire fighter's" have made and, the ongoing saga of John P. Crawley. I can and will only think positively. I have no choice. Going back into the "darkness" is NOT an option for me. Life still means too much to me now. After what was revealed to me on that mountain a few years ago…...NO WAY, am I ever going to throw it all away!

Joyce Mitchell, our close family friend, who originally grew up in India, once told me a story that I will now share with you all:

'You are by a garden with a tranquil, quiet, pond in front of you. There is a light, misty presence about the surroundings. The temperature is neutral, body heat.

You see a piece of paper at your feet and you pick it up. It is a note that reads: "You are in the 'in-between' neither dead nor alive. Just "being."

At this juncture, a man comes from the mist and asks you if you know where you are. You reply, in a somewhat staccato voice, "I, I, d-don't ex-exactly k-know. It says "i-in b-between?"

The man confirms that you have gone from the earth and, that you are in a sort of vacuum, not fully dead and not fully alive. "It's a place of reclamation and redemption," he says. He then asks you to read the remainder of the note. You notice there are more words that were not there when you first read the note: "If you could take one thing, person, belief, or feeling with you, what would it be?""

At this juncture, the man departs and leaves you to decide.

I know what I'd take with me, but it's very, very private. What would you take? It's a good question, because we all must leave this world someday, and I firmly know, now, there IS a beyond.

Part of my life's philosophy has centered around Existential thought and studies. Early on, in college, as part of a contemporary readings and writing class, I was introduced to the likes of Sjorn Kierkegaard, a rather famous, in his day, Existential thinker and philosopher. Kierkegaard believed that a person establishes his or her own purpose in life through the use of "free will." There is no such thing as pre-ordained fate, a set way one's life will unravel, or a "script" if you will. He advocated for independent thinking and, the use of one's mind to overcome obstacles in life

Existentialists, for the most part, do not adhere to "organized" religions or religious thought. I've found, there seems to be two divergent camps here. One camp believes in a "Source" of all our existence; the other denies the "Source" by using terms such as "nothingness", "there is no God," (in this camp are the likes of: Jean Paul Sartre, Albert Camus, Heidegger, and other famous atheistic philosophers). I tend to lean toward the "religious", as they've been termed by such writers as Carl Jaspers and Jack Kerouac. The "religious" Existentialist believes that there is, in fact, a Source of all existence. It's when mankind tries to "define" the Source and uses ritualism to validate it, form it into belief systems, that we get into trouble. That's why, the "religious" Existentialists say there are so many world religions today. To deny such "religions" is not acceptable to the "religious" Existentialist; because, denying such beliefs is a form of denying "self." And, "self" is a large part of Existential thought. A person's "existence" precedes his/her "essence"(purpose). We create our own purposes in life. Purposes are not innate. We are a "part" of the Source; the Source is in us and all around us, all the time; but we cannot "Be" the Source. We can only strive to understand it.

Another tenet deals with "infinitesimal existence"; or, existence that has gone on forever; without boundary. I've expanded this, for myself, into an "infinity of being," with no beginning or end. Most of us have difficulty accepting something such as "infinity." Our brains are "pre-wired" for conceptional "shapes" that have a "beginning" and an "end." Our subsequent experience with our education and environments reinforce beginnings and endings. A sentence has a beginning and end. A book has a beginning and an ending. A chair has a top and a bottom. A day is cycled on a 24 hour clock we use to tell when things start and when they finish. A football game has a start and a finish. A road or destination has an end point, and so on and so forth. We have theorized that the Universe, as we currently know it, has a beginning (The Big Bang) and ends (somewhere). But, to try and fathom something with no beginning and no end is usually mind boggling for most people. Our universe (s) may be infinite. I believe so after what was "revealed" to me a few years ago. One thing I do know, for sure, there IS a Source of all that exists and will exist. We are not alone in all that exits. I don't mean this in the interstellar sense, but in a more "cosmic" sense. Frankly, I believe, if one accepts that there may be many universes, whose to say there aren't other planets that have some "life" form on them? It may be different than what we know "life" to be, but all the same, why shouldn't there be other "existences?" I doubt our species has a monopoly on this stuff.

I know, in some cultures, one's destiny is governed by birth rite, caste, strong religious tenet (Shiva, Sunni, Hindu, Sikhs, Punjab, Catholic, Jew, Orthodox Greek, Shinto, Buddhist, Navajo, Christian, Muslim, and many other religious belief systems around the world; some so obscure, we hardly know them, such as the aboriginal societies in the Australian Outback or New Guinea.) But, these people still have a choice and, more often than not, with the advent of the Internet, smart phones, and television; all of which now encircle the planet, access to "choices" are readily made available. Some say this isn't a good thing, to dilute a culture's mores, practices, and rituals with more "modern" thought and actions. Maybe not. But it is happening and, many people from other cultures, cultures of rigidity and non-conformist beliefs, are leaving their stultifying and suffocating environments to seek a different course for their lives. The world has been changing throughout time and, it will continue to change in this manner. I think this is one reason why we have such conflict around the world today. People are uncomfortable with change. They "like" their comfort zones. 'Mess with "this" Jack, and you may be cruzin' for a bruisin.'Our "comfort zones" are being challenged, confronted, and, in some cases, taken away. For some, this causes great unease, ill feelings, fear, strife, petulance, wars, and dysfunctional behavior in some people (i.e., mental illness and substance abuse, as examples).

During my particular illness, I was "out of the loop" as far as Existential thought and action were concerned. This happened shortly after I retired and became severely ill with diagnosed Major Depression. I fell into what some Existential writers have referred to as the "Existential Void," a place of purposelessness, darkness, despair, anxiety, fear, lack of joy and humor, confusion, and no feelings of security. I was afraid to go outside my doorway and walk down my street, something my wife and I, and our two Corgi pups, loved to do before my illness. I would go about 20-30 yards, accompanied by Susan, and want to turn around and go back. My legs felt weak and I had a distinct feeling of unease about me. The psychiatrist I saw said that this was common to someone with severe Depression such as I. I was so NOT on the right page in life….Hell, I wasn't even in the same library!

My hospitalizations did not help. Nor did all the medications they foisted upon me. All I did was get worse. Especially, when I was placed into a ward that reminded me of the movie, "One Flew Over The Coo-coo's Nest." But, I think, I already mentioned that to you all. It wasn't any fun, but it did reinforce what I'd thought for some time, while working in the corrections field: Our mental health delivery systems and treatment of substance addled folks is archaic, punitive, draconian, and so "out of touch" with what directions the "new science" is pointing. I will cover much of these new scientific approaches in the next chapter.

I worked hard to regain my Existential foundations and practices. They have been my salvation and source of continuous faith and stability. Without them, I doubt I would be here today and, I certainly would not be authoring a book about falling down, recovery, rebirth, regeneration, re-visitation, rejoining society, and rejoicing in the joy of life and being alive.

This is where Existential thought and beliefs can be most helpful. Existentialists believe in tolerance, forgiveness, and compassion. We do not judge, castigate, or ridicule others or their beliefs. As long as the others' belief system isn't "forced" upon us (as in ISIS or ISIL, the barbaric organization that butchers people if one doesn't adhere to its belief and, an arcane system of governance), then, we are pretty "passive" folks. That's not to say we are "bleeding heart" liberals or cowardly. Some of the greatest and boldest people in our Nation and the World have held beliefs that were very close to contemporary Existential thought: Benjamin Franklin, Alexander Hamilton, Thomas Jefferson, John Adams (The Presidents, both of them), Robespierre (The Father of the French Revolution), John F. Kennedy (even though he was a "practicing" Catholic, his writings reflect Existential thinking), Winston Churchill, Karl Marx (though Communism has a lot of drawbacks, the Utopian form has some Existential precepts; an impossible task for a society to reach, but Marx tried), Dostoevsky, J.D. Salinger (read "The Catcher in The Rye" and Existential thought and action practically jumps off the pages), Confucius, Aristotle, and most of the great Greek Philosophers held some Existential leanings in their orations and writings, Michael Angelo, depicting the "other" (a choice) in many of his paintings and sculptures; and, many others. This system of thought has been around a long time, even the Bible and the Koran have some Existential leanings. So, I guess what I'm trying to say here is that most of us are existential. The only problem is, we don't know it yet. Becoming a "fire fighter" will teach us what it's like. Try it...you may even like it.

ON THE HORIZON OF RESEARCH AND DEVELOPMENT

There are some rather exciting things happening over the past decade that I need to inform the readers about. The advent of genomics "mapping" where the human genetic structure, almost 12,000 of 20,000 genetic pairings have been "mapped" as to which "loci" causes what and how these proteins act upon each other is something I'm following; CRISPR techniques, where the DNA is "unzipped" and repaired with a "healthy and viable" sequence has proven to help thousands of people recover from some forms of cancer, debilitating illnesses and diseases (although there are some "moral" and "ethical" concerns here for "selective trait transfer" that flies in the face of "A Brave New World/Orwellian" genetic cloning issues), Theoretically, this technique can produce a viable human, from scratch. There have been some experiments done in China where CRISPR was used to make human eggs ready for development, but the World medical societies frowned on bringing into the world "designer humans," or, a master race that is far superior, in every aspect (strength, intelligence, immune from all diseases, and ageless) or; HBOT studies (as I've previously mentioned) go on to make great strides in helping cure our disabled veterans and others who suffer from PTSD, Traumatic Brain Injury (TBI), and other ailments; Naturalistic (Natural-path) methods that are time-tested and effective, but put down by lobbyists hired by the big pharmaceuticals, big insurance, and hospital consortiums to dissuade Congress from accepting them or funding them, Various and numerous Programs to help the homeless, the substance abusers who want and need help; Police Outreach programs that take with them, on routine patrols, social workers/psychiatric nurses who are trained in the use of intervention and placement of those "walking wounded" in our society; and an overview of what the future may look like. This chapter is dedicated to those "fire fighters" who are doing something to fight the "fire." They are my heroes and they should be yours. And, we can join them in so many ways.

Worth re-visitation is the work Dr. Bennet Omalu and his colleagues are doing in the Department of Pathology at the University of Pittsburgh in the area of Chronic Traumatic Encephalopathy (CTE). In 2008, a CSTE brain trust was created at Boston University at the BU School of Medicine, partnering with the Bedford V.A. Hospital to analyze the effects of CTE and other neuro-degenerative diseases of the brain and spinal chord of athletes, military veterans, and civilians. To date, (2017), the CSTE Brain Bank is the largest CTE tissue repository in the world. Over 250 professional athletes have signed promissory documents to have their brains donated, upon their deaths, to research at this facility. The NFL, finally coming around and acknowledging that CTE did, in fact, exist, donated over 1 million dollars to ongoing research in2010. The Center for Retired Athletes at the University of North Carolina at Chapel Hill is conducting a parallel study on Mild Traumatic Brain Injuries (MTBI) and sub-concussive impacts and, how this relates to ongoing studies of Dementia and Alzheimer's disease. Boston University has also found indications of links between Amyotropic Lateral Sclerosis (ALS) and CTE athletes who have participated in high impact contact sports. Tissues for these studies have been donated by athletes families, upon the athlete's deaths, for these studies.

In 2013, President Barack Obama announced the creation of the Chronic Effects of Neurotrauma Consortium (CENC), a federally funded research project devised to address the long-term effects of MTBI in military service personnel and veterans and it services veterans and others who have served in all recent theaters of armed conflict. As of September, 2015 the CSTE had diagnosed CTE in 96% of NFL players analyzed in postmortem brain studies. (Previous facts in last 3 paragraphs are a compilation of data from Wikipedia and accompanying Bibliography attending thereunto, 2017).

In this chapter, I will also tell the stories of six of my co-patients who I interact with, on a regular and consistent basis, in the Depression and Bi-polar Support Group (DBSA), a National Organization dedicated to education (both sufferer and public), comradeship, support, resource brokering, and wellness. These folks have been kind enough to tell their stories so that you, the reader, will better understand their struggles, their fight for recovery, and their wish for acceptance and acknowledgment for their efforts. I have used "fictitious" names for real people to protect their privacy and hold their confidence in my trust. They have all signed "releases" for copyright and legal protections.

The first person I'd like to tell you about "Katy," is a 50-ish rotund woman who suffered from parental rejection most of her life. She has been with DBSA for over 5 years (more than I) and, from what others, who have been around "Katy" since she joined the group, have told me, she has made great strides. She is diagnosed Bi-polar 2 (mood swings, but not as severe or as long in duration as Bi-polar 1), with Schizo-affective features (mood desensitization and auditory fantasy, or somewhat distorted perceptions of "reality" at times), PTSD (from verbal and physical abuse as a child and young adult), and Dis-associative Affect (meaning, she has had trouble expressing or actually "feeling" normal human emotions). The reason, I learned, "Katy" has had trouble with "feelings," is because she was never allowed to express her feelings in the home she grew up in. She was always "put down" or told her opinion didn't count. She grew up distrusting adults because no one who was supposed to be a role model for her was anything but. She's related, in group, how her mother, who she finally was able to "escape" from by getting married, was "always on me about something, I couldn't turn around before she'd jump on me about this or that." "Katy" grew up learning not to trust, nor did she even know how to trust others. Her self esteem wasn't….she had none. When she first came to Group, she was a quiet, reserved, timid person who sat with her head down and, she avoided eye contact. Her fellow participants and facilitators tried to pull her out of her shell by telling her she was among friends and supporters who would not judge her or put her down for anything she said in Group. One of our rules is that no one has to share if one doesn't feel comfortable;

the idea here is that we try to help people feel comfortable in the setting and not forced.

It took almost a year before "Katy" felt comfortable enough to speak. And even then, it was a quiet, meek little voice saying very short sentences. But, over time and, with encouragement, she is now very vocal and sharing what her therapy and treatment experiences have taught her. In the time I've spent in the DBSA, I've seen vast improvement in "Katy's" willingness to share and help others with what has worked for her. We do not tell people,… "this is what I think you need to do." Rather, we'll preface help comments with… "in my experience, I've done….. to help myself deal with similar issues…" Her whole demeanor is confident, assertive, and motivated to stay well, a good sign for someone who suffers from mental illness. She takes care of a husband who has had some health issues himself, she's help raise two wonderful children, and she has held employment for over two years. These are all positive signs of wellness; but, she's also cognizant of the fact that wellness is an ongoing "management" effort. No one should fool oneself into believing one is "cured."

Another couple, I'll call "Paul" and "Paulette," have both been diagnosed with Bi-polar 2. Paul has shared that he has learned some people in the extended family also suffer from Bi-polar affectations. There seems to be a genetic link in some diagnoses. "Paul" has shared how he sometime gets "set off" in a manic tirade when something upsets him or triggers an episode. Mania is usually exhibited by a shut-down of one's ability to hear what's being said (much like what happens when someone gets very angry), tightening of the muscles and torso, visual "focusing" to where outside influences are ignored or, not acknowledged. A person in a "manic" state will act very strangely, often times walking in circles or pacing and, audibly, saying things that may make no sense to the casual observer. Sometime, caustic or hurtful comments directed at a loved one are made. "Paul" says he's done this to "Paulette." He thinks, and his therapist agrees, that people who behave in this fashion are trying to drive the other person away so they don't have to witness the manic episode. They don't really mean the hurtful things they say. To an unaware spouse, though, it has caused many a marriage to fall "on the rocks." "Paul" has also shared that his thoughts are "racing...fast and furious" when he's in a manic state. Many in the group share this aspect in common (it's a common trait of Bi-polar affectation). The amount of physical energy expended when this happens is enormous. One is usually exhausted following a manic episode. "Paul" and "Paulette" have found an "adequate" medication to help them both, but medications only last as long as the patient is willing to take them and, in some cases, put up with some pretty messed up side effects. Most SSIR inhibitors {causes Serotonin uptake in the brain; thus, hopefully, reducing the effects of an episode or depressive state} (taken by Bi-polar {if they suffer extreme moods of depression following a manic state} and those suffering from Major Depression, can and do cause a severe decrease in the sex drive of a person; so, intimacy is often an additional concern when considering therapeutic interventions). "Paul" and "Paulette" are currently working with their respective therapists to resolve these issues each has. Sometimes, the efficacy of the medication no longer has the desired effect and, the patient has to go through another round of "medication roulette" (as I've termed it) to find another adequate medication. Both "Paul" and "Paulette", as well as others in the group, have experienced this aspect too. No one medication or combination of medications are 100% effective."Paul" and "Paulette" related that they are practicing "breathing exercises" such as those offered by Yoga and other resources to calm themselves; also "mindfulness" (practicing being in the "here and now" as opposed being off on some tangential path) is a method that has been successfully employed by them and others in the Group. They both, as well as others, have found that "taking time outs" are helpful. Coming back, later, when both are "rational," to discuss something, absent the manic feelings and actions, is always a helpful approach. It "clears the air" so to speak. It helps people focus on the right priorities and revisit their goals and shared treatment pathways.

I have suggested in Group, and we've discussed, on numerous occasions, the need to have a "routine" in one's life. This isn't just important for regular, "normal" folks, it's a survival skill for those who suffer from a diagnosis. I have also shared that it also helps me to "journal" and write my thoughts down. Then, I go back a few days later and review what I've written. In this fashion, I can reorient myself, and I can expand upon what is working for me and what is not. For me, this approach has been extremely helpful. When I've shared this, others have told me that they don't feel as expressive on paper as they are verbally. In fact, when our group sessions begin and the "floor is open" for someone to bring up an issue, if there's too long a pause, the void will soon be filled by someone who is Bi-polar. This is a common joke with us, that Bi-polar folks love to talk, and if you give them an opening, they will talk your head off. Hopefully, they are not in a "manic" state when this occurs. I have commented that it isn't the written words or the volume, it's the habit of thinking and writing and, then, revisiting to cross check ones thinking and whether or not our thinking is causing us to be ill or not. We can't remember everything that happens each day, so writing it down, for me, helps. It doesn't have to be, literally, every little thing, just the important stuff (thoughts, actions upon you and what you do with others and how you feel or think afterwards).

For example: The other day, I was talking with a man who has traveled all over the world. He is now retired, but he had a very active career as a merchant seaman. His appearance indicates a man who has lived and relished life. He dresses smartly and has a good taste in fashion. His clothing speaks of someone fairly well-off, financially. He has a white head of hair now. This feature enhances his n rugged looks; a square jaw and age lines about his face and neck. He is of average build, but when I shook his hand, at introductions, I felt the strength of a man whose age (79) was more like that of a 25-year-old. This gentleman told me a story of how he and his shipmates weathered many large storms, at sea, and they were often considered "goners" because of damage to the ships, loss of radio transmission, or actual structural damage to the extent that the ship's sea-worthiness was in question. "Jack" (not his real name) told me the way he and his crew members dealt with what may be their last breaths on earth, was to work together, as a team, each man knowing what he needed to do, to bring their ship back to port. He said some crews were better than others; but, this trait of selflessness in the eye of adversity is very common to those who ply the oceans and seas of this world. So, I wrote this down: "Teamwork is essential for survival." In reviewing this statement, a few days later, I thought of how many applications "teamwork" could work in our daily lives. It usually isn't a matter of life or death (unless one is a fire fighter or policeman or one of the other "risky" career paths), but, sometimes, it could rise to that level of need. In most cases, I concluded, "teamwork" is preferable, as opposed to each individual doing his/her own thing and, often, missing the big picture of what the overall goal is. That's why, sitting in a large circle and telling others what works for them is a form of "teamwork;" to learn which "tools" are effective and successful in "brain management."

One of the other participants in our DBSA group, "Mitch," is diagnosed Bi-polar 1. His mood swings are severe. He has mentioned, on more than one occasion, that his manic tirades are violent and unpredictable. He disclosed that he has spent a lot of time in jail for acting out in public. When "Mitch" first came to group, we saw a very angry young man. "Mitch" is about 23 years old, has a large, muscular frame (he works out doing "cardio"-his word), and he can be very intimidating. He reminds me of some of the angry parolees and probationers I've dealt with who think no one understands them, so they get angry at the world; it's an excuse, but it can be very dangerous to go around, most of the time, with a chip on one's shoulder. "Mitch" has also disclosed the "medications roulette" merry-go-round he's been on since his recent diagnosis. He was first placed on Lithium (a commonly prescribed drug for treatment of Bi-polar 1). He was taking about 1800 milligrams per day but it was not helping. So, his therapist upped the dose to 2000 milligrams. This is dangerous because, if improperly used (as "Mitch" soon found out), one can overdose and require hospitalization for treatment. "Mitch" stated he thought "more" more often would do the trick. He did not consult with his therapist about taking 2 or three pills a day. Nor did he keep a regular regimen of blood testing to ensure that not too much Lithium was in his system. He also continued his "cardio" workouts (raising the body temperature is not advised while taking Lithium). He was admitted to the hospital with a severe case of Lithium toxicity. Not enough to kill him, but enough to experience extreme discomfort, vomiting, fever, diarrhea, dehydration, hallucinations, muscle spasms, headaches as severe as migraines, and almost psychotic delusions. "Mitch's" demeanor left much to be desired. He began his first session by railing on the "system" and how the government is watching everyone and no one has any "real freedom" (his words) anymore. He used his cell phone to demonstrate how he hates to be accountable by having such a technological tool. His attitude seemed to be anti-social and deeply troubled about life in general. He told us he'd been suicidal on occasion, but never felt the overwhelming need to "off myself"(his words) because "that's what pussies do...and I'm not a pussy." Over time, "Mitch" shared more of his personal thoughts and feelings in a more candid, mature, and adult manner. His immaturity was obvious from the onset of his meetings attendance; but, he kept coming back, so, he must be getting something from the group beyond just having an audience to listen to his ranting and illogical ramblings. I spent a lot of time talking with "Mitch" after the meetings when some of us stay around to chat, share more of what has helped us, or just enjoy each others company. I found him to be what I thought: He's a very lonely person who lives with a maternal aunt and his grandmother. He has never held down a steady job (my gut tells me he's afraid to work because of his illness and uncontrolled rages). I've suggested to him that he might benefit from some Yoga classes or transcendental meditation classes, explaining, in detail, what these teach a person to do. Just learning how to breathe to calm oneself down can be a life saver. It was in my case. I've used my own personal experiences, which are far greater than "Mitch's" (due to his age), to expand his "universe" (which is extremely self-contained and egoistic). I'm not doing therapy here, that is between him and his therapist (who he has often castigated in group, without her being present to defend herself); but, I'm trying to open his world to let in some light. "Mitch's" world is very dark, draconian, and servile to what he believes is a government out to "screw" every one. He reminds me of the story of the missionary who goes out into the Amazon, without a map or a guide to show him the pitfalls, and falls into a pit with quicksand in it. As an angry gesture, one of the last things the observer sees is the traveler's raised hand with the middle finger erect over an otherwise closed fist. In other words, "Fuck you world...I didn't like it here anyway."

A lot of time has been spent listening, trying to get "Mitch" to rephrase things and get to the core of what he's really feeling. He has shared, often, and sometimes, there are glimmers of rational thought. Unfortunately, and recently, "Mitch" went on another tirade, in group, to the point of being asked to leave by one of the facilitators (a trained person who modulates the participants behavior and comments). One of our fast rules is to not go into arenas that might "trigger" someone else or cause them to feel threatened. "Mitch" crossed this line by objecting to the facilitators efforts at using an easel with sheets of paper to list topics for the evening. This, apparently, was "too" organized for "Mitch." He stated, "….you're changing the rules on us." When he proceeded to get very hostile, raising his voice in a very angry manner, he was asked to leave. He made a big ordeal of leaving by going the long way around tables and chairs that were the longest way to the large room's doorway. Very childish and, he had to have the last word when the facilitator told him he was welcome back when he had calmed down. "Mitch" then muttered something about... "That'll be the day!," whereupon he exited.

Personally, I think "Mitch" will return to DBSA. Why? Two reasons: 1. He's getting something out of it and he's smarter than what he leads on to be. He can be very rational and thoughtful when he tries. And 2. He has apologized to the group before when he knew better than to go off on someone. That time, the facilitator gave him credit for having the wits about himself to recognize that he was out of line. It was a "learning moment" for all of us. (P.S. He did return to group, the following week, much calmer and more reasoned).

Following "Mitch's" rather theatrical exit, we discussed each others feelings and reactions. One of our group members, "Vic," who had been sitting next to "Mitch," stated he had mixed feelings because he remembered being a "non -conformist" when he was young, rebelling against authority; especially his parents. He recalled where I'd interrupted "Mitch" mid-stream and mentioned how "Mitch" has told us, over and over, that his own, fast rule is to never physically harm any one; but he'd defend himself if he had to. Right behind this he "dissed" his grandmother for being critical of his behavior and saying (in so many words) that no one loved him or cared. I'd told him I know his aunt and grandmother care because they've said so, to the group, when they've attended as supporters of him. This comment probably made "Mitch" even more upset because I could see his rigidity was more emphatic and, his focus narrowed. At that point,

"Mitch" just wasn't "getting it." The facilitator made the right decision because "Mitch" was triggering many in the group with his negativity and angry comments. Those who felt uncomfortable, admitted they felt threatened that evening by "Mitch's" behavior. One member, I recall, even left the room because he was so upset ("Paul"). He later told us that's why he left. So, the group has its moments of highs and lows. Mostly, the group is very supportive, enlightening, and comforting because one does not feel alone in one's diagnosis.

Another example I'll share with you is another couple "Zach" and "Mabel". These folks are somewhat "hippie" in their orientation. Both are probably in their low to mid 50s, with greying hairlines and thin builds. They live on a mini-farm raising, among other animals and gardens, pygmy goats. The goats are reportedly "very smart" ("Zach's" comment), but, "Mabel," being a retired school teacher, just rolls her eyes at this claim. "Zach" was "raised" (in quotes because his story has anything but good role modeling in it) in a rather large family. He stated, "...all we ever did was fight... literally...and with fists, baseball bats, anything we could get our hands on." Fortunately, as far as I can tell from his family stories, no one was murdered. "Zach" is diagnosed Bi-polar 1, Paranoid Schizophrenia, PTSD, and Personality Disordered. "Mabel" is diagnosed Bi-polar 2 and PTSD from her childhood of neglect and physical abuse by a step-father. She has not related that she was sexually abused; however, the way she described her relationship with a mother who never came to defend or protect her, I suspicion she has been sexually abused in some fashion at some time in her life. There's is a bond of common survival in that opposites attract; he's more "out-going" and she is "more timid." He speaks in a rather assertive voice and she, in a soft little voice. They have had their ups and downs. More recently, "Mabel" has not attended group. I found out that "Zach" had been physically abusive toward "Mabel." She took out a restraining order on him and they are now living separately. At our last session, "Zach" showed up and was asked to leave by the facilitator. When "Zach" (within earshot of me) asked "why?" The facilitator stated, "You know why 'Zach'." "Zach" then coyly says, "No I don't...why don't you tell me!" The facilitator then says, "Okay, because you have a no-contact court order and Mabel says she won't attend here if you are also here....we can't let you dictate how she conducts her attendance here." "Zach" then says, "Well okay then!" (in a rather gruff tone). He then left.

I kind of feel sorry for this couple. Their lives have been so full of poor role models, hostility, bitterness, substance abuse ("Zach" has bragged of how, when he's angry, "just light one up {marijuana} and it's all cool man," alcoholism {both}, and despair. They always seem to be struggling to make ends meet. Both are disabled {legally} from their diagnostic and physical ailments; he, macro-degeneration in the eyes from diabetes; she, from a type of intestinal-gastric condition that prevents her from gaining weight and, drains her physical strength to where she often is bed-ridden by mid-day. They have nothing that's working in their favor except co-dependency {not a good outcome in most cases}).

These are but a few of the stories I'm sharing with the readers because, some of these stories may reach "home' with a few of you. We all know these folks, in other lives, we see or experience them every day. Some of them "are" us, just the names and a few circumstances may be a little different; especially if we have a diagnosis.

Not all of the group stories are negative or sad. We have group members like "Teri" who have been in therapy for many years (diagnosed Bi-polar 2, Multiple Personality Disorder {she likes to describe it as "having a lot of 'little friends' inside of me"}, PTSD, and Personality Disorder {her real personality that is}). She has shared her "journey of wellness" (as she describes it) by telling us some pretty strange behaviors she had when she was "popping" in and out of different personas. She told us of the "bag lady" she often emulates when she goes shopping. People feel sorry for her because she's dressed shabbily and walks with a limp. People give her food, money and food stamps even when she's not asking for it. She's a fairly attractive woman in her late 40s who has raised two sons who are now adults. "Teri" has a penchant for the occult and "meditations" cultures. She says these "mantras" help her maintain stability. I say "whatever works as long as it doesn't harm one's self or others." "Teri" hasn't been to group for awhile because she recently purchased her own boutique business and, she runs a shop in a shopping mall near Seattle. It's difficult, now, for her to work all day, go to therapy, and come to our evening meetings, some 34 miles driving distance one way. She tries to attend when she can. Her progress in attaining wellness and managing her diagnoses is astounding. She has said, more than once, "I didn't even like me; how could I expect others to like me?" She has a roommate "Gary" who is also diagnosed Bi-polar 2. "Gary" has also been to DBSA. He's a slightly built man, about age 45, and he works as a commercial truck driver in the greater Pacific Northwest. "Gary" has often described how he and "Teri" sometimes "get into it" when both are "manic" and out of sorts. They have had some pretty severe arguments and fights. Nothing physical....just a lot of verbiage. Funny thing, though, they usually can't remember what their fighting about. Their therapists have stated that this is very common to Bi-polar folks because thoughts and feelings arc coming at rapid succession, like a machine gun firing word/thought bullets. They have learned to call "time out," walk away from it, and come back later when tempers and thoughts have "cooled." Then they have a rational discussion about issues. They have a symbiotic relationship; not wanting marriage, at this time, in their respective lives. They have both played the "medications roulette" game, as has most of us, with "horrible" (both) results until they finally found something that works, Lamictal (usually used to prevent seizures and convulsions, this drug can also be used to treat Bi-polar, and Anxiety, and it often causes dryness in the mouth and blurred vision {so driving a vehicle in unfamiliar surroundings is inadvisable; especially at night}). {Information on all prescription drugs in this book comes from: Physician's Desk References (PDR), DSM-IV or V (Psyciatric Desk Referencing for Diagnoses), Drugs.com, National Institute of Mental Health (NIMH), Center for Disease Prevention and Control(CDC), referenced publications in the bibliography* of this book, personal interviews with psychiatrists/ psychiatric social workers/ and medical doctors, and Wikipedia (ibid. ref.*), and various news articles and on-line, verified, research}.

Most psycho-active drugs have side effects. Some are rather severe (as has been mentioned). Some are advertised on television, in magazines, newspapers and on-line. In all cases, when one is considering taking one or more of these drugs, please go under advisement of a properly trained psychiatrist or psychiatric PRN (Practical Registered Nurse {they are authorized to prescribe}) Since they are prescriptions, they are monitored by pharmaceutical organizations. However, I know of patients who "borrowed" another person's medication to see if it would work better than the one they had. Or, worse yet, they did not have medications and took a friend's prescription to self-medicate without medical oversight. Hospital emergency rooms are full of stories about these folks. Without a proper description of what the person took, it becomes extremely difficult to treat the person. They may not die; but, they usually wish they were dead after having the contents of their stomach pumped out.

When I first joined the local DBSA group, an organization my eldest daughter found on-line, I was introduced to their, then, major facilitator who shall go "nameless" for reasons you will soon find out. This man was very "magnetic." By that I mean, he had a very charismatic personality; someone you'd want to tell your whole life story to. When we first met, he told me he was a published author (something I thought we had in common). I was drawn to him as a leader and co-participant in group. He seemed to be very knowledgeable about mental health issues. He disclosed his name and that he'd been suffering from Bi-polar 2 for many years. We all have the opportunity to give our first name and diagnosis at the beginning of each meeting: "My name is John and I'm diagnosed with Major Depression." Or, "My name is Suzy and, I'm a supporter for John." We also have the option to "pass" and not disclose anything. No pressure.

Over the course of a few months I had the opportunity to observe how this facilitator "worked" people in the group into his "field of control." He was very good at manipulating people. To me, because of my past training and education, this was a "red flag." I tried to discredit my impression, but it still haunted me. A couple other things that bothered me about this man was that he never looked me in the eye when he spoke to me. He looked others in the eye. He knew, from our initial discussions, what my career as a parole/probation officer had been. The other bothersome point was that I'd tried to find his published work. He told me he had authored some successful science fiction novels. There were none; at least, not under his name. I'd previously asked him if he wrote under a *Nom du* Pen (second name) and he stated he does not. These were also "red flags" to me.

A few months later, I happened to be reading the local Everett Herald News Paper when I came across an article in which our "facilitator's" name was in bold print. He'd been arrested by the F.B.I. in a "trolling sting" operation for soliciting child pornography. In fact, our Mr. "Charisma" had a criminal history! He was sent to prison in the 1980s for the Rape and Murder of a little boy in Bellingham, Washington (Whatcom County, Washington State).

When Mr. "Charisma" didn't show at our next DBSA meeting, I and a few others knew why. In fact, most knew why because our group participants have a "phone tree" to call on another when they feel that they are in crisis and need someone to talk them down. The group's general reaction, after they collectively recovered from the shock: ANGER. Angry because they'd been taken in by this miscreant, sick animal. There are women and men in our group with histories of being sexually abused as children. Some of their diagnoses stem from childhood trauma. Some suffer from PTSD as an additional diagnosis.

We spent the whole 2.5 hours that night, after disclosure, discussing feelings, how we'll deal with the aftermath, who we'll nominate for new facilitator. My name came up, but, due to my schedule and authoring this book, I graciously passed. We did, however, demand of the DBSA manager, who was also present, that a better "vetting" system needed to be in place before the next facilitator appointment. These positions are "leadership" oriented and they rely on the trust of the participants. I recalled two women and one man in group who were in tears because, what Mr. "Charisma" had done was violate their trust and confidence; almost as badly as the person who originally sexually violated them! I strongly advocated that the Administration add a Criminal History Records Investigation (CHRI) to their vetting procedure. These records checks are conducted, in Washington State, by the W.S.P. (Washington State Patrol) and they are very thorough. Most States have them. However, they only report "convictions." This means an organization could still hire a pedophile or other criminal if no convictions are extant. Of course, if one knows what to look for ("red flag" behaviors), one can prevent issues before they arise. My problem with this man was that he'd already ingratiated himself with the group. If I had brought up my concerns with the Admin staff they probably would have laughed in my face. I was "new" to the group and, I had yet to establish my credibility. All agreed that CHRIs needed to be done, and that's what is now being done; the same as it is for anyone in a position of trust (teachers, probation officers, police, fire fighters, social workers, psychiatrists, doctors, and the like).

One thing I should add here, something I trained our staff in when I was an instructor for the Washington State Criminal Justice Training Commission: Pedophiles always look for "access." They look for a way to "get into" an organization that has children as its primary clients (day care worker, schools, sporting/athletic venues, church Sunday school teacher, pediatrician, Boy Scout/ Girl Scout chaperon, single moms with victim-aged children in the home {perpetrator manipulates the mom by dating her, sending flowers and the like; but his real focus is on the 5-year-old little girl in the household},etc.), getting into a person's head, ingratiate themselves with your family, your friends, and, of course, your children; especially a kid that's a "loner" or feels unaccepted by his/her peers. The pedophile will go out of his/her way (yes, folks, there are female pedophiles, but they are in the minority population of pedophiles) to be a "friend" to your children. He/she will look for the "weak" link. By that, I mean something that's created to "reel the victim in." It could be a favorite toy, a book, a movie, a type of candy, or just someone to talk to. If your child is bothered by something and his/her behavior or grades change for the worse, be a good listener and ask "open ended" questions. For example: "Sally, I feel as though something is bothering you, do you want to tell mommy what it is?" If the child feels comfortable enough to disclose, always tell the child it's not their fault. Calm, soft speech is best (even if you are seething inside and want to kill the bastard) when talking about these things with your child. One of the common ploys of pedophiles is to cast doubt in the child's mind that their "little secret" will somehow cause the victim-child to get into trouble. The pedophile often relies on the victim's silence by casting doubt and camouflaging his/her intentions. AND, by all means, if something did happen; even if it's done by one of your own relatives (it happens), report it to the police and Child Protective Services because you just "may" be preventing this perpetrator from molesting another child in the future. Child molesters often have more than one victim and/or they molest the same victim over and over until the child is old enough to say "no" and mean it. By, then, it's usually too late; the psychological damage has been done and it takes years of therapy, in some cases, for a person to regain their self-esteem and become a "survivor" as opposed to staying in "victim mode" the rest of their life. Kids don't lie about this stuff and their subsequent behaviors are very "telling." (poor grades in school, unmotivated by things they usually like, poor appetite, complaining of stomach aches or physical discomfort when there isn't any overt sign of a problem {doctors who are trained on what to look for can see if a child has been sexually abused in a matter of minutes}, more shyness around peers and adults, acting out by striking a toy or friend, and other aggressive or "negative" behaviors).

Pedophilia is NOT a mental illness. It is a learned behavior. Pedophiles, at my last reading, do not get cured. Generally speaking, there is no "cure." They have a high incidence of re-offense. A prosecutor once challenged me on the previous statement by telling me that he saw no "repeaters." I told him, "That's because they relocate….to another State, country, or where they have better access." He found out that it's true. States are now keeping better records, since the late 1990s, through the creation of a National Archive Data Base of Pedophiles and High Risk Offenders.

The other thing I often hear about pedophilia is that it's a type of homosexuality. This is incorrect. Pedophiles are not homosexual. Homosexuality is driven by a genetic alteration of XX, XY chromosomes which alter the persons sexual orientation. Pedophiles have no such alteration. They select victims of either sex, usually young boys and girls. Anatomically, at age 5 to 9 (the age ranges where the highest incidence of molestation occurs, {from For Kid's Sake, Inc. and National Data Base Statistics}), most kids look very similar, except for the genitalia. The objective of the pedophile is the "conquest,"; sex is the vehicle. It is habitual, compulsive, and harmful, in so many ways, to a child. Enough said about this; but it is one of my passions to rid our society of as many pedophiles as possible. Lock them up; especially if they are not responding to therapy. We treat for control: to monitor, supervise for compliance, and watch for aberrant behavior patterns. You get one "dance ticket" buster. If you blow it, off to prison you go; for the ENTIRE term of sentence, no credit for the time you spent "playing the system!"

DEALING WITH STRESS IN A STRESSFUL OCCUPATION

During my 37 plus-year career as a Parole/Probation Officer (C.C.O.-Community Corrections Officer) with the State of Washington, I have dealt with some pretty "bad actors." When I began, moving from an adult corrections facility into field supervision, in 1979, I "inherited" a caseload from a wonderful Officer (Eric Leberg), who became a personal friend and mentor, when he promoted to Pre-Sentence Writer for the Courts. The caseload was in the mid 60s; yep, sixty-some people. The risk factors of these men and women ranged from extremely high to fairly low. In order to "manage" such a large caseload, one must have very good time-management skills. Mine were good, so I had to "hit the ground running." Eric had done me a big favor by writing out where each person was at in terms of compliance with Court or Parole Board conditions of supervision, manageability, risk, cooperation, and achieving goals that had been previously set (getting off supervision is a given, but one must "earn it.")

My first day on the job was a real challenge. I had a Superior Court appearance scheduled with a fellow on the caseload who I had yet to meet. On top of this, the fellow came from a financially fairly well-off family; the man's father was a successful dentist in town. The "violation" action on this man's report, authored by Mr. Leberg, was "1. Failing to Obey all laws {a standard condition of supervision, parenthesis mine} by committing DWI on June 23, 1997 in Snohomish County, Washington."

The official report, which I only briefly had time to read, gave the official version, as written by the arresting police officer and a synopsis of the event, as written by Mr. Leberg. There was a "Defendant's Version" section in the report where the probation officer interviews the defendant/probationer to get his/her side of the story to report to the court. In this case, the defendant denied he was drunk while operating his vehicle and that the officer's breathalyzer testing machine (BA) was in error when the defendant blew a .12 mg/gl (.08 blood to alcohol percentage, or lower, being the legal limit in Washington State). He had no proof of the BA machine being faulty. In fact, I recall, there was a statement of "re-calibration" on the BA machine that was less than a month old.

The defendant's attorney, hired by the boy's father (I say boy because he was only 21 years of age), no doubt (the defendant had no visible means of support, did not have a job, and lived at home with his parents), was a rather well-known and flamboyant, theatrical jurist in the court room. When it was my turn to take the Oath and take the stand, I nervously did so. I'm sure the defendant's attorney cued in on my stress and obviously shaky voice and body movements. Attorneys are virtual experts at reading body language, inflection, and the mood of people they cross examine. In fact they "play" with these things to get a defendant or, person giving testimony flustered or contradictory so the case will run in their client's favor.

So, here I am, first day on the job. I mention this to the Judge as I'm sitting down, within earshot of the defendant's attorney who pipes up: "Oh, so Mr. Crawley, you haven't actually met my client yet?" I affirmed his statement with a nod. The attorney then went on into a formal introduction with all the panache of a Shakespearean bard. He obviously did this to throw me even more off-guard; but, in kind, he had not worked around me and he did not know me either. His actions actually made me angry, and in a controlled manner, it actually allowed me to become more focused.

I began my testimony by reading from Mr. Leberg's very well-written report. I got about two sentences into the report and the defendant's attorney stood up and vehemently objected to the manner in which I was presenting evidence to the Court. When the Judge asked him what it was about my testimony that bothered him I recall these words,"…because I'm cross examining a Report your Honor, not a person! He's just reading!" At this juncture the Judge requested the attorney, "Bear with it, this officer has not had the opportunity to know this client or his case." The attorney grumbled something I could not hear and, I was then instructed, by the Judge, to continue with the reading of the Violation Report into the court record.

We finally arrived at the place in the Court proceedings when a recommendation is given on a finding of guilt; which, in this case, was affirmed (with the defendant's attorney's objections noted throughout…he earned his money that day). The Judge asked for my recommendation and all I could think of was, knowing this defendant's drivers license had been suspended, automatically on conviction, to recommend that the defendant not operate a motor vehicle unless properly licensed, registered, and insured in this State. At this point, the defendant's attorney asked: "…and on what form of logic do you make that recommendation, Mr. Crawley?"

There was a dead silence in the courtroom. I remember the Judge looking down from his bench, glasses pulled down on his nose so he could see better, and nodding as if to prod me into saying,…. "the statistics on our Nation's highways." At this juncture, the Judge tapped his gavel and stated, "Good enough for me…let's have a recess." The Court Bailiff stated, "All rise." And that was my first success as a Parole/Probation Officer. However, I do remember being very nervous and stressed at the time. Probably because everything was new: new surroundings, new job, new duties, new staff to work with, new clients, new office location, new commute, etc.. When I was in therapy, I recalled this event as something, I think, many of us have to deal with in life. I call it "baptism by fire." You either sink or, as in my case, you swim for dear life (career).

As I became more familiar with the Courts and Parole Board settings, and the subsequent training and teamwork by some of the finest, dedicated, and self-sacrificial, professional people you'll ever meet, my 'comfort zone' in the job grew to that of a confident, well-rounded Officer.

But, there are cases that stick out as "exceptions:"

One in particular was not to long after I'd been on the job, for about 6 months I believe. I had a fellow "Jerry" who had just been released on parole from the local Work-Release facility up the street from our office. Prior to Jerry's release, the media was filled with some horrific murders which had occurred a couple days before. A woman, in her early 30s, her 7-year-old daughter, and an elderly neighbor friend were killed by someone who violently cut their throats with what was thought to be a butcher's knife. These victims were cut so deeply that they were almost decapitated (according to the coroner's report).

It was learned that "Jerry's" roommate in Work Release, one Charles Campbell, was a possible suspect because Campbell was in prison for 1st Degree Rape....rape of the 30-year-old woman victim of the murder, some 6 years prior.

"Jerry" came to my office on the third floor of the Commerce Building in Everett, Washington for his Intake Interview. Upon first meeting "Jerry," I noticed this frail-looking, rather meek individual nervously moving around in his chair as we sat down to go over his paperwork. I recall stating something like, "You seem pretty nervous today Jerry, are you okay?" At this juncture, "Jerry" just looked at me as if he was carrying the whole world upon his shoulders. I'm pretty good at "reading" expressions and body language, so I took my shot and said, "Well, it seems like you've got something to say to me, but you can't or someone's got you frightened."

"I'll tell you what, Jerry. You got back out and sit down in the lobby and think on it some more. You have a couple choices here....you can tell me and I'll try to help you...or, you can live with it the rest of your life." Jerry got up, went out the door, and was back in my office in less than 30 seconds. He began by stammering something about "b-b-eing t-there."

I recall saying to him, "It's okay man, just calm down, we've got plenty of time here...just talk to me."

Jerry then began relating how he'd been with Campbell when Campbell had him drive to the Snohomish River, within about a mile of the Work Release, and dispose of a bloody set of clothing wrapped around what Jerry recalled as a "b-big K-KNIFE!" At this juncture I stopped Jerry and told him to "hold that thought." (remembering we have to read people their Miranda Rights if they have anything to do with a criminal act). I then went to my supervisor's office, Glenn Greer, and told him he needs to come to my office, next door, and hear what is being said. I then read "Jerry" his Rights and he proceeded to tell us how he went with Campbell to the river to dispose of Campbell's clothing and promise Campbell, on the threat of his own death, never to tell anyone. Campbell told "Jerry," 'I have people on the street...an all I have to do is point at you and you are dead meat.' (not a direct quote, but close from what I recall.)

To bring this story to its proper conclusion, it was Jerry's testimony at Campbell's murder trial that nailed the coffin on Campbell's guilty verdict, 3 Counts of Aggravated 1st Degree Murder, which, at the time, carried an automatic death penalty in the State of Washington. According to the jury, they found "no compelling redeemable quality" in Campbell's life (quoted from the Everett Herald's news article accompanying Campbell's verdict) which, in essence, sealed Campbell's fate. It took the State over 12 years to execute Campbell, by hanging, in Walla Walla State Penitentiary. This was due to the extensive filings of one appeal after another by Campbell's attorneys. Some years later, the death penalty, in Washington, was overturned by the Supreme Court, so we now have life sentences without the possibility of parole as the maximum punishment.

As an aftermath of this case, work release programs in our State suffered greatly. Everett's Work Release closed down a few months after the Campbell incident and we have yet, to this day, to have another work-release in Snohomish County.

So, years later, I was on a committee with one of our Department of Corrections (DOC) Administrators, Joop Dejong, trying to convince the public, at hearings, that work release criteria and safeguards were in place to prevent what happened, in Campbell's day, would never happen again. In fact there were some politicians who questioned how Campbell even qualified for work release in the first place. I think a few people were either fired or severely reprimanded over this. Criminals convicted of violent acts weren't supposed to be considered for work release, even in Campbell's day. I've termed this loss of a usually viable program: 'Campbell's Nemesis.' He ruined it for a lot of deserving inmates.

One other event I found to be particularly stressful was a case involving a middle-aged man "Mr. D" (since he's still alive, I think) we'll use anonymous names, and his paramour, "Ms. Z", a middle-aged woman. They both had met at a social club for single middle-aged folks where they dined and danced and established relationships. "Mr D." and "Ms. Z," initially, hit it off fairly well. Unfortunately, as I learned later, "Mr. D." became rather "controlling" and possessive in his behavior and he was alcoholic. "Ms. Z," an independent woman who owned her own interior decorating business in Enumclaw, Washington was also an avid equestrian who owned her own horses and stables. She lived out in the countryside. "Mr D." a slightly built man, had been an engineer at the Everett Boeing Aircraft Plant, the largest air-frame assembly plant in the world. He had to retire early due to (again, I found out much later) diagnosed mental illness (Major Depression).

What placed "Mr. D" on supervision with the State of Washington was an incident where "Mr. D" was told by "Ms. Z" she was no longer interested in them being a couple and, she wanted to move on with her life, absent of him. "Mr D," apparently didn't like to be rebuffed and he went to her home, while she was gone, let himself in (earlier in their relationship, she had told him where she hid the key), and he hid in the bedroom closet.

Upon arrival home, "Ms Z" went upstairs to take a shower. As she was disrobing, "Mr. D" came out of the closet and confronted her. He was holding a firearm in his hand. He demanded she lie down on the bed so he could make love to her. Being a resourceful woman who was in the early phases of menopause, "Ms. Z" smelled alcohol on "Mr. D's" breath and she deduced he was not thinking very clearly. She then told him she was with her period and it would be too messy for him and her and, not very enjoyable. She invited him downstairs for a cup of coffee. Taken aback by this sudden gesture of kindness, "Mr. D" complied.

After "Mr. D" apologized, profusely, had his coffee and left, "Ms. Z" phoned the Sheriff and reported the attempted 1st Degree Attempted Rape. She told police she was in fear of her life, and she knew "Mr. D" had a temper. It could have gone south in so many ways, but it didn't. She considered herself very lucky that day.

"Mr. D" was arrested at his residence in Arlington. He had a nice lot on the river (Jim Creek) where his double-wide trailer sat. He plead guilty, in King County Superior Court, in the early 1990s (I don't have the exact date here, just the decade). The crime was "Attempted First Degree Rape WAWADW (while armed with a deadly weapon, a 2 year enhancement on a prison sentence, at the time, had he gone to prison.) "Mr. D" received a probation sentence with a year in jail. His supervision with me began upon his release from jail. I supervised him because he lived in my territory, even though the sentence emanated out of another county.

Our first meeting was congenial and I reviewed his Conditions of Supervision (which were substantial), and he griped about having to jump through so many hoops. I told him he could easily have been sentenced to prison, but, had it not been for his victim's compassion in requesting probation and counseling, he was still able to have a type of "freedom." I recall that my comments seemed to fall on deaf ears.

Two months later, "Mr. D" was "down the road" on me. He absconded from supervision and I issued a Violation Report wherein I claimed 5 separate violations of what the Court and DOC had ordered. He was, eventually arrested, following the issuance of a warrant from the Court, and placed into the King County Jail, where he awaited a scheduled hearing date. I went to the hearing, as the supervising officer, and "Mr. D" was found guilty of all violations. In other States, one can have probation revoked and be sent to prison. Washington State had just changed their laws, prior to "Mr. D's" conviction, to where the most he could receive, in jail time, would be 60 days for each violation. The judge had the option of doing a "partial finding", a total finding of guilt, and he could sentence the defendant to 60 days running concurrently (for all 5 violations) or, consecutively, running 60 days each. The Judge chose "consecutive." So, in essence, "Mr. D" would go back to jail for almost a year before I'd see him on my caseload again. His file was archived to the King County Records Vault.

About a year later, I was sent an assignment noting that "Mr. D" had, again, been released and he was required to re-report to my office for Intake. He did so, in response to my letter requiring a mandatory appointment. I could tell, from the onset of our meeting, that "Mr. D" was not a "happy camper." He had booze on his breath (one of the issues I had with the court on this case is that they knew he had a drinking issue and they did not impose a "no consumption of alcoholic beverages" condition of supervision on "Mr. D"). It is extremely frustrating for a C.C.O. to supervise a person when certain conditions, we know should be in place, are not. On top of this, I recall, the file was still in the other county and, we didn't receive it until just before "Mr. D's" second abscond. We reviewed his conditions off a printout I received from our records office, again, and I told him I was setting up an appointment, with the Catholic Community Services (CCS) counseling program, for him in the hopes it would cover two bases (alcohol assessment and the required Court-ordered treatment/therapy he was required to do). I knew CCS had a contracted psychiatrist available who might be willing and able to work with "Mr. D." I encouraged him to comply and told him that things go much easier when one is "with the program." He left my office grumbling under his breath.

"Mr. D" did attend one session that I was able to document with CCS; however, one week later, he was "down the road" again (absconded). I also received a phone call from "Ms. Z" stating she'd been receiving "hang up" calls. She thought it might be "Mr. D," "because that's what he did before" (prior to the instant offense that put him on supervision). I recall asking "Ms. Z" if she had a "safe place to go...one that "D" knew nothing about." At this juncture of our phone conversation I recall "Ms. Z" saying something about not letting "this man run my life...I have a gun too, and I know how to use it!"

This time, I phoned the King County prosecutor (Don Raz) and, I requested he "walk a warrant through" to the Judge," because I did not want to wait the approximate 30-days it took to get a warrant from another county (knowing how slow these things take). Three days after the warrant hit the system (law enforcement APB), "Mr. D" stalked "Ms. Z" to a place where she was getting her vehicle serviced and he shot her, paralyzing her from the waist down, for life. The police/sheriff and office of criminal investigation grilled me, by phone, for a good hour (each), wanting to know everything and anything I could tell them about "Mr. D" that would help in apprehending him. I disclosed what I knew and the fact "Mr. D" had not stayed around, long enough, twice, for me to really get to know him. I did recall that he once had said that he frequented casinos where he liked to drink and gamble. I also found that he'd traded in his ford truck and camper and bought a new Chevrolet, maroon, Impala vehicle at the Arlington Dealership. This was after my seeing his neighbor on a field visit to try and get additional information to give to the investigators. I wanted "Mr. D" caught just as badly as they did.

This case went on to gain notoriety by being placed on "America's Most Wanted," a popularized television program in the 1990s and early 2000s that financier Rupert Murdoch Enterprises bankrolled. I believe, to this day, had it not been for the exposure of this horrendous crime on the media, "Mr. D" may not have been caught; at least, not caught as soon as he was. As it happened, a couple weeks after his criminal act, near Reno, Nevada, in an outskirts Motel, some room cleaners had left a motel door open while they went to clean another room and "Mr. D" took the opportunity to lie down on the bed that was being changed. He fell asleep and, when the cleaners came back and saw him, one of them recognized him from the television show. Police were phoned and "Mr. D" was, again, arrested. Under a pillow in the bed he was sleeping on, was a loaded pistol; the same weapon he'd shot "Ms. Z" with. I, of course, learned all of this via the subsequent police information line, television news, and the newspapers.

All the staff who subsequently reviewed this case (a formal inquiry and review is always required when a C.C.O.'s client commits another heinous crime) informed me: "You did everything you possibly could have done, John; and more than most of us would." It was a nice sentiment; true, but it still didn't help me with the depression and feelings of unworthiness that came afterward. I had done everything I knew to do; absent standing guard at the victim's home, some 100 miles away, which was not "practical" because I had other, even higher risk, clients to supervise.

The victim sued the State and the King County Sheriff's Office for not responding to my phone calls warning them that I had good reason to believe that "Mr. D" was, in fact, stalking "Ms. Z" and they needed to keep a close eye on her residence, vehicle, and I recalled even giving them the make, model, color and license plate number of "Mr. D's" new car.

Preparation for the trial took almost a full year. In the interim, I had my regular job to do, but much of the week was spent being "coached" and reviewed for my testimony and deposition (as it was, a 4 hour process where I had to go over all the notations, Judgment and Sentence, why I did what and when, chronological records, etc., etc. while the victim's attorney continually peppered me with questions so, I guess, I'd trip up or contradict myself. I was told later, by the Attorney General (A.G.) assigned to me that I'd done well. But, that doesn't quell all the stress and additional anxiety one has to deal with as a result of this long, drawn-out process.) My doctor put me on Paxil, a relaxant and anti-depressant. I thought to myself, as I was dealing with this, now I know why attorneys delay and ask for "continuances" (reschedule of hearings) is not so much for preparation as it is for defendants and those who testify to "forget" or "mix up" dates or times or events. We cannot remember every little detail, in minutia, all the time. And, time has a way of eating away at our memory bank. This is true of most people; even those who are said to have "photographic" memory capabilities.(from Psychology Today)

In the end, after three days of sitting at a table by myself, in a King County Court room, with the A.G. to my right at a separate table, with all his paperwork stacked in bunched, organized "presentation stacks," the State decided to "settle" the case. When these things go on, in a back room, during recesses of the Court, a "Risk Manager" from the State is negotiating with the Plaintiff's Attorney, on possible payouts. The theory, I was told by one adjudicator, is the more often they meet, the longer the delay, the further apart the potential amounts diverge. In other words, as the State went lower, the Plaintiff's Attorney went higher.

In testimony, the Plaintiff goes first. It really boils down to, what my A.G. "coach" told me, "whoever tells the most believable story wins." "Ms. Z's" was excellently portrayed, with a lot of personal "the life before" and the "life after" show, a power-point presentation. They spared no expense. She sat closest to the jury in direct view, wheelchair and all. The jury was in tears following her attorney's initial presentation and her testimony. It was a completely believable story, with all the right "buttons" pushed.

I'll never forget my A.G.'s first opening sentence to the jury. His name is John Kershner, a man I still admire, even today, for his insight, wit, and knowledge. He was one of the Washington State Attorneys General senior jurists. His opening statement: "We do not give our Community Corrections Officers a crystal ball." He waited a long pause so this could sink in. There are ways to predict human behavior, and we did a fairly good job of it; but nothing is certain, and we cannot be 100% accurate all the time. Psychology is an imperfect science. These are facts.

One other thing I learned from this case is that if you are a victim of a heinous crime and the perpetrator is on an F.B.I. want list, you can legally seize his/her property (as was done in this case...remember?, the nice double-wide on the creek, about 1 acre, his new car, and anything else of value), sell it, and use the proceeds to hire one of the top notch law firms in the State.

So, as I told my wife, who graciously sat, by herself, in the gallery of the courtroom, after 3 days into all of this, "They (the State) are going to settle, I won't even get to tell my side of the story." {which, by the way, I prepared for over a year to tell....it WAS worth telling} So, my prediction came through about an hour later. Proceedings were stopped, the jury was dismissed, and we all went home. I did get one ounce of solace though: I learned, later, that the victim, "Ms. Z" never blamed me for what happened. She actually demanded that my name not appear on the list of defendants. So, in a way, I guess that was a little piece of vindication for my efforts. I did try....hard. It was a "system failure" where better communications may have saved the day. One can only speculate on this. Nothing is a "given."

"Mr. D?" He received 444 months in Walla Walla State Penitentiary. He was in failing health, about 57 years old, the last I heard. I don't know if he's alive today. Frankly, I really don't care.

Another little "fix" came soon after this: C.C.O.s are now allowed to issue their own warrants and put them, almost immediately, into the system. But, remember, just because there is a warrant out for someone's arrest, there is no guarantee that it's going to get served. There are hundreds of thousands of warrants, as I write this; some of them have been "in system" for years.

So, folks, that's just some things about having a stressful job. But, now, looking back on all of it, I wouldn't have traded it for all the tea in China (as is said.) I met some real quality people along the way. I was fortunate enough to have great staff to work with, both as cohorts and, later in my career, as a Supervisor. I did a lot of traveling, and, once in awhile I'd run into an old client who said, "Hi Mr. Crawley...do you remember me?" (as I'm thinking, should I?) And this fellow introduces me to his lovely wife and beautiful children and he tells me I helped him "'clean up my act' and now I'm a shift supervisor at Fluke Manufacturing." Someone once told me, 'you never can tell much about a person until you've walked a mile in their shoes.' My dad used to kid about this phrase by saying, "Yep, but you are a mile away and you have HIS shoes!"

SO, WHY DON'T WE HAVE SOCIALIZED MEDICINE?

Well, a couple of "reasons" come to mind: 1. Congress and the FDA (Federal Drug Administration) have been in legion with Big Pharmaceuticals, Big Medicine, and Big Insurance for many years. It's like a "brotherhood" of conspiratorial traditions not to "rock the boat" and change things. And 2. There's a lot of money to be made by keeping the "status quo." So, why change it? I have reams of text, and video presentations, and documentaries to prove these claims. Some will be in the bibliography of this book. Many in Congress have pharmaceutical stock investments, so do prominent doctors and hospital administrators, as do insurance CEOs. They all have stock in each other's endeavors. So, why give that up?

I'll give you a few reasons why we need to change the current system. We are the only civilized, modern economy in the world that does not have some form of socialized medicine. We cannot afford to keep on going down this path because our citizenry is dying and in ill health. Our "patient base" is growing each day and our providers are overwhelmed with work. We treat people who cannot afford to pay because it's mandated by law, but we put them right back on the street to suffer again. It's a "revolving door" of apathy and neglect. Our tax payers are spending a fortune for this, and they don't even know it. Our State and Federal taxes have a "built in" sum that each of us pays toward the care of the homeless, the mentally ill, substance abusers, and the veterans coming back from harms way. The "fees" we pay on "out-services" and add-on surcharges go for these costs. The provider is certainly not going to pay the freight if they can get out of it.

Our current Administration (2017) wants to dump Obamacare, the closest thing to "socialized medicine" this country has ever seen. But it was flawed. It did not "build in" enough profit for the providers and they opted out. So, now, we're faced with a "change the system" attitude in Congress. Change to what? They aren't sure. They want to keep some of the "better" or "more popular" coverage like allowing a son or daughter to be covered in the family home until the age of 25 ; and, pre-existing conditions will allow one to have coverage. But, it seems that the "profit" incentive is still the driver in all of this. The Administration wants a "market driven" (read: profits) system. A "single payer" system has been floated out to see if it will fly. Many are skeptical of such a system because it has too many "outs" for the payer. So, as of this writing, we are "stuck." No one seems to have a solid solution. What we may, eventually, wind up having is much like what we're trying to ditch; only, we'll be paying more for it. I do not see our country going much further, economically, unless we adopt some form of socialized medicine. It just makes sense, and we could reduce some of the exorbitant profit gouging that the big medical and pharmaceutical corporations now demand. They are swimming in profits and they use the excuse of research and development costs to ward off criticism. If that's the case, then have a tax deduction for it; don't stick it to us for your mistakes and failures in the lab! And driving up the cost of certain drugs and preventative devices (Epipen @ $6,000 when it costs less than $300 for the same thing in Canada) should be a criminal act. Or the recent hedge fund young man who bought the patents on some organ transplant medicines and drove the price from $400.00 to $8,000.00, over night, was criminal. In fact, he was called before Congress over this to testify as to how hedge fund managers "play the market" so they can get rich at our expense. People die because they cannot afford these drugs. People suffer because some company decides to "jack" the prices up so far that one has to mortgage his/her home to afford medical care. Recently, diabetic insulin prices were jacked up to budget-busting proportions for most middle-class families. What's wrong with this picture? EVERYTHING!

So, I'm a big proponent of socialized medicine and health care that's affordable, obtainable, and effective. Our medical/pharmaceutical/ insurance conglomerates are way too fat with profit and, many have forgotten the basic tenet of the Hippocratic Oath… "first, do no harm." Harm to the pocketbook, in my opinion, is harm because the patient cannot afford treatment. When people die because they cannot afford to see a doctor, I get very upset. We do not need to have a system that prevents the average citizen from having adequate medical care. Personally, I believe it should be written into our Constitution as a God-given right: "No person, who is a citizen of the United States of America, shall be denied medical care and treatment due to their station in life." So basic, so simple, so RIGHT.

This advocacy is also part of the "fire fighter" mantra. We need to stand up to the profit takers and say, "ENOUGH." We need to demand our right to "…the pursuit of happiness," as is guaranteed in the Constitution. It's hard to "pursue happiness" when one is sick or diseased, and they can't afford treatment.

I recently watched an old DVD of Crosby, Stiles, Nash, and Young (CSNY) from the 2009 era. They were song writers and entertainers who were popular during the Vietnam era. They decided to go on tour to rouse the people up to the wrongs of the first Iraq invasion; an invasion that was predicated on lies and innuendo; much like those that put us into Vietnam.

I remember reading a book, when I was in my teens, titled "The Ugly American." It was a fiction about a man who traveled to South East Asia and found himself in a morass of deception and corruption. He was in charge of a quasi-military operation that tried to sway the local population toward the Western ways and "assimilate" these folks into the more "modern" culture of the West; much like our efforts with the Native Americans. And we know how badly that turned out. Except for the tycoons and politicians of the day. They made a lot of money and drew great prestige from their exploits (General Custer comes to mind here; in real life, he was an asshole.)

Anyway, CSNY asked … "who are the men who run this land?"… "peace is not a lot to ask for if you've never been shot or shoot at someone." Their message was for the fathers and sons who pass their habits on to the next generation and the awful results that entail war, suffering and pain. "What's goin on...Do you know....Don't you wonder?" "Down under.... the ground." And do you remember? "Stop...what's that sound...everybody look what's goin down....there's a man with a gun over there....he better think...you got to beware...paranoia strikes deep....into your heart it'll creep....." They were trying to deliver a message. One that resounded in the protests that, eventually, caused our government to quit the carnage, and profit taking, that was Vietnam.

In 2009, things were different. Their message had mixed reviews. We were fighting "evil" in the form of Saddam Hussein and his henchmen. Unfortunately, we were also creating the seeds of ISIL or ISIS, the caliphate of a 13th century belief system that was far more dangerous and lethal than anything Saddam thought about or could conjure up. There is a reason why the Middle Eastern populations do not trust the West. All one needs do is study the Crusades to see why. Every Crusade was a total failure, but a lot of people died as a result; most of them were Muslims.

"Lawrence of Arabia," the movie in which Peter O'Toole did such a superb job of playing the role of "Ah-rence" (as the Arab tribesmen called him), was a depiction, during the First World War, in which the Turks and the English and the Tribes of Saudi Arabia fought to "drive out the infidels." The British were on the side of the Arabs. At the end of the conflicts, the Middle East was divided up into three sections: Syria, Saudi Arabia, and Iraq. The one caution I recall from the story was that "Lawrence" felt it was the wrong move on the part of the axis powers. He felt that the Tribal Leaders should determine their own boundaries. There has been strife in these regions ever since.

In a time of war, with the advent of the media and "Close Up" photographs and film, we have been indoctrinated to "accept" what is happening as a part of the routine of daily existence. Our video games depict violence as if it was just another "dink of water." Our children are fed this pablum daily. Then they go off to the "real war" and, they come back injured in more ways than anyone could imagine. Or, they don't come back at all. We have an average of 22 veterans and active service personnel committing suicide every day in this country (I already documented this fact earlier). "No one sees them coming home that way….buried in the ground...scarred for life...we had a chance to save their lives...we had a chance to change our lives..."(Young, Deja Vu').

We do have returning veterans who have gone on to careers in medicine, counseling, and successful coping with the PTSD that many suffer. But, it takes a lot of people, in many places, to help a soldier recover. They are the "fire fighters" I speak of. They are the unsung heroes who do good each day. We do not see them because they choose to be "invisible" and, they are "present" only to those who suffer.

I know this chapter is about "socialized medicine" and how we can achieve a state of "homeostasis" (balance) among those who approve and those who object; and I'm trying very hard NOT to interject "politics" into the picture. But, it seems, with all that the current Administration (2017) is trying to do by using a "business model" to deconstruct everything this country fought for, died for, and strives to protect, I just can't sit by, idle, biding my time, without saying something.

Tonight, April 4, 2017, I went to listen to an audio tape and power-point presentation of Dr. Martin Luther King's speech: "Beyond Vietnam---A Time to Break Silence." I had heard excerpts from this speech after my return from my military service in 1968. This speech wasn't as famous as Dr. King's "I have a dream" speech at the Lincoln Memorial in August 1963, but it was just as profound...and relevant; especially, in today's (2017) political climate. In his speech, Dr. King related how we supported the French in their battles in Vietnam during the 1950s. The French did not want to give up their colonial hold on this country. Even when they lost in a very decisive war, we still supported a "puppet" government run by a ruthless dictator (Diem) who was instrumental in sucking our country further into a morass of greed, corruption, military quagmires, and eventual killing fields we knew as Da Nang, Ke Son, Bien Too, Na Trang, and many, many others whose innocent people suffered our wrath and napalm, and carpet bombings in what was felt to be a never ending Conflict. Congress never declared war on Vietnam. It was said to be a "police action"; "to bring the people out of strife, pestilence, and misery"(Richard Nixon). In my opinion, it was far from a "bringing;" more like Armageddon. I know....I was there....I saw it.

Doctor King said, in his 1967 speech, "The greatest purveyor of violence is my own government." He echoed the words of John F. Kennedy who said, "A country that spends more on military defense than it's own social needs and programs is a country approaching spiritual death." We have been going down this "slippery slope" for some time now and, we are paying dearly for it. Our jails and prisons are overcrowded because we have virtually no "continuum of care" programs. Our veterans are coming home to a detached, I-pod world where one's worth is not measured in their character, but how much "bling" is in his mouth or around his neck. Our children and bombarded with info commercials, Nintendo, X-box, and violent video games that dull their senses and offer little in the way of cultural values and substance. We have incubated a culture of "entitlement."

Dr. King's message was right on for today's world. He was murdered exactly one year later, 1968, and the celebration I went to was in honor of the 50 year anniversary of his eloquent and poignant speech. It rings just as true today as it did 50 years ago; even more so because we are just now beginning to question what we've wrought in the recent Presidential Election. I will leave history to play this out; but, we should all voice our objections to being treated as if we are ignorant of our inherent rights and Constitutional guarantees that are currently being gutted, trod upon, and challenged in place of an oligarchical form of government; a fiefdom if you will, where a "police state" could easily be created if we stand by and do nothing. It happened in Rome. It happened in Nazi Germany. And you can bet your bottom dollar, it can happen in the good 'ol U.S. of A!

Dr. king, and others, (Gandhi, Jesus, Mohammad, Confucius, Alexander the Great, Socrates, Plato, etc.) have all alluded to the "spirit of love that shines through the darkness (in human failings) and brings about a new generation of peace and tolerance." If it were not for most people believing that the previous statement had merit, you and I would not be here. We must have hope, conviction, and values to live by, or we will perish from the face of the earth. Extinct….like the dinosaurs.

Some one once said that, 'insanity is doing the same thing, over and over again, expecting a different result.' We do this when we go and fight a war, spend lives, billions of dollars, kill a lot of innocent people, destroy the economy and infrastructure of a country, and expect the people of that country to welcome us with open arms because we "liberated" them from whatever WE decided to tell them was their enemy. In this respect, we are our own worst enemy; because we have yet to learn that compassion isn't at the toss of a coin into a beggar's cup; nor the giving of foreign aid to people who only want us to leave them, and theirs, alone to be what they want to be, without our "help." It's called "self determination," something our country, I hope, still cherishes.

John F. Kennedy also said, "Those who make peaceful revolution impossible will make violent revolution possible." History proves out that statement. Dr. King said, "Silence is betrayal...we must speak up when wronged." "We cannot and should not be mesmerized by uncertainty, a vocation of agony, nor a society who sends its poorest citizens off to a war, some 8,000 miles away, so that the better off can profit by their deaths and suffering." "Jesus gave us the word...Gandhi gave us the pathway." "We are deeply in need of a way out of the darkness (Vietnam)." "Let no man pull you so low as to hate him." "We are in need of a symphony of brotherhood." "Darkness cannot drive out darkness...only light can do that." "Hate cannot drive out hate...only love can do that." "We cannot continue in our own arrogance." Sound familiar?

If it doesn't, you haven't been on this planet long enough. In my opinion, with what I see going on in our country right now, we are headed for a major upheaval….and I don't mean that in a good way. If we haven't learned from our enemies by now, we'll never learn and we are doomed to make the same, stupid mistakes that cost people their livelihood, their family, their possessions, their home, and, for many, their lives.

We have time to correct the course we're on. But we need "fire fighters" to do this. If we stand by and watch the "fire" consume what we value, then we are as guilty as those who are too myopic to see what they are doing. Greed and corruption "blinds" people. They lose sight of what's really important: their family and loved ones, their health, their ability to solve problems with favorable outcomes, brotherhood, peace, and their faith. How does it go?... "He so loved himself that he sacrificed everything to gain the world, but, in the end, he got nothing..." or something like that... you get the point I'm sure. Right?

FISHING WITH JIM

On to a more "lighter" topic. Rather, a true story that I relate to you, dear reader, because I think you may enjoy it and it may give you some sense of the peace and solace I derive from one of my favorite past times: fly fishing.

Jim and Judy Johnston are my best friends. Actually, they are more like a "brother" and a "sister to me. They know my complete story and they have been constant, loyal supporters. We went to high school together, graduating in a fairly small class (less than 200 people) in 1961, from Marysville H.S. Judy and I attended the same university (Western Washington University in Bellingham). Jim attended the University of Washington as a fisheries biologist major. He went on to obtain a Master's Degree in this field. He also earned enough money, during high school, tying gorgeous flies, to buy his first car, a 1958 Chevrolet Impala. This vehicle made many a fishing expedition to British Columbia where Jim taught me how to perfect my skills at fly fishing. Jim and Judy were "sweet hearts" throughout their later high school and college years; eventually marrying and having a family: a son, David and a daughter, Laura. Jim and Judy are fiercely "independent." I was often the "mediator" between these two in a somewhat "rocky at first" courtship.

On one occasion, I recall coming back through Bellingham, after a weeks-long fishing trip to Canada. Jim wanted to stop and see Judy, who was finishing up her teaching degree, because he had departed for Canada with some "words exchanged" between he and Judy. He intended to apologize (this was huge for Jim because, as Valedictorian and President of the student body in our high school, one is humbled by having to apologize). Anyway, we "stunk." We had not bathed for a week and we were dressed in clothing that reeked of fish guts, camp fire smoke, and sweat. I suggested it might be a good idea to bathe first. But Jim was adamant; like a fish rising to the fly, he was committed to seeing his true love. So we stopped at the old house Judy lived at with her fellow classmates. I remember Jim waltzing up to the door and knocking. I waited in the car, sensing a "storm" brewing. And storm it was. Jim got an earful that day and, he sheepishly returned to the vehicle. I remember asking him, "So, how'd it go?" He just looked at me with a look of disgust on his face and told me, "I'm going home to take a bath."

Jim and I would probably not be picked, by the average observer, to be close, lifetime friends and confidants. Our personalities are juxtaposed, but different. We developed opposite/ different interests and activities in school. Jim was a natural leader. He was very academic, rising to the school's honor roll at an early age. Judy, the same. He became an officer in the United States Navy soon after graduation from college. He has always been a scholar, an Administrator (he once held the position of Assistant Game and Wildlife Administrator for the State of Washington), prior to his retirement.

Jim was a track runner in high school. I was a football and baseball player. Jim was always "independent" in his thinking and behavior. He was not resistant to compromise, but you better come prepared with you point of view and justifications. He was also, pretty much, a "loner," being very selective with who he held "close to the vest." We had some really interesting "debates." I learned a lot.

Judy is the much more social and out going of the two. She won more than her fair share of beauty pageants in school. I was a solid "B" grade student while both Jim and Judy garnered "Honor Roll" positions early on in their academic pursuits. I tended to "play" while Jim and Judy tended to study and involve themselves in wholesome activities. I was a "party animal," collector and promoter of "classic" automobiles, and I spent most of my earned cash on dating, guitars, and car repairs. Jim and Judy saved their funds for college.

Looking back, the only things I recall Jim and I having common interest in was fishing and art. I've already told you that Jim tied great flies; he also was a fine artist. He should have been an architect because he designed and acted as his own contracting consultant on three homes he and Judy later built. I was lucky enough to reap the benefits of his labors at fly tying. Jim would give me his "seconds," flies he did not consider worthy of selling. As a result, I never had to buy a fly in my life. When we graduated from high school, Jim owned the newest car in our class; bought with the proceeds of fly tying.

Jim also liked visiting with my parents. As I've previously written, my mother, Angie, was a gifted artist and Jim would often bring some of his art work to show her and ask for her critique' or comments. Jim also admired my father, John L., and they would sit and talk for a lengthy time. Jim has since told me that he considered my parents as his "second mom and dad."

Fly fishing was a passion Jim and I both embraced. In addition to being taught about the finer points of casting, Jim taught me about the cycles of fishes lives, their marine habitat, what supports a viable ecosystem, and natural selection. He taught me about the various diseases and parasites that fish succumb to, and he showed me different ways to look at Nature, with depth, and ecological understanding. He was also a superb photographer who, in my opinion, could hold class with some of the best professionals in the field.

Jim and I once planned a fishing trip to British Columbia soon after we graduated from high school. This trek became an annual ritual for us around the end of May, each year, until we were called to serve our country in the military service.

When we fished together, we usually caught a lot of Kamloops Rainbow Trout. These fish ranged, usually, between 2-5 pounds. However, once in awhile, we would catch a "monster" at 10-12 pounds. For those of you who are not familiar with Rainbow Trout, they usually average below two pounds. Our first trip together in the second week of June, 1961 was memorable to me for a number of reasons. We did a lot of planning and collection of gear we'd need: Coleman camp stove, pots, pans, paper plates, eating utensils, cups, fresh water, two coolers packed with food such as frozen bacon, eggs, frozen sandwich meats, ketchup, mustard, frozen butter, mayonnaise, bread, pickles, pop, and other items; not to forget the rolls of toilet paper! We would usually go sparingly on the vegetables and sweets; although, I had to have my home-made chocolate chip cookies! Judy also made cookies for us too.

Jim and I took inventory of our fishing gear at least three times. He was always very thorough. Our fly rods and reels, lines and various and numerous tied flies, were paramount to a week-long trip to the great North land. Everything had to be "just right" as Jim would say. I usually packed my stuff without much of an inventory. As a result, I often had to "borrow" a leader or "tippet" material (very thin extension of mono-filament line extending beyond the end of a leader). Somehow, I knew all would work out in the end. I was an "optimist" in those days. My Depression never seemed to raise its ugly head when I was with Jim, fly fishing some pristine high lake in Canada.

Jim was the methodical one; I wasn't. He'd lay out the sleeping gear, tent, foam rolled-up mattress pads, ropes, stakes for the tent, ax, bow hand saw, anchors for each end of the 18 foot Alumacraft canoe we carried on a rack that sat atop the 1958 Impala, canoe paddles (with a "spare" just in case one got lost or broken), flashlights, spare batteries, dry matches sealed in a waterproof container, newspapers and dry kindling wrapped in the papers and bundled to take up less space. Jim was also very thorough in what we took to wear; taking a change of underwear for each of the seven days we'd be gone. He planned to dress in "layers" in the event warmer weather appeared. I figured I was good to go with three pair of under wear because I intended to wash clothing, as needed, and dry the clothing in the sun (please remember this). I was the fisherman "optimist" and Jim was the fisherman "realist." It remains so to this day. If I'm the yin, Jim's the yang, and then some. Jim is tall and lanky. I'm shorter and heavier. We're now, both, gray/white haired on top; although Jim has much more "on top" than I do. I began balding (as my father had) in my fifties.

As I recall, on this particular fishing trip, we departed Marysville, Washington on a cloudy day. We were headed for the Kamloops Plateau, about 250 miles northeast of the Canadian border crossing at Sumas, Washington. Jim usually liked to leave before dawn. I like to sleep in. At about 3:30 A.M. I hear rapping that eventually became pounding on my bedroom window.

"Get your lazy ass out of bed Crawley....or I'm leavin' in three minutes without ya!" I do believe I had my clothes on and my stuff in the Impala in less than three minutes that morning. Off we went. Now, Jim is the "quiet, intellectual" sort most of the time. He usually leaves it up to me and my loquacious genes to get a conversation going; something like this (Note that Jim's use of the King's English is usually very proper. He only deviates from it, as far as I know, when we're on a fishing trip):

"Did you get the car filled up with gas Jim?"

"Yep."

"Did you remember to bring the maps?"

"Yep."

"Do you have a lake in mind to go to first?"

"Yep."

Wanting more scintillating conversation, I decided to ask a more "in depth" question...a "two-parter." I then asked him which lake and how long it would take us to get there.

"English Lake, about four hours away, and the fish are bitin' early in the morning."

Note: As time went by, Jim, having done a Master's Thesis in British Columbia, got to know most of the Provincial fisheries biologists. He'd phone one to get the latest fish report prior to our departures. So we kind of had a "lock" on the good fishing; but, at times, the water would be "off the bite" and we'd have to move on.

I remember asking Jim, on this particular trip (being our first together), how he knew the fish would be biting early in the morning. His reply: "They just do...trust me."

Getting a little tired of the "Gary Cooper (the actor who said little)" responses, I decided to catch up on some shut eye. We drove for about two more hours, crossing the border while I tried to sleep. The Canadian authorities were very kind to me. They didn't even try to wake me up (although I was awake because I heard actual conversation between Jim and the border guard). Unlike today's Homeland Security scrutiny, all they asked for was Jim's driver's license and what our purpose was in Canada. It was a foregone conclusion, seeing the canoe on top of the car and fishing gear stashed in the back seats. Fishing was, apparently, an acceptable activity. We were given the "go ahead" with a wish for good luck on the lakes. Great people those Canadians!

Another 2.5 hours of driving and I was half asleep when Jim turned off the main highway. I could barely see the sunrise in the East, so I knew it was still very early in the day. I was immediately greeted with a road, if one wanted to call it that, or a very bumpy, potholed, and rutted cow path which would be more apropos. My kidneys began to dance with my lower lungs, and my butt, when I came down from the car's ceiling, felt as if I'd been slammed into a wall. From one jostle to the next, each breath I took was forced from me with the tossing and bumps. We were on this "road" for about 45 minutes, I guess, because I lost track of time.

Suddenly, we came to an abrupt stop. After the dust cleared, and I coughed myself silly, I notice a patch of silvery, shimmering water to my right. "It's...it's... a lake!" I exclaimed. "English Lake to be exact," in his usual deadpan, was Jim's reply.

We soon began setting up our campsite. I noticed that there were some semi-fresh and some very fresh "cow pies" (cow poop to you city folks) laying about. Fortunately, there was now enough daylight to see and smell these stink bomb land mines. We made every effort to find a "clean" area where we could erect the tent and have some space. We found a site nearby, among the scrub pines and rocks, about 300 feet from the water's edge. Much of the Kamloops is "open range." So, we were prepared for bovine visitors. Jim had some firecrackers to scare them away.

While Jim went about pitching our tent, yours truly went about trying to find some dry firewood in our general vicinity. I noticed that the air was pretty chilly, even for June. We'd climbed up to a plateau, about 4,000 feet above sea level. The late Spring's frosty mornings were still upon us.

After we set up our camp site, I noticed the morning sunlight was just beginning to strike the tops of the taller pine trees at the far West end of the lake. I stood by the edge of this pristine lake, watching the swallows, on gliding wings. They dipped and soared over the glass-like surface of the water, catching invisible bugs, and creating concentric rings as the very tips of their wings barely touched. What grace and beauty to behold. A moment of tranquility and peace which soon was broken by a voice:

"Common Crawley...are we fishin' or not!?"

In haste, having been woken up from my reverie, I turned around and stepped, full force, right into the middle of a fresh cow pie; my neatly greased Brogans now covered in cow poop. I ran down to the lake's edge and, holding onto the branch of an overhanging snag, I attempted to douse my boot into the water and wash off my shoe.

It was here that tranquility parted company with reality and suffered the pangs of defeat. I heard the crack of the branch overhead, and, as I fell into the lake and went for an early morning swim, all I could feel was "numbness", and then, almost immediately cold...EXTREME COLD! I was in a numb "daze" for what seemed like an eternity, clawing my way back up to the surface. This lake probably saw an ice thaw about two days prior to our arrival. I almost came up out of the abyss walking on top of the water, sputtering something about "GGGGODDDDDDAAAAMMMMMMMMN IT.............CCCCCOOLLLLLDDDDD!!!!!"

Jim, in his calm, stoic, and educated wisdom yells, "It's too early for a bath Crawley. Now you've scared all the fish away!" I could swear that there was a gleeful chuckle at the end of his comment.

It took the better part of an hour to thaw out by the camp fire. One pair of underwear down and two to go. I hadn't planned on my doing laundry with me still in the clothing!

We finally were able to get on the lake a couple hours after my disaster and, a warm change of clothing, and having a warm breakfast in our guts helped....at least it did me. Our canoe weighed all of 78 pounds, so it was fairly easy for two people to carry to the lake. The canoe had a V-shaped bottom and Jim and I, over the years, had perfected a method whereby we each could stand upright and cast from opposite ends of the craft. It took good balance and a steady center of gravity...no quick moves or bending over. It was an act of sheer bravado.

We took turns casting and retrieving line in a slow, deliberate retrieve called "mending" the line (in fly casting jargon). There are many types of "mending" line. Some prefer short, little jerks that make the fly "twitch" and dance at the other end of the line; while some prefer a slow, steady pull with periodic "breaks" to let the fly sit. We were using flies, this particular morning, that floated on the surface of the lake. I was using a "caddis" imitation and Jim was using a "dragon fly nyph" imitation. Each fly was said to be "deadly" at catching Kamaloops Rainbows.

In fly fishing, there are usually two types of lines (sinking and floating, and the same goes for flies: sinking or floating). Of course, there are many variants among these two types: slow sinking line, fast sinking, sinking tip, dry floating and "wet" floating where the line floats just below the surface. There are tapered, weight forward, and other variants and weights for lines and there are virtually tens of thousands of fly patterns; a new "find" or creation every day. Many anglers tie their own flies. It saves, they say, on cost. I doubt this because I've seen and priced some really expensive fly tying materials like peacock feathers and marabou dubbing, the elk hair variety. Anyway, it's definitely an art form and one that takes many years to perfect. I have a kit, but I rarely use it...as I said, I've been spoiled by one of the best. Usually, most fly fishermen enjoy using floating lines because they can actually see the "take" or strike when a fish takes the fly. The sheer joy of playing a fish with only you, the rod, and the line separating you is a real adrenaline "rush." A natural high that I never get tired of.

Anyway, back to my story. Late in the day, I was able to catch one very small fish (about 10 inches in length, barely enough for a meal). So much for the "early bite." But, I think Jim attributed our bad luck on English Lake to my early morning dip in the drink.

After dinner, we packed everything up except the tent and sleeping bags. We intended to leave in the morning for a lake where Jim was sure we would have better luck.

The next morning, for me, came way too early because all I remember hearing, again, was, "Crawley, get your lazy butt outta the sack...the fish are bitin'!"

So, off we went, bumping down the washboard, cow path pretending to be a road. My kidneys and butt ached, my teeth were chattering, and the grit and dust were chocking me with each gust of wind that blew dust our way; whether the windows were rolled up or not. Canadian dust has a way of finding you, even if you are ensconced in a zipped up tent with all the flaps down!

By the time we hit pavement, I was ready to get on my hands and knees and kiss the ground; ever so thankful for smooth asphalt. All Jim did was grunt.

It took us about 20 minutes to reach another lake Jim was interested in. Fortunately, this lake, Corbutt, was just off the main highway. What a relief! The lake wasn't much to look at, about 28 acres with lots of reed beds and vegetation growing out in finger-like shoals that were just under the surface, about 5-7 feet deep. There appeared to be "pockets" or holes in the vegetation where large fish might lie in wait for an unsuspecting fly or morsel to come withing striking distance.

Jim pitched our tent on what appeared to be an old boat ramp with a gravel surface. This, apparently, was the only "level" surface he could find because the edge of the lake was overgrown with brush and detritus. Did I mention that this spot had a downhill pitch of about 18 degrees? No? Well, it did and I was met with the choice of sleeping with the blood running down to my head, or having my heart work overtime pumping blood back up to my brain. I opted "blood downhill to head" so I wouldn't be comatose when Jim yelled in the morning….well, you know the drill by now.

After a restless sleep, mine, Jim and I went onto the lake. We had no breakfast because we were anxious to catch something…anything! There was a light breeze and some cloud cover moving in from the West. The clouds looked dark and ominous. I felt a chill in the air.

Jim made the first cast, a perfect figure eight glide of the line, poetry in motion, landing his dragon fly nymph about 70 feet away, right over the top of one of the big holes in the vegetation on the lake's shallow bottom.

At first, we looked at the big wake coming toward Jim's fly in disbelief. Was it a fish or a lake monster? It was a fish…a REALLY BIG FISH. The fish struck with such force that Jim's fly rod immediately bent down and the race was on!

Jim let out a "Whoop!" and I began pulling up the anchor. The fish, we assumed, was very large because we could see its flash below the surface some 40 feet away. The silver flash alone appeared to be at least 20 inches or more in length; this would not have included the fish's head or tail which have a darker hue. The bend in Jim's rod was about 180 degrees to the surface of the water, arching downward. This monster was actually dragging us, boat and all, toward the middle of the lake. Jim was very adept at "playing" large fish, and his "drag" (brake) on his reel was, at times, screaming as the fish took many runs away from us. Jim is an excellent fisherman and, in my opinion, he could "play" an elephant on a piece of thread if he had to. But, this fish was a real challenge. We didn't know exactly how big it was! This trout (we thought it was a Kamloops) took all of Jim's line and almost 90 feet of backing before tiring enough to where

Jim could begin reeling the fish toward the canoe. I sat ready with the fish net, a rather puny piece of equipment that had nylon webbed netting that measured, maybe, one foot by two feet, with a wooden handle of about 2 feet long.

When this fish finally surfaced near the canoe, all I could do is fit the head of the fish into the net, up to the fish's gill plates and a little beyond. Clearly, the net was too small. Eventually, after some rather colorful, expletive language from me, I was able to slip my hand around the crux in the tail of the fish, while forcing the other end of the fish into the net. Leaning a little over the boat's gunnel, I was then able to catapult the fish, net and all, into the canoe. Unfortunately, the force and weight transfer caused me to change seating arrangements with the fish. He was out of the water and in the boat...I wasn't. Back into the drink I went. This was getting to be a sorry situation I did not relish at all! When I came up for air, all Jim heard was, "GGGGOOODDDDDAAAMMMMMNIT.... CCCCCOOOLLLLLDDDDDD!!!"

At this juncture, it was all I could do to hold onto the back of the canoe, paddle my legs, and hang on while Jim paddled to shore. When my feet finally touched bottom, I was able to climb out of the lake, through some brush, and back onto the roadway nearby. Our camp was a short distance away, but it was no solace for me to have a slog back to camp. I probably looked like a wet rug with two feet, dripping my way back to our campsite. Under ware: two down...one to go.

After drying out, again, I was determined to get a fish and not go swimming for them. I had my last clean pair of shorts on and, I had no intention of getting them wet. We noticed a weather change, and we'd donned rain gear. When the barometer falls, the fish usually go deeper. So we switched to sinking lines with imitation fresh water shrimp and Chronomids (small aquatic organisms, usually red or black in color, that fish eat at depths). Fortunately, there were no cow pies this time so my boots stayed wet, but clean.

The rain turned to hail and a windstorm began. I recall Jim's silhouette, in his rain poncho, looking as if he was a giant sail at the end of the canoe, being blown down the lake. It reminded me of Horatio Hornblower, "my captain...my captain," skimming the water at about eight knots (about 10 m.p.h.); too fast to fish unless one was trolling for sea Marlin in the Bahamas. And this weather was not Bahamian by any means! The day ended with a return to shore: 1 very large trout, 2 wet fishermen (dry shorts though), no fire, hail/rain/wind, and an early bed time without dinner (just cookies and pop).

We did manage to catch a goodly amount of large Kamloops Rainbows the next day when the weather turned sunny and warm. Our fish ranged in size from about 2.5 pounds to over 10 pounds; eight fish in all for three days of fishing. We broke camp on the third day of our arrival and drove North to Merritt, B.C., the nearest town that had a cold storage. We intended to put our catch on ice and travel to some other lakes. When the cold storage proprietor saw our fish he exclaimed, "WOW! Where'd ya get these beauties?" Jim, in all of his best, stoic reverence, and abiding by every loyal fisherman's credo, looked this fellow straight in the eye, leaned closer to him and replied, "South." Whereupon, we departed.

Jim never discloses where he catches fish, except to me. He knows I will never break our trust and loyal bond. This pact has lasted a life time. Jim is the brother I never had, and Judy, the sister. They are both confidants, teachers, reciprocal, loyal friends who I love very much. They understand what it's like to suffer mental illness. They are "fire fighters."

We are all retired now, in our 70s, and I remember Jim phoning me the other day to suggest we celebrate our 75th birthdays by doing one last trek to the great North land. He wants to go back to Corbutt and Courtney Lakes (sister lakes) to "catch another whopper" like we did years ago. I didn't have the heart to tell him that there are no "old time sake," just the here and now, and if we get blessed with a miracle, as we did that week in June, 1961, it would surely be an epiphany and, a sure sign that God truly blesses us (In That, I do believe, I'm thankful for each day)...... "Whatdaya say, John?"

I replied, "I'm 72 Jim, you're 73 goin' on 74, remember? I was the one who was skipped from the start of my 2nd grade year to 3rd grade when we moved to California. How in the world are we going to do our 75th Birthdays at the same time? I think we should go before we get too old and feeble to cast a fly or carry or paddle a canoe."'Jim just chuckled and said, "I always knew you were the smart one Crawley, but ya can't swim worth a shit!... All ya do is step in it!"

We're planning a trip BEFORE our 75th Birthdays as long as we both can paddle, drag, not carry, the canoe to the lakes. I'm also planning on taking a whole suitcase full of under ware.

I'm also entertaining the idea of a complete "fly in" trip, Jim included, to Kamchatka, on the Eastern Russian peninsula where the fishing is fantastic, sightseeing stupendous, volcanoes active, Arctic surroundings lush (tundra, but in the summer there are trees and green as far as the eye can see), and no "civilization" for 1,000s of miles, save a few Native people. I'm going to have to sell a lot of books to make this trip a reality.

THE RATIONAL THOUGHT

Now, some of you, who have read thus far are probably thinking, 'Where is this all going to?' Right? I don't blame you. I'd be thinking the same thing about right now. Well. here's the deal. We, and I mean <u>WE</u> need to get on board with our Congressional Representatives and tell them we're sick and tired of being used as "guinea pigs" for the National trough of continuous payment and sacrifice. We need to stand up and say, "Enough is enough!" "We're tired of all this bullshit, hyperbole, and innuendo. We are tired of paying, every year; we're tired of purchasing "nothing" just to say we are "purchasing" something that even comes close to solving the issue of mental illness/ substance abuse/ and care. In this country, We are tired! Period.

The solution? Is found, "partially", in PARITY of treatment plans that are funded, in perpetuity, and offered to everyone who is willing to "clean up their act." If you were given a chance to start over again, no strings, no encumbrances, would you take it? I think most rational people would; even those who are considered to be "mentally ill," would jump at the chance to "get well" or, at least, get to a place of "balance" in the universe. We do not like pain, in any form (physical, mental, transcendental, existential, spiritual, or by some sophomoric upstart). We are creatures of "habit." We don't like to be put into uncomfortable circumstances. We usually avoid uncomfortable events or, we find a way to avoid unpleasant feelings. Our very existence is predicated upon a world of "pleasure" v.s. "pain." Most of us will try to avoid "pain." Many will actually go out of their way to avoid being thrust into painful experiences. I understand this...I know this; but what I do not know is why some of us habitually and continuously, go forth to harm ourselves.

We do this in many ways: Through drug and alcohol abuse, through continually down-putting our fellow workers or friends, over-criticizing others we come in contact with, withdrawing love and affection from those we know we should love and care for, intentionally disabuse what we thought to be wrong about ourselves or someone else; and then go out of our way to make false accusations about someone we feel has wronged us in some manner. We only wind up hurting ourselves in the end. A wise man once told me: "When you cast hatred onto another, you are doing the same to yourself." This is true, but we refuse to acknowledge it at the time we do it. We are so upset that we forget how much anger can do to us, spiritually, physically, and emotionally.

For a short period of time, following my retirement, I taught "Anger Management" classes for the District Court liaison service. During the process of learning the topic and researching information, I learned how much destruction anger will create in us. Beyond the object/person one wants to vent upon by either breaking it or breaking a relationship, we often heap a lot of self-loathing onto ourselves. I also learned that we don't hear so well when we are angry. In fact, auditory senses actually have a tendency to "shut down;" hence the term "he had selective hearing when he got mad." Our blood pressure rises, and people have had strokes as a result of letting their anger, literally, get the best of them. Our digestive system also reacts by pumping a lot of hydrochloric acid into our stomach. Too much of this stuff, too often= peptic ulcers. Our sight becomes extremely focused and we often hear that people who are angry seem to have "tunnel vision." That's because they do tend to zero in on the object of their disdain. There are a lot of negative hormones and limbic system detractors that really mess with our ability to reason, act with restraint, or think in a logical manner. Anger, if gone unchecked or corrected, for lengthy periods of time will kill you, literally. Sometimes, uncontrolled anger leads into mental illness and hospitalization. Another thing we don't do, when angered, is breathe. In fact we usually take in very shallow breaths, resulting in a lack of oxygen to the brain, causing even more agitation and irrational thinking. Part of the curriculum of the Anger Management class was teaching people how to breathe; to relieve stress. The 5-second rule applies here: breathe in for 5 seconds, hold for 5 seconds, release out and repeat. People who properly do this technique often mention that they feel "really relaxed" afterward. It does work. It has scientifically been shown to reduce stress and anxiety in most folks (Psychology Today, NIMH studies).

So, to bring all of this into perspective, I'll quote an article, written on December 24, 2016, that appeared in The Journal Gazette out of Indiana, one of our "middle ground" States that reflects on what we're up against as a Nation:

'The Indiana General Assembly and Governor Eric Holcomb's administration begin work next month. Investments will be prioritized and probably limited based upon predicted tax revenue. One investment that should make the list is the medical care of veterans. Traumatic brain injury/ post traumatic stress injury (PTSD, parenthesis mine) is the most significant issue facing veterans today; thousands of Hoosiers have this. The current VA care is not working; how can we change this?

Nothing supersedes evidence/ good data/ and science. We need $2 million in funding for a world-class hyperbaric oxygen therapy treatment program, conducted in existing Indiana clinics. The Indiana Veteran Recovery Plan, a clinical trial, treats and gathers scientific data so the treatment can become a standard of care for everyone. The Military/ Veterans Coalition of Indiana is trying to get Indiana to initiate this statewide clinical trial.

Ironically, The Indiana "poster child" for hyperbaric oxygen therapy treatment is Josh Speidel, a non-vet. Josh was an outstanding basketball player at Columbus North High School a few years ago, but he was in a terrible car wreck and sustained an extensive traumatic brain injury.

Several doctors told his parents to plan on sending Josh to a long-term care facility for the rest of his life, as his broken brain was repaired as well as it was going to get. Josh might improve a little bit, but it could take up to five years.

His mother investigated alternative medical treatments. She discovered Carmel's Wellness Origin. There, Josh had more than 50 one-hour hyperbaric oxygen therapy treatments and dramatically improved. Josh also received craniosacral massage, occupational therapy, physical therapy, and cognitive rehabilitation training.

Josh improved so much that he started the University of Vermont this fall and participated with the basketball team in training and attends varsity games. Josh is vastly improved and doing fine in college, and will not be going to a facility for the mentally diminished.

Seventeen years ago. Dr. Paul G. Harch discovered that hyperbaric oxygen therapy treatment, conducted at 1.5 atmospheres of pressure, could repair a chronic traumatic brain injury. Dr. Harch, director of the Hyperbaric Medicine Fellowship at Louisiana State University's School of Medicine, has used the therapy, (successfully -parenthesis mine) on more than 700 patients and taught the technique to hundreds of doctors.

In 2008, Dr. Harch applied his technique to five combat veterans with traumatic brain injury and post-traumatic stress disorder from concussive blasts. So far, all have significant recovery (Actually, parenthesis mine, according to subsequent documentation via "The Oxygen Revolution" 3rd edition, 2016, Harch has an average 83% success rate where no symptoms and, sustained "cures" are replicated in over 3,000 patients).

Other studies suggest there is sufficient evidence to support the use of hyperbaric oxygen therapy treatment in mild traumatic brain injury// persistent post-concussive syndrome. Reported positive outcomes and the durability of those outcomes have been demonstrated at six months post-treatment (actually, parenthesis mine, the sustained results have been documented well beyond five years without any relapses or occurrence of mall-adaptive behavior patterns, "Oxygen Revolution", Ibid.).

Even more convincing, the battle-tested Israeli military uses hyperbaric oxygen therapy as the primary means of treating their most precious asset—their wounded soldiers. We don't.

Parts of Josh Speidel's brain were so damaged they didn't survive. However, other parts are now repaired and healing continues. Josh does still have some limitations that include short-term memory issues and a tremor on his right side. Josh may never get back to 100 percent in all areas, but there is hope. His broken brain can and will continue to heal and grow better thanks to hyperbaric oxygen therapy treatment.

Josh's treatments were not covered by insurance; they were paid for by hundreds of worldwide donations. There are thousands of other people just like Josh out there, suffering silently with no donations to cover their expenses. They are our veterans (and others), and they deserve our care.

An Indiana veteran's recovery bill could help hundreds of veterans, and eventually the evidence cold help make this life-saving treatment approved by the Food and Drug Administration and a standard of care for everyone in Indiana (read: the U.S.A.) and across the Nation. Insurance then would cover this treatment, and perhaps the Federal V.A. would use it as well (they are now, but on a very limited scale though)....'

Again, here is compelling evidence that Big Insurance, Big Pharma, and Big Medicine have yet to "get on board" to help this "train of hope" move forward. They stand to lose billions of dollars if this one application is implemented (no more pills and lengthy treatment sessions). They stand to lose even more if it is not.

So, What Works?

Today, 4/17/2017, I learned of a program in Connecticut (APT Foundation. Org), founded in 1970, that is now sponsored by Athena Insurance Group wherein "long-term continuum of care" treatment is being offered to drug-addled folks, as well as those suffering from mental illnesses. There are also some psychiatric components to this program. The cost of the average patient in this program is $38,000.00; well beyond what most middle-income families can afford. They are having a 72-79 % success rate (free from drug use) per year. This is phenomenal when one considers that "science" and "success" are not, usually, mutually congruent terms where drug addiction and successful treatment are paired. There are many, many relapses in the drug world. People often enter rehab and drop out or they succumb to further addiction issues soon after leaving the rehab center.

The reason for the Connecticut program's success is based on the fact that the "program" is intensive during the first few weeks. Once a patient has began to use the program's resources toward his/her wellness and "clean" living, the program monitoring and close supervision begins to drop off, but NOT completely (as is the case with most treatment programs now in existence throughout the U.S.A.). Herein lies the "success" of said program….the "continuum of care" element. Besides providing each patient with a caseworker and "coach" to advise and tailor the program to each patient's specific needs, there are support group elements and peers to aid in the evaluation process, and to help the patient learn the tools that are necessary to cope and overcome their drug addiction and manage their mental health needs. In my book, the people who had vision beyond the "bottom line" here are "fire fighters."

There are many other programs throughout this Country in which successful re-rehabilitation and successful pathways to a drug-free and managed mental health care are extant. For example, there is a program in Arizona (Sierra Tucson, 844-215-1400, Sierra Tucson.com), sponsored by the Combat Warriors organization, wherein veterans (and civilians) are placed into an isolated environment, in the desert, and are given constant attention to their needs for health care, medications, counseling, psychiatric treatment (as needed), continual support by family and friends who also may attend the program with their loved one, exercise, diet management, and limited medications so that a "natural" balance, eventually, occurs. They have been in existence since 1983. There is horseback riding, hiking in the desert wilderness, camping, cookouts, journal entries, and group therapy sessions to acknowledge that "we are not alone" in our suffering and willingness to gain wellness. Their philosophy of treatment is grounded on the "holistic" approach to body wellness and connectivity to self and one's environment. One-on-one therapy is also available. All the veteran (patient) need do is apply. There is a "token" fee for these services and, if the veteran cannot afford them, they will be covered by the Organization, no strings attached! Insurance coverage is also available.

Another "horse identified" program exists near Vancouver, Washington State where equine care and "bonding with one's assigned horse" takes place. This program, "Windhaven Therapeutic Riding, www.windhaventherapeuticriding.org/, is run by former military people who have hired ex-veterans, nurses, and therapists who have expertise in such service-connected maladies as PTSD, TBI, and other mental illnesses associated with combat and traumatic events in the veteran's life. Horses actually "pick" their partner. It seems that horses seem to "know" who they will be able to work with. The interactions between horse and veteran are amazing. The feedback one gets out of this experience is awesome. Signs of PTSD (sleeplessness, night sweats, nightmares, over consumption of drugs and alcohol, anger, anxiety, depression, etc.) seem to melt away through these contacts with the equine family. The program, above, in Arizona, also sees similar results when vets are paired with horses. We see "in kind" results when therapy dogs are brought to retirement homes to interact with the elderly shut-ins; and, the cancer ward "pet therapy" advocates tell us of how a "healing presence" occurs when people interact with animals. One common aspect of all of these programs is the fact that the animals take a patient-participant out of his/her element and provides an "other than me and my problems" atmosphere. The interaction with the animals gives the patient/participant a sense of purpose and worth; the fact that an animal "cares" enough to "interact with me," gives the person a sense of personal value and self-esteem (often lost in the toils of war, disease, and aging). The V.A. Hospital in Vancouver, Washington makes referrals to Windhaven; so, not all V.A. providers are messed up (source: Veterans Health Administration Newsletter, 5-23-17 retrieval).

These are examples of what some folks are doing, as "fire fighters," because they are looking beyond the status quo. They are visionaries and risk takers, but they are betting their efforts on known science and, the proof that longevity in treatment, with a "safety net" is the most productive and "positive results" way to go. The factual successes of these programs are a matter of record.

We need a conscientious effort by the public to advocate for these programs…,.many of them. The Federal government is remiss in not funding such programs because they are caught up in the "profit-taking" morass of Big Medicine, Big Pharma, and Big Insurance, who don't really have these patients' best interests at heart. If they did, they would fully fund or advocate for such funding as I've suggested. In my opinion, they are extremely short sighted and wrong-headed in not funding long-term care programs and the "safety net" continuum (s) that need to be in place so that this Nation will be healthy and productive beyond what currently exists. A healthy Nation is a prosperous and productive Nation; ready to match or beat any competitor, world-wide.

I also believe that the Federal Government stands to lose a lot of tax revenue, they are now receiving, if said "continuum of care" programs were put into place. I've already addressed the individual tax, fee, surcharge, etc, savings each individual would save if "continuum of care" was adopted as the "gold standard" of care for this Nation. Patrick Kennedy's, "A Common Struggle," has also underscored the various political and corporate entities who object to such implementations. His ideas parallel mine, but his treatment of the Governmental "stonewalling," outright rejections without adequate, substantive reasons; and, counter manipulations of facts supporting "continuum of care" are frustrating and baffling at the same time. It's really amazing how our own Government, when faced with the facts, can become such "ostrich imbeciles" who won't see the light or acknowledge that there is a better way. Our current dilemma over "climate change" denials (as a political ploy; without any scientific basis to back up the denials) is another example of Congressional "bottom line" myopia. Maybe we need to ask them how long they think their grandchildren can tread water. It's really sad that this country, which I dearly love, can't find some risk takers and visionary thinkers to take us to the right path. Many of them seem too busy raising funds for their own party's next elections. Many of them, in my opinion, have lost the meaning of "representative government." They seem to be more focused on their own, self-serving political ambitions than "…...for the good of the people." We can change this if we study where the money for campaigns comes from and, vote those out who are "owned" by the "company store." This is not an impossible task. You will be a "fire fighter" if you do this. We need people who can not only think, walk, and talk a good game, but people who are committed to the welfare of ALL citizens, not just the select few. We have such people waiting in the wings…...all they need is your vote to give them flight.

I've already mentioned the wondrous use of HBOT, CRISPR, genetic mapping, and CTE prevention techniques and helmet design (now there's a project worth millions for some engineering graduate student: design a helmet that reduces the chance of concussion/CTE by more than 70%). One of the other, innovative, approaches to these issues is in the form of community volunteer groups who have offered to help the poor, the dispossessed, the mentally ill, and the substance abusers in their community by helping staff the shelters, the Missions, their church kitchens, remodeling old warehouses into small apartment-like dwellings for the homeless, providing medical/dental care via community clinics that are staffed a couple days a week by local dentists and doctors so that the overall health standard in the community is good. No one likes to be around sick (cold, flu, etc.) people any more than I; so, these voluntary medical/dental stations help with preventative medical/dental care. It pays dividends in the long run because there is less illness and, it puts people back on their feet with a job, a roof over their heads, and what's most important: a sense of self-worth. People will usually work their tails off if someone gives them hope. Those too ill to be cared for in the local community could go into health care facilities (hospital-like clinics) for short stays until they are well enough to return to the streets. By then, maybe, they'll have a lead on a job or some legal form of earning income to pay for their basic necessities. We have a woman in our community (Marysville/Arlington) who goes around giving homeless folks clothing to help with their, often, limited or worn out wardrobes. She also gives them references to the local shelters, soup kitchens, and where they can sleep, safely, for a couple nights. She is a "fire fighter."

We have a team of local police officers who are relied upon by the local school district and who are appointed as school resource officers. These folks took time to go to local merchants and get donations so they could bring a couple "experts" to the schools to talk to the students about bullying, harassment, and improper texting. These people are all "fire fighters" because they are doing something pro-active and preventative. We had a couple of devastating school shootings within the past 3 years and it really affected most of the schools. Kids were afraid to go to school. Things have changed thanks to the intervention of these fine officers who volunteered most of their time beyond their regular call to duty.

We have a mayor who will not allow the "immigration" fiasco, that was recently signed in the White House, to interfere with children in our community, many of whom were born in this country, from continuing their education. Police have been instructed not to harass or pick up their parents if no warrants exist. He is a "fire fighter" because he knows the stress put upon immigrant families when one or more of them is undocumented. He has been working with local lawyers to find pathways to legalization for these folks. They are a part of this community and they can be and, in many cases, are "fire fighters." We should not shun people who, for lack of proper paperwork or the knowledge of how to obtain same, are doing their very best to work, pay taxes, abide by laws, and provide for the cultural diversity of our community. After all, isn't that what America is all about?

Have we grown so callous as to reject the very people who help us clean our homes, do housekeeping at major hotels and motels, pick our crops, roof our houses, build our houses, care for our lawns and gardens, and who are restaurateurs, doctors, lawyers, dentists, chiropractors, teachers, plumbers, welders, water treatment plant supervisors, garbage truck drivers, railway employees, pastors and priests? I think not. There are ways to "legalize" these folks if the Government really wants to help. In my book, most of these folks are already "fire fighters" because most of them contribute, in some fashion, back into their community.

If we really want America to be great, we don't bite the hands that feed us, cleans us, or cares for our children. We embrace them and make them welcome citizens! If the current Administration in Washington D.C. (2017) continues to go down the path of xenophobia, then our country will suffer the consequences, and it won't be pretty folks. It will surely add to the "fire" of which I speak. We will have more sick people, more mentally ill folks, more substance-addled people, and broken families who will do nothing but drain our resources even more that they do now. Someone once said, "... power corrupts….but, absolute power corrupts absolutely." So, least we be less mindful, perhaps it is time that the three branches of Government take heed and, adjust the disastrous course they currently find themselves upon.

I know this chapter is about "What works," but I think what works also includes diagnosed people being advocates for themselves. As an example of this, I'll use an incident that was disclosed at our last DBSA meeting (April, 2017). One of our participants, "Kelly"(not her real name) mentioned that she'd gone to her local drug store to pick up her prescription for Lithium Carbonate, a commonly prescribed drug for the treatment of Bi-polar 2. While at the store and waiting for her prescription to be filled by browsing the aisles, one of the clerks announced her full name and "….prescription for Lithium Carbonate is ready for pick up." Normally, the full name of a patient is not mentioned nor is the name of the prescription when announcing such information. In fact, it is a violation of the HIPA (Health Information Privacy Act) Federal Law to do so. "Kelly" went to get her prescription and embarrassingly mentioned to the clerk that she felt wronged by having her private information broadcast throughout the store over the PA system. The clerk, apparently, reacted gruffly and stated something to the effect, "What do you want me to do...come and get you?"

"Kelly" went home and told her father about this incident. Her father stated, "We're going back to that store and talk to the manager about this." "Kelly," at first, didn't want to go and "cause problems," she likes the store and staff and she was trying to rationalize the incident as something to pass over, hoping it won't happen again. Her father insisted that the store management needed a reminder. So, they went and talked to the store manager. "Kelly" received a sincere apology and, a statement that such an incident would never happen again. By being an advocate for herself, I feel she helped quell some of the "stigma" that often gets associated with the mentally ill. In this sense, it is something that "works" for the sufferer and builds self-confidence and self-esteem.

Note: I Hope that you all can see where I'm going with this book. I'm not after the people who provide us with medical care, pharmaceutical needs, or insurance coverage if they are sincerely applying their care to all who are qualified and in need. I'm not about denigrating the people who provide the services and wonderful care of our sick and dispossessed folks. What I'm getting at are the poor methods we are using to help these sufferers and, often leaving them stranded to cope, without resources or a pathway, to success; just because they cannot afford the freight of what's needed. We can and should do better where caring for the sick and infirm are concerned. We have the greatest medical and provider services in the world. We should not be squandering them over the "bottom line" arguments we hear from the providers. Their "vision," in my opinion, is myopic and without merit. We can and need to do better when providing for our citizens in this country. Most countries in the world do better at caring for their populace; and they prosper because of it. Who cares if someone can't afford a bypass operation; it should be done the same for the person who cannot afford it as that person who can. We should value life on an "equality" basis (as is proposed in our Constitution). The dollar sign should not be the guide post of whether we treat someone or not. The dividend payback on this stuff is enormous. By investing in our people, we are giving them the confidence and courage to move forward and become even better citizens. Trust me...this works...I've seen it work on both a large and small scale during my

*career. People, who have been helped, thrive, they prosper, and they give back.
to the programs (society) that helped them. I am convinced of the preceding
statement because I've seen it in operation with my own eyes.*

In fact, as an example, we had *a* work/resource development program *at*
one of the offices *I'd* worked at in Everett and Marysville, Washington. The
program was designed to use probationers to perform community service
hours in lieu of jail time. These individuals were on community supervision
for various crimes, but they were eager to perform and gain recognition
from their supervising parole/probation officers. We were more than happy
to provide these work crews with the basics (water, sack lunches, and
encouragement to get the job done). We had a van and the "volunteers"
had to show up at our offices by 8:00 A.M., just like a regular job, and be
dressed for work. We supplied all the tools, gloves, etc. If a "volunteer"
was late, he or she would "miss the bus" and be left behind. Two misses
and you were off the crew, no excuses (except for documented illness or
doctor/dentist appointments and per-arranged meeting schedules). We
took these "volunteers" to the woods so they would gain true appreciation
of Mother Nature and all that she has to offer. Part of one project I recall
was the crew's work at a nature preserve that was managed by the city.
They were tasked with clearing brush and making a stream bed more
navigable for salmon runs. The city had partnered up with the Washington
Department of Fish and Wildlife for oversight on this project. The crew
did such a good job that they were honored by the mayor at a local
city hall public meeting. Another project we undertook was the painting
of local business buildings that had been "tagged" by 'wanna be' gang
members. The merchants supplied the paint and rollers/brushes and we
supplied the labor. It was a "win/win" situation. The buildings exteriors
were enhanced and the probationers got credit for community service
hours. I also recall that a couple fellows were later hired by some merchants
because the merchants liked the men's enthusiasm and willingness to do
a good job. Most of the folks we had on these work crews had issues with
drug abuse and/or mental health. They all did well because we gave them
the encouragement and recognition for a job well done. It's amazing how
far a little acknowledgment and support will go to help someone overcome
some character deficits.

BACK TO THE FUTURE?

I recall one of the "Back to the Future" movies predicting that the Chicago Cubs would win the World Series in 2016. Well, guess what? They did, and in the same year as predicted. Who would have thought? It had to be a miracle right? Nope, not so much a miracle as a coincidence. It so happened that the Cubs had been building a powerhouse team since 2006. They were "primed" and ready for a big win. The fact they made it in 2016 was coincidental to the prediction in the movie. Stuff like this happens every day; it's just that we don't see it or recognize it because we're either not interested or not aware of the facts that contribute to the circumstance.

In this sense, I'm predicting that Congress will, eventually, see the light and pass fully funded parity laws (where Medicaid and Medicare are inclusive) for our mental illness and substance abuse treatment folks. It just makes common sense. We can't go much further with lack of care for most of the afflicted in this country because our jails, prisons, streets, social worker caseloads, schools, colleges, and hospitals won't be able to handle it. We have burgeoning institutions who are crying out for help. Our Veterans Administration Hospitals have "wait lists" a mile long, our "farming out" soldiers to civilian care is mammoth, and we haven't even scratched the surface of our sick street people. Something has to give...and soon!

I'm sure Congress will allow for "subsidy" funding to Large Medical Consortiums, Big Pharmaceutical Corporations, and International Insurance giants. They could be "partners" in all of this "IF" they decided to put the "profit motive" in the back seat for awhile. First, they need to focus on the needs and service delivery. The profits will come later. There will be enough to go around for everyone...and then some. As a result, we will have the most effective, efficient, and prosperous medical/ preventive/ and health care system in the world...bar none!

Once the word gets out and a service delivery system is in place, we won't need to put more money down the "rat hole" of negligence, discouragement, disappointment, and futility as is the case now in many areas of our country. Care, only for those who can afford it, has never worked in the history of the world. And when it did work, it didn't last very long (Greece, Rome, England, France, Russia, China, Japan, Australia, and South America are historical examples of how the rich rode roughshod over the poor and paid, dearly, in later years, for it).

Medicine and psychiatric science are making great strides in the discovery of new pathways to wellness and continued care. To not fully fund them at this point would be anathema and, a great dis-service to humankind. Science and technology, if applied in the right formats, can and will help us all. Applied in the wrong arenas (i.e. for political control and usury) and it will be the undoing of mankind. We need great leadership, foresight and vision for the pro-social and positive results to happen. In order to do this, we must elect people who are capable of seeing into the future and not those who just rely on the next donation from some conglomerate, corporate shill. By the same token, we must "un-elect" those who have lost sight of "...we the people", and are no longer representing the "majority of the constituency."

THE BUCKET LIST

I have a bucket list. I've had it for about two years now. I will share some of what is on my "bucket list" with you and the status of same:

1. Get up, get out, move, and exercise. (even with Arthritis in my hips)….. …….doing it daily
2. Play my guitar…………………………………………….. " " "

3. Journal and/or write in my book…………………………… " " "

4. Drive my car (I didn't drive for 6 years after my diagnosis)………….. doing it daily

5. Eat properly balanced meals (no sugar, little carbohydrates), fruit, meat, fish, salads " " "

6. No alcohol (I'm alcoholic so drinking is out of the question)……… doing it daily

7. Take up fly fishing again (was a favorite of mine over the years)…..done last Summer and this

8. Share time with friends and family (I enjoyed time with folks, but fell away)…..doing daily

9. Take a Summer road trip besides regular trips to our beach house in Oregon…….planned

10. Fly in Jim's Bi-plane again (went two Summers ago, GREAT!)........ planned

11. Take the canoe up into the estuary and river between Seaside and Gearhart, Oregon.planned

12. Go on a fishing trip, in British Columbia, with my friend Jim....... planning

13. Go on a fly fishing excursion on the Kamchatka Peninsula in Russia (dep. on book sales)

14. Play my violin again.. in the "trying" stages

15. Share more experience and gain more insights via my time w/ DBSA... ....3x month

16. Read at least one book a week... trying

17. Continue to do research and note taking at the local library........... daily

18. Learn how to prepare more meals for myself (I got some early lessons from wife)...in works

19. Make better use of my time and resources.............................. daily routines

20. Take my medications, use medical info to my advantage, see doctor, etc......as needed

So, as you can see, I'm keeping fairly busy. As compared to the 6 years (2008-2014) I was a "vegetable" (assumed the per-natal position, in bed, with the electric blanket turned up to "5") who thought it was an effort to pee, bathe, shit or eat, I've come a long way. Depression can do so much damage, psychologically, that a person doesn't even want to live. I know, I was at a very low point at one time that I'll never revisit again. I've made a pact with myself; even if I have a grave illness, to never go back...no matter what.

I saw a special on television the other night. It was about Scott Hamilton, the all-time Olympic figure skating champion. He has had to live with one tragic situation after another. First, he was born with a human growth deficiency (hence, his smallness of stature). Second, he's been diagnosed three times with inoperable brain tumors! He has a great sense of humor, is always optimistic, and he's sponsoring a clinic for budding hockey players in his home state. He visits kids and people in the local cancer wards, giving them encouragement and hope. He has a beautiful wife and kids who love him very much, and he's just a kind, generous, human being who is gracious under fire. In my book, Scott Hamilton is a "fire fighter" because he's been knocked down a number of times, only to get back up, dust himself off, and get back in the fight. When asked, "why or how is it that you're never depressed or down about life?" Scott's reply was, "Why not...what else is there? I've come this far in 47 years and, if I'm granted another 47, I'll be 94 and still a happy man." Now...THAT'S attitude!!

We have many "fire fighters" in this world. They are the "angels" among us. We often don't see them, but they are there, helping us and guiding us if we just lift our eyes to look and see. We can be them, we can try and we can succeed. I know this to be true because it took me a long way around to become one myself....I'm just stubborn, I guess, but I know now what it takes and I have it, and I will never let it go.

A Political Animal I'm Not

I have tried in earnest to keep "politics" out of this novel But, it seems, the current Administration is "hell bent" on fucking things up. First we have the Obama Care Snafu where the Republican majority has promised to rid us of the foibles and high costs of the current program. Never mind that this program saves people money and actually puts profits into those companies who stay with the program. Never mind that it's the best health care system we've ever had in this country. Sure, it has some "glitches."

Social Security had a lot of faults before it was finally adjusted. Any new Government program always has faulty implementation and "roll out" issues. It's just too big and cumbersome not to have issues. But to 'can it' and destroy most of the helpful aspects, in my opinion, is asinine and totally irresponsible of our Congressional leaders. They are pandering to the Big Insurance Companies, Big Pharmaceuticals, and Big Medical Consortiums who lobby to have their way with Congress and the health care of these United States of America. Congress, in the main, and in my opinion, is "owned" by the "company store," lock, stock, and barrel. If you doubt this, Google where the money is coming from. It's pretty obvious who's paying the freight for Congress to pass laws and amendments that favor the rich and the business elite. This "IS NOT EQUAL REPRESENTATION" under the Constitution of our United States of America. This is pandering to the few, the richest, and the most "influential" (by choice of the Congressional representatives), and NOT FOR THE PEOPLE IN GENERAL.

As an example, recently, (April, 2017), of "pandering" and "looking the other way" (by Congress) I will use the example of our President using his private Mar Largo Estate and "members and guests only" golf course, in

Florida, on a Government website to promote his personal business interests. This is not only illegal; it's a violation of the Emoluments clauses provision of the United States Constitution. No acting office holder, including the President, can use his/her office to promote private business interests. To do so is a potential cause for impeachment. And what are our Congressional representatives doing about it? Nothing! They are touting their "party line." 100 days ago (as of April, 24, 2017), many of them were saying they did not support the President elect (he did not win the popular vote, no matter what he has claimed). So, the old adage is true, "politics makes strange bedfellows." Unfortunately, in this case, it may very well be the undoing of this country's Democratic Model and system of "balanced" governance.

If we want equity in health care in this country, then we're going to need some major players come to the plate and hit some "home runs" for all of us. Giving "play" to the select few is not going to get it. We need "major play" involvement, dedication, and ownership. If we do not step up to the plate, our health care, delivery systems, and profits (eventually) will surely suffer; and, we will become a second-class nation in the eyes of the rest of the world. As I've said, most civilized countries have been working on providing their citizenry with complete, comprehensive health coverage for decades. Most have it….we don't. What's wrong with this picture? Are our priorities fucked up? (I think so). Are our focus and strengths being squandered? (I think so). Can and should we do better? (most definitely!).

If the Congressional members had to pay for their own health care and did not have the "golden parachute" of lifetime care once they leave office, I think we'd all see a major change in this aspect of National care. They really don't give a shit because, they have it all. So, how do we make them care? Vote them out of office is one way. Another is to get on "grass roots" campaign committees to badger the providers with petitions, speeches, town meetings, and community forums that offer a "block watch" of your representatives intentions and actions that really serve YOU, and not some backroom cronies who fund the Congressman's/Congresswoman's pockets. As I said, and I'll say it again: "Follow the money." It will lead you to the culprit and those who do not have our best interests at heart. On the other hand, sometimes it does lead to altruistic good. We need to be aware, informed, questioning, and actively involved in the political arena; otherwise, the "assholes" will take over. In my 73 years on this planet, I know the previous statement to be true. If we (I) don't get involved at any level, then, I (we) deserve what I (we) get.

As it stands now, I do not agree with the current Administration's viewpoints, actions, and ill-thought motives for changing our Nation's health provider-ship. We do not stand to benefit from what is currently being proposed. The additional suffering, lack of care for the homeless, substance abusers, PTSD-addled veterans, victims of sexual abuse, and general lack of continuum of care, for most of us, will be readily evident if the current changes in the health system are implemented. Too many people "fall through the cracks" in what is now being proposed.

What we need is a comprehensive, "safety net" system that covers everyone, regardless of their ability to pay or not. Funding for payments can be derived from the populace in some fashion (via taxes, fees, or sur-charges to the general public, equal-share taxes for big business and off-shore accounts, or {for example, bottle/can returns at, @15 cents apiece, with the money going directly into the "care industry" fund, without "administrative siphoning."}) Something as simple as this would generate millions of dollars so that the taxpayer would not be burdened with the lion's share of the cost. There are many innovative, creative, and supportive ways in which we can and should do this. Why we haven't started yet is beyond me...other than the fact that the "Big Providers" want their "profit margins." They are myopic and shortsighted. They do not see the vision I see or, anyone who is a "fire fighter" sees. We could have the best health care service delivery system in the world if certain corporations would let go of the purse strings. They stand to prosper greatly from this. All they need do is take the risk. The odds of losing are minimal; the odds of winning are phenomenal. Obamacare was visionary, but flawed. It was a start in the right direction. All we need do is "tweek" it and make it a viable system for all. If Congress "throws out the baby with the bathwater" on this, we would not be remiss in voting every one of those out of office who were party to the demise of the Affordable Care Act. We need comprehensive, "parity" health care in this Country. We need people in Congress who really care for our best interests and, who act accordingly to fully fund those programs that benefit the majority. Now I've said it...and it's my truth!

THE "HAVES" AND THE HAVE "NOTS"

When I was growing up, I was led to believe if one worked hard and studied, one could succeed. I believed this axiom and acted upon it. For the main portions of my life, it worked. I began working, at age 12, picking strawberries to earn money for my school clothes. My parents could afford the clothing, but I was always independent, wanting to "pay my own way" in life. I went to school and earned two degrees, one in Psychology and the other in Sociology. I became a Parole/Probation Officer, Supervisor, and Trainer for the Washington State Criminal Justice Training Commission. After a successful career spanning 37.6 years, I retired. Now, most of my time is spent with friends and family, writing, researching, interviewing folks for the book, my music and taking road trips in the Corvette.

When my wife retired, in 2010, she bought herself a brand new Hyundai Santa Fe SUV. When I retired, I purchased nothing. I got sick. After spending over 6 years in treatment and recovery for a number of deficits (previously mentioned), I learned how to better manage my life. Not having driven a car for over 6 years, I decide to purchase a vehicle I always wanted, a Corvette. So, I did. Some have said it was a "mid-life" crisis that drove me to buy this car. I say, at age 67, one is well beyond "a mid-life crisis" and more into quality of life and symbols of success,. The Corvette is much more to me than a status symbol. It represents "survival", "dedication", "resolve", "re-birth", and "perseverance."

I was listening to a radio program today (April 26, 2017) on NPR (National Broadcasting Radio) wherein the narrator and his guest were discussing "plutocratic philanthropy" and the "ownership, by the extremely rich," of certain aspects of our Democracy. Names such as Bill and Melinda Gates, Steve Balmer (Gate's former business partner at Microsoft), Warren Buffet (Berkshire-Hathaway Investments), and Michael Bloomberg (former 3 term Mayor of New York city and CEO of one of the largest information gathering/synthesizing/coordinating systems in the world) were brought up as examples of those who's philanthropy affects and effects our Governmental actions or inaction. I'm not one to denigrate Bill and Melinda Gates for the work they have done, via their world-wide Foundation in helping to bring vaccines and other medical services to third-world countries that would not have the same care if they depended on their own governments. Nor would I fault Steve Balmer's very recent offer to provide millions of dollars into an effort to provide housing for homeless families in the Northwest.

However, there are concerns over how much power and control we are delegating to others for efforts our own Government has failed at or, taken (as in the current Administration, 2017) funding away from. We do not need to create an "oligarchical" form of Government and, our legislators need to set limits on what and how philanthropists can donate. Besides the media attention and tax breaks, these individuals enjoy further Government "perks" in the form of additional tax breaks (eventually) while the rest of us get the bill.

One of the examples I'll use here is the purchase of railroad companies by Warren Buffet a few years ago. Mr. Buffet's mantra, a few years ago, was, "buy what people are going to use." It's good investment advice, nothing illegal about that. But, when the trains are loaded with mid-west coal to ship to China and oil for the Asian market, I feel a "moral exception" has been breached.

On the other side of this is Michael Bloomberg's efforts at closing down the coal industry as one of the world's largest producers of "green house" gasses and CO2. He has also had successful campaigns against big tobacco and helping people quit smoking. He has given millions to the Sierra Club to promote the Natural Environment in this country. In my opinion, his efforts are promoting the health benefits to our human brothers and sisters, and it is worthy of "fire fighter" status. However, one questions the "moral" application of someone using his/her wealth to "shut down" a viable business and put thousands of people out of work. Bloomberg says that he's willing to help fund technological training for these folks if a program, he feels worthy, is presented to him (CNN interview, April, 2017)

We know, for example, that climate change is a real thing (beyond what the "nay sayers" and pundits for the Right-wing have said). There is incontrovertible proof. Winds, mostly, travel from the East (think Asia) to the West, across the Pacific Ocean. Aside from Pacific weather, storms, etc. there are CO_2 deposits that are reining havoc on our oceans. Any shellfish (think clams, crabs, lobster, prawns, scallops, etc.) is affected by the CO_2 because it breaks down the carbon molecules in the shell and exoskeleton of the organism. As a result, the organism either dies from a disease or, of outright exposure to elements its system cannot tolerate. This is also true for coral reefs. The Great Barrier Reef off the East Coast of Australia has been decimated by CO_2 infusions. Over 30% of this reef has been destroyed by CO_2 infusion from "acid rain" and other pollutants that affect the ecosystem (example: runoff from fertilizers at sugar cane farms, where forests once stood, during torrential tropical rain storms, Nature Channel Special 2016) have caused massive reductions in the coral populations. Coral provides a habitat for other creatures that we eat (fish, crustaceans, mollusks, etc.). So, as the oceans go...so do we.

Limiting the amounts of investments that enhance global warming and pollute the air, I believe, are worthy efforts by those in Government who really care about our future on this planet. Philanthropy can be a good thing that helps many people. Philanthropy that detracts from the welfare, health, and ecosystem should be placed into check. The Government's function in all of this is to act as an overseer and governor of intent and purpose. If the results are harming the people, the planet, and our survival then the Government needs to step in a close these practices down. Profit can be a good thing, but profit at the expense of our health, wellness, and future generations' survival is not. It's pretty simple folks, we need to "watchdog" our industries and corporations much better than we have been doing. Frankly, under the current Administration, (2017), and from what I'm seeing and reading about, I have little faith that they have our best interests at heart.

For example, just today (April26, 2017), I learned that one of the budget proposals in the Trump tax plan is to cut "Meals on Wheels" for seniors across the Nation. I'm sure the Republicans won't tell you about this because it would drive most voters to the point of being furious. "Meals on Wheels "is funded by Federal Block Grants and they fed over 137,500, 000 people last year. Many shut-in seniors depend on this program for the only really balanced and nutritious meal they get each day. Volunteers do the "heavy lifting" (preparation, delivery, and check ins on people who are often bedridden). Therefore, we need to keep a close watch and take appropriate actions (legal, petitions, town halls, "grass roots" organizations, partnering with those organizations that fight corrupt entities and organizations who do harm to us and our planet). It has been done, and, with the help of "fire fighters" like you it will continue to be done. I do not give up hope on my fellow mankind. We WILL, eventually, do the right thing. There are reasons we are still here; but we need to take better care of each other and the planet we live on. And we need to hold our leaders accountable when they fail to abide by their oaths of office.

Isn't Anyone Looking
Up Anymore?

With the advent of our current technology, we are now inundated with cell phones, I-pads, I-phones, Smart Phones, X-boxes, I-tunes, App after App after App to where most of our time, if we let it, is taken up by some electronic device; be it the television, "streaming", "binge" watching, texting, and other forms of what we've been sold as "communication." All at a cost. I'm not talking about what it costs us, in money, to have our devices each month.

There are "social" costs embedded with this stuff. We talk about "social media." What, exactly, is that? Is texting someone across the State a way to really communicate with that individual; or, would calling them on the phone be a better way of actually sensing, from the inflections and tenor of their voice, even with a "picture" format, be a better way of communicating? In my world, nothing beats face-to-face communication. Texts don't "feel", they are impersonal, and emojis just don't do it for me. Somehow, I think we've "dummied down" our populace and sold them on what's "hot" and the latest "upgrade" to where we're like a bunch of lemmings, running over a cliff, to the next Application or new device with more "bells and whistles," and a bigger price tag.

The tech companies and programmers are lovin' this shit. They're making loads of money at our expense. But, what I see is many people who are devoid of feelings and, a sense of making "real" contact in a meaningful way. There's a lot of superficial contacts going on in our world because everything is moving so fast. Technology is said to be our answer to what ails us; but, is it really? Or, is it robbing us of our humanity? Our being? Our time? Our purpose in life? It's something to think about.

Alvin Toffler, the author of a book titled "Future Shock,", circa 1960s, wrote about the age of technological expansion and invention. He predicted much of what we see in today's world. I particularly liked the analogy he used with the old fashioned ink-well pens; the ones that lasted a lifetime if one took care of them; as opposed to the Bic pens of the day. He stated that "our personal relationships seem to be based on the moments of usury and, like the Bic pen, when our relationship is no longer useful (pen runs out of ink), we discard it or throw it away." We seem to do this more often now than in the past. Relationships are not as "long lasting" as in the past. Our dating and intimate relationships are often temporary and fraught with angst and disillusionment. We have a lot of people going around with the air of "entitlement" because they've never really had to struggle, fight for their country, or made a commitment to someone beyond who buys the next round. I'm not saying that this is true for all of our current populace; but, I see it...I see it a lot.

One example I've seen quite often is when a young couple comes into a restaurant with their child and the parents spend most of their time on their Smart phone, ignoring the child until it comes time to order. They order and go right back to whatever they are doing on their respective devices. I saw this last summer and, in my opinion, the couple should have been spending "quality time" with their kid, while on a family vacation, but they did not. I wanted, so bad, to go over to their table, grab their Smart-phones out of their hands, and ask them why they weren't talking the time and interacting with their child. But, out of courtesy and respect for others' privacy, I did not. It's a "free" country, right? They had the right to do whatever they wanted to do. I just felt sorry for their kid because he was left to fidget all by himself while his parents "played."

I've seen people walk into telephone poles while doing stuff on their Smart phones. I've seen them fall down hills and off of drop-offs while playing "poke'-man" last summer (2016). I've seen people drive into the back end of the car ahead of them because they were too distracted by the App on their phone. And, I've seen folks walk right off a curb into oncoming traffic when the "Don't Walk" sign is flashing. The National Traffic Safety Board (NTSB) recently, (2016), came out with some pretty scary statistics. Instead of DWI/ DUI as our leading causal factors in fatality collisions on our Nation's highways, it's now "distracted driving" (ie. texting, App use, e-mails, and e-searches) or just, generally, not paying attention that's causing more and more wrecks on our highways. It only takes a fraction of a second, at 50 miles per hour, to cross the center line on a two lane highway (the most common road system in the U.S,A).

We have a whole industry predicated on "connectivity" and finding one's inner self so they can find a soul mate to share their lives with. How in the hell did things get so fucking complicated? What ever happened to boy meets girl, asks girl out on a date (or girl asks him), they both have a great time, talk and share common experiences, and, eventually, they get married and raise a family? Or, not. Now, we have to go through sensitivity training and group dynamic profiling to find a mate, or purchase a "dating service" app. We must be cognizant of LGBT folks so we don't offend someone; and we must be "politically correct." What the fuck does that mean? I can't say Donald Trump is an asshole? Or that God wasted his efforts by giving Trump opposed thumbs? Or that his hands are too small? You know what they say about people with small hands?; they have small _____ (you fill in the blank). Or that his Press Secretary, Mr. Spicer, is an idiot for claiming that Hitler didn't use chemical weapons during the Second World War when comparing it to what Assad is doing in Syria (Press Conference, April, 2017); he seemed to conveniently forget about the 8,000,000 Jews, Poles, Czechoslovakians, Hungarians, Serbs, Russians, French, Dutch, etc. that were gassed to death in a number of Nazi concentration camps.

We now have what George Orwell referred to as "double speak" in his famous novel "1984." Only, in today's Washington D.C. world it's called "alternative facts." There are only facts folks….there are no such things as "alternative facts." It's bullshit...pure and simple; and, it's politics. Since when have "bullshit" and politics been mutually exclusive entities? They haven't. We have some very active prevaricators in the current

Administration. It doesn't take a genius to figure out who they are. So, I guess, the guide post here is "buyer beware." Be aware of what is being sold to you as "truth" and "honest" information; especially on the Internet and Smart devices; and, at White House Press briefings. Do your "fact checks"...and do them again, using a different source. If you are still in doubt, go to the source and question the findings up close and personal. Sometimes people will lie to you on "social media" but they have a really hard time doing it in person because they haven't had much practice at it; depending on their age and, how often they use Smart phones. I'm pretty good at telling when someone is lying to me because I've been trained in what to look for; especially definitive body language clues. Someone has to keep it together for a long time, with me, before I'm going to believe what they are claiming is true. Most people can't keep it together that long when they are lying...there always will be a "tell" when they are lying. If you play poker you will know what a "tell" is.

Part of the "solution" I'm getting at here is based on an old adage: "Tell the truth the first time....you won't have to remember as much." We should strive to be truthful in all that we do...even when it hurts. Honesty is the lubrication that turns the wheels of Justice and fairness in our democratic society. Without it, we would be on the way to Armageddon. Most of us, I believe, are honest, faithful citizens who try to live honest lives. Some have strayed from the path of righteousness and some are totally lost; some are called "career politicians." So, you can see I don't hold much trust with "career politicians." I've caught them in too many lies over my 73 years on this planet. Unfortunately, I think, the higher one gets in political office, the rarefied air seems to lack the oxygen content that allows for clear thinking and, they succumb to the most virulent and contagious of corruptions that come along: money. If we'd take money out of the equation, we'd probably get some really fine representation from those we elect. I've seen some really fine people go down to Washington D.C. and come back political hacks who have "sold their souls" to the highest bidder. Those who withstand the onslaught of lobbyists, conglomerate infusions of "soft" money, PACS, and "party liners" are a very rare breed. I have few that I would say meet this test. I could, maybe, count 5 in all my years who I greatly admired for doing the job they were sent to do. I don't fault the others, much; they are human just like you and I, and they should be held to a higher standard, but they often are not. Maybe they just need to look up more often and see the real world instead of a 5 inch by 7 inch screen.

The other point I wanted to make here is that "fire fighters" do use social media, but sparingly. They are usually involved in other pursuits and voluntary endeavors like working for the homeless shelters, working at the local food bank three days a week, playing music for those who cannot get out of their adult facilities, volunteering at their local hospital, church, synagogue or mosque, and spending quality "face time" with family, friends, local leaders, and (yes) politicians. We advocate for the good, the "better angels" in all of us, and we seek solutions rather than being part of the problems. We don't have time to gripe...we're too busy. We also "look up" from what we are doing, quite often. In this manner we keep "connected" and aware of the moment. We practice "mindfulness" (being in the here and now as opposed to some fantasy world provided by some of the "social media" stuff...not that an "escape" isn't bad once in awhile, but a steady diet of the stuff soon turns Johnny into a rather dull lad).

And, finally, I want to tell you about another person I consider to be a "fire fighter." Her name is Tracy Bowdish. She is a "music therapist" who works out of the Norfolk, Virginia healthcare system. Primarily, Bowdish helps people, who have suffered a stoke or memory loss, regain some of their ability, through songs she plays on her guitar, by singing lyrics while she encourages them to sing and sings the lines with them. She doesn't use "social media" because she's blind. She says she can "feel" a person's soul and willingness to bring out their sound, so her gift is in her lack of sight, perfect pitch, ability to listen and really "hear" people, musicality and, her ability to reach into a person's being and bring out some of what was lost in the past. (read more about Bowdish in the Everett Daily Herald. Com "Focus" section for senior citizen resources or Norfolk News).

THE ON-GOING SAGA OF PROTEST AND DISSENT

I know this information will probably be "old news" by the time this book is published, but what I'm writing here is a matter of history and, you need this information to make intelligent, informed, decisions:

From an NPR (National Public Radio) broadcast on 4/27/2017:

I learned of a Mexican citizen, undocumented because he did not know how to get the proper paperwork for a work permit, who lived in New Mexico for 27 years, raised a family, worked and paid taxes and recently got a speeding ticket (no other criminal history). When it was discovered that he was an "illegal" he was given the choice to go into the ICE (Immigration Customs Enforcement) detention center or "voluntarily deport." He chose the later. Unfortunately, he had other options he was not informed of. One who is given this "easy fix" is not informed, by our government, of their "DUE PROCESS" rights (as we inform all other citizens who are arrested). He had the right to seek assistance from the Mexican-American Consulate, a right to attorney representation, and the right to a fair and impartial hearing. He got "screwed." Pure and simple. Now, he's back in Mexico, a country he has little, if any, affiliation with and his family is trying, desperately, to get him back. So much for the "Trump policy"…. There are many others like him, who have committed no crimes.

Another issue is the current Administration's desire to "roll back" so called benefits to Mexico and other countries due to the "bad deal" (Trump's words) we made in the NAFTA agreements with trade and businesses in Mexico.

Yes, a lot of jobs went south, but the respective economies, in the main, benefited. Now, our current President wants to build a wall between our two nations. What's wrong with this picture? In my opinion, many things:

1. There are more than 1,000,000 Americans now living in Mexico. Do we want to foment the Mexican populace by antagonizing the "base" and causing riots? I think not.

2. Think about the tourism dollars and exchange of good and services, as a result, between our two countries. If a wall is built, the symbolic nature, alone, would discourage tourism and free trade.

3. Think about how our economies are interdependent (as we are with Canada), and we really cannot afford to "bash" this existence and profitable (for all) situation. We can use our technological advantages to train displaced workers. If you want to put Federal funds into something that works...this would be the place Mr. Trump.

Another issue mentioned on this NPR broadcast was the bro-ha over the former General Michael Flynn's acceptance, unapproved by the State Department, of 10,000 of thousands of dollars from various entities in Russia in the past few years. For what? This has yet to be determined because, as a plea offer, the State Department is considering an "immunity from prosecution" standard for Flynn if he testifies, truthfully, as to who put him up to this nefarious ploy. What were the Russians after? And, who was to benefit from the information Flynn was to share? He was warned, the Government official site says, but he did it anyway, as if he was a "rogue" agent. Personally, I doubt this guy was that foolish. Someone put him up to it with a promise of more prestige and wealth. We may never really find out, but, as in the Watergate Scandals, Congressional hearings have a way of getting to the truth as long as all the "players" are dedicated to the higher moral and ethical precepts of the Constitution and their oaths of office. Flynn may have to "fall on his sword" for the betterment of the American Democracy. I hope so, because I believe there's a lot more to this than what we are being led to believe. It may actually go to the Presidency, as it did a few years ago with Nixon. If it does and we survive the fallout, then it will be a good day for Democracy and our "balanced" form of government. The "truth" IS FREEDOM, never forget that.

The other issue on the NPR presentation that I have some very real concerns about is our current Administration's (2017) intent to limit or reduce the Antiquities Law, passed during President Teddy Roosevelt's time, in which he created the Grand Canyon National Monument. It appears that there is a movement, by certain business (mining, timber, coal, oil, natural gas, etc.) interests (mostly in Utah), to reduce the land mass or nullify the National Monuments that have been in existence, unfettered by any former President, for over 100 years. Now, the current Administration (2017) is voicing an interest in reducing or eliminating, altogether, these Monuments because (their words) "There is too much control, by Government, of Federal lands." This is poppycock, unadulterated bullshit! The only reason a sitting president would attempt to do something so egregious is because his cronies and business friends have stock in mining, timber, minerals, oil, and natural gas exploration. These lands are protected from such pillage and desecration. Shame on Trump and his ilk for trying to ruin our National Heritage and Natural Habitats that future generations desire to enjoy and appreciate. The tourist dollars alone provide more than adequate revenue for the protections of these Monuments. These invasions of our protected lands cause people unwanted stress and anxiety. They contribute to the "fire."

If the Federal Government really wanted to help out, the Congress and the President should advocate for a "full parity" law, fully funded in perpetuity, that would, eventually, save taxes and the enormous expenses of building, operating, and funding prisons, jails, social service networks, overburdened hospitals, and other entities that are grossly affected by our lack of "continuum of care" in this country.

Do I have a "beef" with the oil industry? You bet; even though we have been conditioned to be dependent on the oil teat in this Country. Oil is not infinite. We are gradually learning to convert to "electric" vehicles. Though the initial outlay of purchase price is rather steep, in the long run, we'll save money and the environment; regardless of what the "climate change deniers" say. "Green Revolution" and sustainable energy is the wave of the future and there are many small companies who are getting on board with these innovative and energy-efficient technologies (like solar roofing tiles that produce up to 80% of the power needed for the average home in America).

Another reason (reasons) I have dislike of the oil industry in this country is because every family of largess and influence, who had Congress' back, some years ago, stole land, that was producing oil, from our Native Americans. In fact, they even had some Native Americans, who owned land, murdered (Check out what happened in the mid-west and southern states if you don't believe me; it's readily accessible on the Internet).

My own Mother and Father, God rest their souls, had a run in with Big Oil. My father purchased about 2.7 acres of land in Texas a number of years ago. He was pretty savvy about real estate investments. The land was surrounded by large corporate leases, owned by oil companies, for the exploration of oil and natural gas. Guess what was found? You guessed it. Oil and natural gas deposits. The old woman who sold the property gave my father an "easement road access" to the property that crossed over the land leased by Big Oil. When my parents went to check out the property a few years later, they found a "NO Trespassing" sign on a large locked gate that blocked the road to their property. When they inquired as to the "easement," the oil company told them, "What easement?" So, my parents spoke with their family attorney and were told, in so many words, 'The big oil companies rule; they'll keep you in court for years.' The oil conglomerate offered to pay my parents the same price they'd paid for the land some 10 years prior. Their attorney told them they were lucky because, in Texas, apparently, land can be taken for "imminent domain," and Big Oil IS imminent domain in Texas! So they took the money and ran. They got screwed because the oil leases on the adjacent land were worth millions of dollars!

As I've said, at the onset of my book, there are many entities and issues that affect the "fire" we are facing. It's not just about health care and guardianship of our Constitution and Civil Rights. It's about our continuing survival on this planet! We need more "fire fighters."

Now don't get me wrong, I don't dislike all Republicans. I have very close friends who are Republicans and, we have some very interesting and lively conversations about what this Government needs to do and not do. Someone once told me that Republicans hate Government so much that, when they get into office, they use Government to really fuck things up and then, the Democrats have to come back in and clean up the mess. Just sayin'.

I also have Democratic friends, very liberal Democrats. And we argue too. So I guess I'm an enigma, a unique political animal. Remember? I'm an Existentialist, a person who has to "acknowledge" others' beliefs and traditions, even if I disagree with their arguments and tautologies (logic). I must accept them as equal beings on this planet and, I learn from them so I may expand my own universe. I accept, unless they are trying to kill me (ISIS) or force me to believe as they do. I guess one could say I'm independent, but that may not allow for "acceptance" nor "understanding."

Anyway, recently, on NPR (April and May, 2017, broadcasts) a couple commentators had government officials on and, both questioned what the current Administration is doing to mess things up. One issue mentioned was the budget fiasco. Apparently, in crafting the new budget, current Administrators decided to cut the "Meals on Wheels" program, which is funded through Federal grants. This program feeds shut-ins and elderly folks their, mostly, only one nutritious meal a day. Last year they fed over 300,000,000 meals to people who were on fixed, low incomes (Source: Meals on Wheels statistical report for 2016). Now, most of the Congress will not "fess up" to this boondoggle because, if widely known, some (most, I hope; if you have a heart) would string these Government people up or, run them out of Washington D.C., tarred and feathered. These are our parents or grandparents folks! What in God's name are these idiots doing? Don't they have any compassion at all? Are they so egregious that they must have their wealthy supporters line their pockets with gold and/ or provide more power and control over the rest of us so that we all are suffering? Personally, I think it's time to "clean house." Many, who are now in Congress, do not have altruistic or good intentions for most of the populace of these United States of America. I'm sure of it.

When a sitting President uses his private property and golf and country club (Mar-a-Lago in Florida, NPR broadcast May, 2017) to advertise on Government websites, so he can get richer, in violation of the Emolument Articles of the Constitution (No Government official, including the President, shall use his/her office toward personal gain, financial or otherwise), and no one seems to be doing anything about it, we've got a serious problem and lack of leadership here. These acts are potentially cause for impeachment. Is anyone in the lofty city of Washington D.C. listening or, do they even care? Have we lost out to greed and corruption? If so, I don't hold much shrift with those who are currently sworn to uphold and defend our Constitution. Nor do I have much faith in them doing the right things when our health care is at risk.

Again, this is exactly why we need to be "fire fighters." Things will get worse if we don't stand up and fight for our rights and fairness in how our Government operates. We ARE the Government. People forget that. We are supposedly the "bosses" of those we place into office. If they aren't doing the job right, leaving most of us "out of the loop" and treading all over our Constitutional Rights, it's time to fire them and find someone who really believes and acts in ALL of our best interests, not just for the few! So, will you join me, and others, on the front lines? Do you think you'd make a good "fire fighter?" I think so. You read this book didn't you? That means you have interest and ambition, and, hopefully, inspiration to do what's right. I've given you many pathways to success. You are free to find your own. But first, do your homework. Know the enemy. Know where he/she gets their funding from and who they act for. If they have pharmaceutical stock or off-shore accounts, that might be something worth using in later challenges of loyalty to their oaths of office. Not that owning stock in a successful company is bad; but, if they are playing favor at the expense of the rest of us, then they are not fulfilling their sworn duties to serve the "will of the people." They are serving their own greed and what certain CEOs and Bankers want them to do. That, my friends,

IS NOT REPRESENTATIVE GOVERNMENT!! Again, "follow the money," you'll learn a lot and have something substantial to base your challenges upon. I'll get off my "soapbox" now. I thank you for your consideration of this challenge and, I wish you the best in undertaking it. Your anger and the energy it generates will motivate you. It won't be ill spent. Change comes slowly, most of the time. We don't leapfrog history very successfully. It reminds me of a poem I once heard:

> 'Children throw rocks at frogs in jest,
> But the frogs do not die in jest.
> They die in earnest.'

We need you to rid the "children" from Washington D.C. and, from anywhere else where greed, corruption, waste, lack of care, ignorance and wanton disregard for the sick, mentally ill, and substance addled are common place.

WHAT CAN I DO?

When I've had discussions with folks about the lack of "continuum of care" in this Country, they often balk and say that there's just too much bureaucracy and greedy infrastructure in the pharmaceutical, insurance, and big medical consortiums to bring about the changes I suggest.

Well, there are people, right now, who are doing something about it. I've identified some of those folks in this book and, I know of many more who will not give up on trying to bring about the type of coverage in providership we all need.

You can help out by: 1. Question your Congressional Representatives, congressmen/women and Senators, and any other government official who can have impact on the quality/sustainability of care. See where they stand on these issues. Ask them if they would support "continuum of care" medical coverage for all if it could be shown that a significant tax savings would occur. If they aren't interested or, they "nay-say" the issue, vote them out of office. Find someone who does care and work to get them elected. You'll be doing the Country a great service!

2. Get involved. There are numerous organizations and "grass-root" political movements, right now, in your area, who are in support of changes that would provide "global" medical coverage from cradle to grave for everyone. All you need do is look one up on line. Use your Internet for the common good. If you don't or cannot join a movement; try donating to their cause. Money always opens up doors; it's just how and when it's spent that makes a difference.

3. Stay "connected" because this stuff moves along very quickly. There are new developments in the science of it every day. Your local providers can fill you in on what's working in your local area. If there's interest, start up your own organization or, become a "chapter" in an existing National organization like DBSA (Depression Bi-polar Support Alliance). You can be a "fire fighter" in your own community who enlists other "fire fighters" who just need a direction and some motivation and structure to get the job done.

4. Volunteer at your local food bank, homeless shelter, "Meals on Wheels," Mission, Church, Synagogue, Mosque, hospital, social services network, school district as a mentor for "at risk" kids, drug treatment facility, mental health outreach program, or "shadow" a caseworker for a couple of days to see what enormous tasks they face each day. You will not only gain knowledge and experience, you will have even more "ammunition" to bring about the type of changes in our medical/treatment service delivery system to convince our leaders that the "continuum of care" model is the most efficient, effective, and least costly (in the long run) way to go.

5. At the end of the day, you will feel accomplished and happy to have been a part of changing the paradigm that this country currently suffers. Trying to capture a cure for the opiate epidemic we're now facing continues to be illusive because we aren't providing the "safety net" for those who suffer. Throwing money at a broken V.A. system isn't the answer. Changing the Affordable Care Act into another form of egregious greed and corruption won't get it, and we'll be left with more "kindling" and fuel for the "fire" that is now, pretty much, out of control in this Country. Remember, a sick Nation is not an effective Nation on many fronts: economically, monetarily, internationally, functionally, spiritually, knowledgeably, militarily, judicially, institutionally, personally, family, and just about every other "lly" you can think of.

You can be a "fire fighter." The time is now and our future, as a society and survivors on this planet, depends on it. I do not lie. I wish you the best results in all that you do in life. I will leave you with a prayer I say every day:

Bless me indeed (for to be truly blessed is not selfish)
And expand my territory ("territory" being knowledge, wisdom, love,
compassion, understanding, communicating, etc.)
And let Your hand guide me,
So that I do no harm to myself and others. Amen.

BIBLIOGRAPHY

References

1. Wakefield, Jerome C (2013-15-22) "DSM-5: An Overview of Changes and Controversies" *Clinical Social Work Journal.*

2. Welch, Steven; Klassen, Chrisse; Borisova, Oxana; Clothier, Holly. "The DSM-5 controversies: How should psychologists respond?" *Canadian Psychology/Psychologie canadienne.*

3. "Coalition for DSM-5 Reform". Coalition for DSM-5 Reform. Retrieved October 31, 2013.

4. *Anger Management,* course syllabus and instructor's manual/handouts/ literature 2008, Court Services Institute, Seattle, WA (John P. Crawley was a Certified Instructor of this course as a provider for various District Courts in Northwest Washington State. The course was taught as a Diversion project, part of a Court sentence, in lieu of jail time for various defendants).

5. American Psychiatric Association (2013). *Diagnostic and Statistical Manual of Mental Disorders (Fifth ed.). Arlington, VA; American Psychiatric Publishing. ISBN 978-0-89042-555-8.*

6. Hathaway, L.M.; Boals, A.; Banks, J.B. (2010). "PTSD symptoms and dominant emotional response to a traumatic event: An examination of DSM-IV criterion A2". *Anxiety, Stress, and Coping.* doi:10.1080/10615800902818771.

7. "Diagnostic Ethics: Harms/Benefits, Somatic Symptoms Disorder". *Psychology Today*. Retrieved January 29, 2015.

8. *Child Abuse: Symptoms, Intervention, Reporting Requirements*, course syllabus and instructor's manual, course # 7813-A, Washington State Criminal Justice Training Commission, Burien, Washington, 1990-1992. Mead, James J. (M.A., Ph.D., For Kid's Sake, Inc. original copyright 1985, La Brea, CA Trainer's Manual/ handouts and publications{John P. Crawley was a certified instructor of this course}).

9. Harch, Paul (physician/researcher), <u>*The Oxygen Revolution; (2nd Edition and 3rd Edition),copyright 2010 & 2016 respectively,*</u> Hatherleigh Press; ISBN 978-1-57826-326-4.

10. Kalb, Claudia; <u>Andy Warhol Was A Hoarder</u>; Inside the minds of history's great personalities: (Frank Loyd Wright, Marilyn Monroe, George Gershwin, Abraham Lincoln, Princess Diana, Christine Jorgenson, Betty Ford, Charles Darwin, Fyodor Dostoevsky, Albert Einstein)

11. Lane, Christopher (July 24, 2009). "The Diagnostic Madness of DSM-V". *Slate*.

12. Cary, Benedict (May 8, 2012), "Psychiatry Manual Drafters Back Down on Diagnoses", *The New York Times,* nytimes.com, retrieved May 12, 2012.

13. *New DSM-5 Ignores Biology of Mental Illness* (http://www.scientificamerican.com/article.cfm?id=new-dsm5-ignores-biology-mental-illness); "The latest edition of psychiatry's standard guidebook neglects the biology of mental illness. New research may challenge that." May 5, 2013 Scientific American.

14. "National Institute for Mantal Health abandoning the DSM". Mind Hacks, Retrieved May 23, 2013.

15. DSM-5 Update: Supplement to Diagnostic and Statistical Manual of Mental Disorders. Fifth Edition" (PDF). *Psychiatry Online*. American Psychiatric Association Publishing. September 2016.

16. *Roots of Wisdom*; Native Knowledge. Shared Science. Hibulb Cultural Center, Tulalip Tribes of Washington State; mytyl@hibulbculturalcenter.org

17. Depression/ Bi-polar Support Alliance (DBSA), Snohomish County Chapter, 424-405-0786, Facebook.com/DBSAsnohomishcounty. (Also DBSA National on line).

18. Infectious Madness; Washington, Harriet A., Ph.D., Shearing Fellow, University of Nevada, Black Mountain Institute; research fellow at Harvard Medical School; National research scholar for the National Center for Bioethics at Tuskegee University; and, visiting scholar at Depaul University College of Law; visiting fellowship at Harvard School of Public Health and, John S. Knight Fellowship at Stanford University; a comprehensive study of the organic sources of mental illness and how we "catch" certain diagnoses., Back Bay Books (Little Brown and Co.), copyright 2015, ISBN 978-0-316-27780-8 (hc)/ 978-0-316-27781-5 (pb).

19. International Hyperbaric Medical Association; http:www. hyperbaricmedicalassociatio.org/ various research and PDF files on longitudinal studies from 2005 through 2016.

20. The Brain, a story of you; and as seen on PBS documentary, Eagleman D., Ph.D. neuroscientist and professor at Stanford University, CA; copyright 2015, Vintage Books (subs. Penguin Random House LLC), ISBN: 978-0-525-43344-6.

21. The complete and revised daily journals of John P. Crawley from June, 2008 through March, 2017. Also, professional training guides, literature, notations from a 37.6 year career as a Washington State Parole/Probation Officer {now known as Community Corrections Officers}.

22. The complete medical history, including prescription records, diagnostics, treatment notations, and overviews of John P. Crawley's two hospitalizations in 2008, Swedish Hospital Psychiatric Ward, Seattle, Washington; and, 2009, Northwest Geriatric Psychiatric Ward, Northgate Hospital, Seattle.

23. <u>The Other Side of Normal</u>, How biology is providing the clues to unlock the secrets of normal and abnormal behavior, Smoller, Jordan (M.D., Ph.D., associate professor of psychiatry Harvard Medical School and associate professor at the Department of Epidemiology at Harvard School of Public Health), copyright 2012, ISBN: 978-0-06-149219-8.

24. <u>A Common Struggle</u>; by Patrick Kennedy, copyright 2015. Blue Rider Press, a subsidiary of Penguin Random House LLC. ISBN 978-0399-17332-5.

25. NEHST *"Cut, Poison, Burn,"* a DVD documentary of how the Federal Government (specifically Congress and the FDA) collude with large pharmaceutical corporations, insurance conglomerates, and big medical provider-ships to thwart meaningful and effective treatment modalities because other "players" (we, the people) are "marginalized" and, we, the taxpayers, are looked upon as not having a stake or ownership in same. Copyright 2005. Featuring: Congressman Dan Burton (Indiana); Dr. Stanislaw Burzynski (Burzynski Clinic, Houston, Texas); Dr. Julian Whitaker (Whitaker Wellness Institute); Dr. Leonard Zwelling (Vice President of Research Administration and Professor of Experimental Therapeutics, Maryland Anderson Cancer Institute); Dr. Vincent DeVita (Professor of Medicine at the Yale Cancer Institute, former director of the National Cancer Institute); Shane Ellison, M.S. The People's Chemist; and G. Edward Griffin, author of <u>World Without Cancer.</u>

26. <u>On Looking</u>, Horowitz, A. The Walker's Guide To Observation; Scribner (Simon & Schuster). Copyright 2013, ISBN 978-1-4391-9125-5.

27. <u>Writing Through the Darkness,</u> Schaefer, Elizabeth M (Ph.D.), easing your depression with paper and pen; copyright 2008, Celestial Arts Publications. ISBN-13:978-1-58761-319-7.

28. <u>The Power of Memoir, How to write your healing story,</u> Myers, Linda J. (Ph.D.); copyright 2010; Josey Bass, A Wiley Imprint Publication. ISBN 978-0-470-50836-7.

Note: Various periodicals, news stories (Seattle Times, The Oregonian, U.S.A. Today, New York Times, etc.) and data, publications (Time, Newsweek, Atlantic, Harpers, Psychology Today, AMA Journal, etc.), personal journal entries, personal interviews, and outside source work (example: PDF files/clinical studies by Dr. Paul G. Harch; and others noted in text) was obtained for additional documentation and validity of statements made within this novel. Where appropriate and needed, you will find the source described at the end of a paragraph or, in related data and subject's matter, at the end of a chapter.

Printed in the United States
By Bookmasters